THE UNIVERSITY
WINCHESTER

Martial Rose Library

Inspiring Writing in Art and Design
Taking a Line for a Write

Inspiring Writing in
Art and Design
Taking a Line for a Write

Pat Francis

intellect Bristol, UK / Chicago, USA

MIX
Paper from
responsible sources
FSC
www.fsc.org   FSC® C020822

First published in the UK in 2009 by
Intellect Books, The Mill, Parnall Road, Fishponds, Bristol, BS16 3JG, UK

First published in the USA in 2009 by
Intellect Books, The University of Chicago Press, 1427 E. 60th Street, Chicago,
IL 60637, USA

A catalogue record for this book is available from the British Library.

Cover designer: Holly Rose
Copy-editor: Heather Owen
Typesetting: Mac Style, Beverley, E. Yorkshire

ISBN 978-1-84150-256-4

Printed and bound by 4edge Limited, Hockley. www.4edge.co.uk

Right to write

Think write
Doodle write
Hear write
Talk write
See write
Draw write
Do write
Make write

Write about
Write in
Write through
Write on
Write below
Write round
Write right
Write wrong

Write
Write re-write
Right to write

CONTENTS

Acknowledgements

Very many people have unwittingly contributed to this book over a period of years.

All my one to one students continually challenge me to find ways of explaining something and developing methods for taking the fears out of writing. For specific ideas, thanks to: Kim, Nina, Gay, Jess, Sophia, Ayla, Sarah, Ashley, Nathan, Emma, Minne, David, Laura, Louise, Dan, Edward, Jack and Rhiannon. But my thanks are to all those I have worked with.

Many tutors at the different places I work at have supported me and enabled me to extend ideas and I am indebted to them. Particularly: Lynne, Sheelagh, Jemma, Michelle, Anne, Emily and Terry.

My connections with the BA Illustration course at UCA Maidstone go back many years and the encouragement from Neil, in particular, is truly appreciated.

Writing PAD is acknowledged elsewhere, and provided me with professional expertise, friendly advice and huge encouragement. Harriet Edwards has been most helpful to me personally and I also would like to thank Julia Lockheart, Nancy Roth and George Marks.

Felix Lam at Cltad initiated the delivery of workshops which laid foundations for this book. The participants of all these workshops are thanked for their feedback and their feelings that the book would be useful.

Special and warm thanks are due to:

- Mike for advice, Lucy for early inspirations and Pauline for support.
- Alex has given me great encouragement and thoughtful discussions and, of course, his illustrations.
- Helen has shown great enthusiasm, taken up thoughts and made me laugh so much, and then provided lovely drawings and inspiring writings.
- Fernando, over the years, has given me the opportunity for much creative writing and he provided some illustrations for this book (this time the words outweigh the visuals!). Pilar has had joyful conversations with me about puppets and teaching.
- May, Sam and Holly at Intellect have given great help, support and inspiration.

Nearly finally: my friend and colleague Sarah has been the outstanding support for this book and my deepest thanks are to her for patience, honesty, laughs, inspirations, revolutions, and wonderful examples of teaching.

And finally to my Mum and Dad whose support, interest, encouragement and discussions, have kept me going through this project.

This book is dedicated to R and S.

Résumé of the Book

⮑ The Introduction gives a brief explanation.
⮑ 'Connecting Inspiration, Theory and Practice' contains the ethos of the book.
⮑ 'The Process Visual' underpins the practical approach to writing.

The book is then split into three sections.

Section 1 is about Principles:

■ this explains the methods and the ideas behind this book.

Section 2 is full of short and useful exercises I call Practicals:

■ this has subsections so, if you are focused on a task, you can go to specific areas
■ if not – dip in
■ or take a title that intrigues you
■ or start at the beginning and see where it takes you
■ the early ones are warm ups and fun.

Section 3 is full of Examples

Here there are all sorts and styles of pieces of writing which explain or give further thoughts. They contain a lot of spin-off ideas and reflections, and this is where I have shown my methods of idea-generation and how my thoughts fly off at tangents. It also reveals how different styles of writing work in different ways. And I break lots of rules.

There is a short **Conclusion**, because every story has an end, but within which there also lies a beginning.

The **Bibliography** is subdivided so that you can find good books to help with writing, or the books that inspired me with ideas, and the reference books that help expand your knowledge of words and vocabulary.

The **Index** is the place to go if you want to go straight to specific points.

The **Contents Pages** help with the detailed listings of all theories, activities and examples.

INTRODUCTION

Inspiring Writing in Art and Design: Taking a Line for a Write is a deliberate play on the words of Paul Klee who encouraged artists to take a line for a walk – getting them to loosen up their drawing and to observe what the line became and where it went.

Writing, too, can be seen as a process of the exploration of thought, through lines.

John Berger emphasizes the question and dialogue that lies at the heart of drawing:

> Image-making begins with interrogating appearance and making marks. Every artist discovers that drawing – when it is an urgent activity – is a two-way process. To draw is not only to measure and put down, it is also to receive. (Berger 2005b: 77)

In taking two artists talking about drawing and using them as the first words in a book on writing, I am purposefully laying out my pitch.

The writing process parallels the stages of working in many of the arts. Just as rough sketches and doodles begin an art or design process, and are then backed by research, reflection and constant adjustment, so too the writing process. Practice involves a rehearsal of the parts of the whole; focusing, re-focusing, exploring points of view, talking writing, hearing writing and writing by doing. Writing may be a dialogue between writer and their thoughts through the medium of words written by the hand.

In the educational programmes for the visual arts there are a vast number of writing requirements, but students often feel that they enrolled to do their subject: to design, to draw, to make, but not to write. And then they find that they have to undertake a wide range of writing assignments. It could be said that visual students have a wider variety of writing tasks than those studying other subjects: they are required to be visual and verbal, whereas many other subjects just ask for the verbal. There is not much in terms of published practical help, and little that takes this visual preference into account.

The premise behind this book is that while there are many books on how to write academically in all subjects, and a few on how to write academically for art and design, they all take a similar approach: you have to be relatively confident in writing already, and also feel that academic writing is really the only sort of writing that counts.

This book offers a different focus. It uses ideas from *creative writing practice* which incorporate fun, exploration, experimentation, development, reflection, memory, experience, visual metaphors, and many other strategies.

Creative writing techniques lie nearer to the creative practices of the studio and therefore may be familiar and more approachable, and they also have profound implications for the academic writing styles often required in theory studies. The writing skills may build more incrementally towards the finished pieces, or may add depth and context and questioning, as Berger mentioned, to the process itself.

So this is a practical book. It does not dwell too long on theories behind why something is, or how something works; there are other books that do that.

This book presents a range of ideas to reflect on and to develop. It is based on activities that have worked with many different people on differing occasions and for vastly varying purposes. I was encouraged to compile it by a number of people: either those who had read all the theories and found no practical solutions, or those who found some of my methods helpful to them in unblocking their own, or others', writing.

Much of the developmental work behind the practices put forward in this book came from working with individual dyslexic students. Many students responded, developed and contributed to the ideas shown to them. In workshops, the ideas have been presented to a wider audience of those who fear writing, as well as those looking for new approaches in their work.

It is hoped that this book will prove of use to students – working by themselves; to support tutors as a fund of ideas to help in their work with a range of students who struggle with writing; and to academic tutors – both theory and studio, who will find a number of strategies that they can use or adapt to their own subject and practice.

There are key principles behind the ideas presented: primarily, that writing needs to be *practised*, but that practice is both fun and creative, and also has a function in itself. In addition, the ideas that evolve throughout the practice can help *develop the skills* to meet the demands of the writing tasks. Underpinning these are that some writing tasks need to be *broken down* in order to clarify the focus, then the writing can be *built up* in a number of ways.

Research is a very loaded term in education today, but in this book it is used in the simple sense of the explorations, readings, interviews and reflections on material that writers need to do to inform their writing. It can vary in complexity, depth and originality at different stages of a course.

The book is split into three sections. Firstly, there are a number of short pieces, some formal, but many informal in form and content, and all about ideas and inspirations behind writing. The second section consists of 'exercises' – practical ideas for developing specific areas of writing. The third section shows some examples of writing that are presented with annotations to give further ideas, reflections on processes, and notes relating the principles to practice.

The layout of the book is varied according to what is being presented and to underline the overall themes that there are no rules, just possibilities.

This approach leads to an eclectic variety of styles of writing and this is deliberate in order to underpin the subject matter, and to show how different voices relate the author to the reader. The book is not an end in itself; it is intended as a point from which readers and writers can develop their own styles, ideas and preferences.

this book tells a story that is
playful
provocative
not definitive
suggestive
corrosive
melancholic
delightful
irrational
logical
decisive
whispering
elusive
illusive
contradictory
active
gestural
emotional
wistful

Fig. 1: Multi-faceted.

Connecting Inspiration, Theory and Practice

This section aims to connect the various threads of influence which inform the writing of this book. I have tried to justify my approach by supporting it with principles of learning, the embedding of skills, and creativity; but I do not want to dwell for too long on this – the important part is the getting on with it.

In underpinning the relationship of writing to reading, I have spent some time referring to the key writers who have inspired the writing approaches I advocate and who offer insights into the processes of writing.

Writing and Learning

Riding and Rayner (1998: 9) have created a simple visualization of a matrix for the determining of learning preferences. One dimension extends from the Verbalizer to the Imager, and the intersecting dimension, from Wholist to Analytic. How we prefer to process, organize, absorb and represent information determines where we see ourselves located on these. Many visual artists may gravitate to the wholistic / imager sector and many writers might locate themselves firmly in the analytic / verbal quadrant.

This way of representing the process of taking in information, and the method of organizing it, could also be used to explain the approaches to writing taken in this book. Many manuals of writing aimed at education concentrate on the form of the essay or dissertation. However, what this book concentrates on is the richer and broader range of writing activities that can surround the essay/dissertation. It also reflects on the folio of writing that could support the portfolio of work undertaken on the course as a whole, and which is more realistic for the range of writing that has to be produced in life. In addition to looking at a wide range of writing styles, this book aims to use creative strategies to underpin most of the practical exercises.

Sketching and doodling in writing, not just in visual work, and finding visual metaphors for ideas, which is proposed throughout this book, is related to the visual end of Riding and Rayner's scale, whereas work on essays and dissertations is usually seen as purely in the realm of the verbal. The verbal end of the scale is often the frightening part for many reluctant/fearful writers and therefore, by approaching tasks from the preferred way of absorbing material, it is hoped that strategies will be strengthened and all areas of work will benefit.

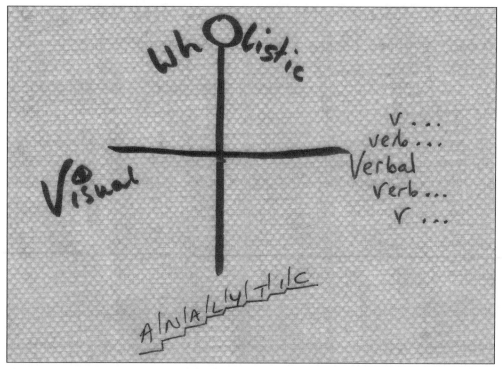

Fig. 2: Author's adaptation of the Riding and Rayner scale of learning preferences for writing.

The emphasis in both teaching styles and in requirements for pieces of work, towards either wholistic or analytic, and either verbal or visual, could be one of the reasons why some students have difficulties in writing. It is also where tutors may have difficulties in bridging what is *required*, with what is *preferred* by the students.

The approach here is to oscillate between the extremes, and to gravitate to the preferred style of process of working and absorbing and organizing information and then to use a mixture of techniques and inclinations to deepen writing skills.

Creative writers often talk about seeing the whole picture in their minds and then working on detail to build up to and create that whole. Thus they move from wholistic to analytic, and probably back to wholistic again. In addition, creative writing often employs visual methods throughout the writing with, for example, the use of metaphor, analogy and description. Thus creative writing could be said to clearly illustrate the use of the *whole* Riding-Rayner scale.

Hands on writing
One of the main reasons for this book's emphasis on starting many of the writing activities with issues of feeling and exploring two and three dimensional objects, is to inspire thoughts and questions and to engage with the materiality of writing.

In experiencing the texture of materials, whether fabric, wood, stone, metal or paper, what is created is another aspect of the two dimensional: one is the thing being written about; the other is the writing itself. So you write about something: *about* the fabrics, as well as *on* the fabrics, not as finished pieces, but as experiments. Then you reflect on the process and the effects and results – and this gives further ideas.

This approach to the writing process and its materiality gives ideas of the **what** to write about and takes away the blocks about the **how.**

In Lee Hall's play *The Pitmen Painters* (Hall 2008a) the miners filled their non-work time with going to and commissioning WEA (Workers Education Association) classes, in order to fill the gaps in their truncated education, and to broaden their knowledge of the world. They had done Evolutionary Biology, Introduction to Psychology etc., and one of the classes now on offer was Art Appreciation. Some were cynical about this, preferring to do economics. But others wanted to know how to understand the meaning of painting, how to approach a painting. The lecturer showed a few slides of Renaissance paintings. He was met with incomprehension. They wanted 'to know about proper art, and to know what it means, the secrets behind what is going on'.

They argued fiercely about what 'meaning' meant, and why they might need to know about 'feelings'. The tutor is floored, but then decides to get them to create some art and then discuss from there. He set them to do a lino cut. The play depicts how, in the next meeting, two miners showed their lino cuts. The others were too ashamed to bring their work in, or had thrown it away – because it didn't mean anything.

The discussion explodes into life and comments come out about meanings and feeling from the very people who questioned the validity of these in art. The play, a condensing of several years of the work and development of the Ashington Group of miner painters, is a crystallizing of what learning about art is really about. Amongst other things, it has to be learning by doing and then reflecting on the doing. As the playwright comments: 'they were profoundly concerned with creativity and how that linked to personal growth and collective understanding – how you learn and the relationships, with teachers, with peers, in that process' (Hall 2008b: 32).

This is what this book is expounding as being a way into writing: writing is about doing, and learning from the doing. This is behind my constant repetitions about starting from the self, writing about writing and the materiality of writing. This is about the feeling – in both senses – of textures and emotions, and that the best way of *learning about writing* is by *engaging in writing*.

This link with how we learn also relates to elements of time. We do not instantly write in a deep and reflective way; we have to build to it gradually. Knight and Yorke (2003: 53) argue that 'complex learning is almost invariably slow learning, taking longer to grow than most modules last'. Thus writing should be part of the ongoing process: not bolted on to parts, but running through the whole. This can particularly be related to the need for the keeping of ongoing reflective journals – where the journey can be explored.

One of the frustrations with all areas of learning is the element of forgetting, and Phil Race, in reflecting on this, provides good justification for the elements of practice and repetition which underpin study and development.

> The most complex ideas probably need to be grasped then lost several times before they are gradually retained more permanently and safely. Learners, however, often feel frustrated and disappointed when they have mastered something one moment, and then find that it has slipped shortly afterwards (Race 2005: 15).

This is what happens in writing – sometimes you can write about something succinctly; then you become clumsy and miss the mark of what you are trying to express.

Again this can link to reflective journals which are private – the journal is the place where you can do, forget, try again, and constantly practice. You can, over time, embed skills, ideas, thoughts into your practice. This is a slow process, and often private. As Race also writes, learning is about the learner taking ownership of their learning, so reflective writing is where they take ownership not only of the writing but of their own reflective processes. Reflection is the process of embedding, and learning not to forget. So the light bulb comes on and then, frustratingly, it seems to go off, for no apparent reason, but later it comes on again, at a different wattage, and spotlighting a different subject.

Race's 'five stages of learning' is described as the 'ripples in the pond model' (Race 2005: 26–41) and this analogy is very similar to many that underpin the writings in this book.

This process of learning, the process of doing and writing, may seem to go round and round in circles, and the circular shape is one that seems to constantly occur throughout many of my visual approaches to the teaching of writing. But I also would want to clarify this. It is not a closed circle: it is more like the quick doodle of a circle which you sketch down – and frequently the line does not join up. In this process you create an open circle, or one that actually fluidly transforms into a spiral. The sense of movement, then, is much more akin to steady learning.

This learning spiral, or cycle, is propounded in many theories of successful learning. Firstly there is a want to do something and a need, then learning by doing, and then developing learning from feedback, and finally the reflection stage of making sense of what has been learnt.

If there is no need or want, then it is difficult to progress, but something can happen when you are doing something, even if the motivation comes from outside yourself, as in a workshop perhaps, so that you then want to carry on and try something for yourself. If someone is reluctant to write (therefore having no want) then the act of doing can create the climate for something to happen.

Feedback, often from others, can also come from within. A major aspect of writing is that it is to communicate and this provides a great stimulus to learn what works and what does not, and what is appropriate for which occasion – all points to be reflected on and then acted upon.

Using Writers as exemplars
In the writing of this book I have quoted from a number of authors who inspire me. In workshops I might use examples of their work to show what I mean, to inspire, and to elucidate a point. I have to state that these are *my* inspirers. They are not used for any particular academic points, nor always for the art or design debates that emerge, but for their writing. It is about the way they write: their voice, their use of metaphor, their use of creative forms to discuss ideas, and so much more. These are some of the best communicators in writing.

John Berger is one of the main writers I use as an example, and indeed some of his words opened my introduction to this book, and his work can relate to all visual art subjects. He has written poems which crystallize a feeling and show the soul of words; he has written essays – some short reflections on one idea, some analytical and academic in their references; he writes about ideas; he contextualizes; he is writing today. His writing is sometimes very deep, but the energy and passion in it almost always attracts the reader to work at the language and the articulation of the ideas. It may be that some tutors will have different reactions to Berger's ideas, but it is his *writing* that I am drawing attention to here, and the discussion that can lead from the ways he writes about these ideas could be most valuable to stimulating students into writing themselves.

The following is the final part of a short piece called 'Once through a lens' from the book *and our faces, my heart, brief as photos*. Berger's use of metaphor is matchless in the layers of meaning it can set off in our minds:

> Those who read or listen to our stories see everything as through a lens. This lens is the secret of narration, and it is ground anew in every story, ground between the temporal and the timeless.

> If we storytellers are Death's Secretaries, we are so because, in our brief mortal lives, we are grinders of these lenses (Berger 2005a: 31).

Berger's book, written with John Christie, *I send you this Cadmium Red* (Berger nd), is a wonderful source of writing about inspirations and the way ideas spin off from a starting point, bringing in references, feelings, memories, perceptions and ideas through linking to all forms of visual art, performance and literature.

It is also a prime example of the idea of dialogue writing – one person writes about something (in this case a colour) and sends a letter to the other who responds to what is written, and then goes off tangentially to other ideas. It encompasses analysis and academic knowledge and also is about the stories of human beings and colours.

I also use, as an example of reflective writing, a piece from the artist Josef Herman, where he thinks about the process of drawing:

> I don't know how to begin. I will begin with the obvious. I am alone in the studio. I stand in silence. I am undecided. On the easel there is a large sheet of cartridge paper pinned to a board; on the table, a small white page. My eyes go from one to the other. I have to choose between two different physical situations; the physical situation is part of the way my mind works. I know from experience that if I sit hunched over the small page on the table, I will make a different **kind** of drawing than when I stand in front of the large sheet of cartridge on the easel. Hunched over the small page, my drawing is likely to be intimate, reflective and involve me in a greater inward concentration. Standing in front of a large sheet, I am likely to give outward things priority; the arm's length distance between the paper and my body makes also for a space which encourages a greater use of energy and a display of gestural sweeps. When I sit, I condense; standing, I expand. The compulsion to begin work on either is equally urgent, hence my confusion ... (Herman 1985: 1–3).

Certain key words leap out to me in this reflection, principally the 'gestural sweeps'. This began the process which ended in my writing about writing as gesture. That piece was fuelled by many other readings and reflectings, my interest in drama and the physicality of words, but Herman's words here were the trigger. That is what reading does – it sets off fireworks in your mind.

George Perec, with his use of lists and inspirations, provides some offbeat source material to show where something mundane can go. Three essays from *Species of Spaces* (Perec 1997) filter into my ideas for practicals. His 'Notes Concerning the Objects that are on my Work-Table' reflects the inspiration behind the idea of the object as subject, which forms the basis of my exercises in observation and stimuli to writing. He also wrote an essay 'Think/Classify' that relates to material I have written about classifying and clumping. He was an archivist and brings this detailed inventory and patterning tendency to fruition in his work, which can be hypnotic in its creativity. 'Two Hundred and Forty-three Postcards in Real Colour' is in the form of a list, but is also about the inspirations that flow from the postcard. Sometimes, even in a title comes an idea and it can be about *how* you read the title, not even what it is meant to be about. That serendipity is at the heart of reading and your own writing.

Helen Cixous writes reflectively about her own processes of writing and noting and keeping memories, and in books such as *rootprints* (Cixous 1997) gives inspiration about the detail of writing. Her particular approach comes across in her words: 'All biographies like all autobiographies like all narratives tell one story in place of another story' (Cixous 1997: 178). She finds the story in all forms, and this is a patterning that underlines many of the practical ways into writing that feature in this book. She also writes of her process of writing which starts with silence and is 'as if I were writing on the inside of myself' (Cixous 1997: 105). Her insights into this process filter throughout my attempts to explain or justify activities.

Margaret Atwood, the novelist, essayist and poet, has provided many ideas and images for this book and I use her writing as examples in workshops. She has illuminated the writing process, particularly in *Negotiating with the Dead* (Atwood 2002), and her image of the difficulties of writing being akin to 'mice in molasses' was a key inspiration for my own reflections and subsequent writings.

In a similar vein, Virginia Woolf was, in her reflective journals and diaries, revealing about her process of writing, and her methods and observations corroborate many of the approaches to practice. This keeping of a diary, and using it as a warm up and practice for writing, lies at the heart of what I am advocating.

Monday April 20th 1925

One thing, in considering my state of mind now, seems to me beyond dispute; that I have, at last, bored down into my oil well, and can't scribble fast enough to bring it all to the surface. I have now at least 6 stories welling up in me, and feel, at last, that I can coin all my thoughts into words. Not but what an infinite number of problems remain: but I have never felt this rush and urgency before. I believe I can write much more quickly; if writing it is – this dash at the paper of a phrase, and then the typing and retyping – trying it over; the actual writing being now like the sweep of a brush; I fill it up afterwards (Woolf 1987: 79).

Her use of the phrase 'sweep like a brush' reveals an example of the common vocabulary of writer and visual artist, reminiscent of Herman's words above.

The physicality of writing is encapsulated here.

Julia Cameron, in books such as *Right to Write* (1998) and the *Sound of Paper* (2004), and Natalie Goldberg in *Writing Down the Bones* (1986), have inspired ideas for exercises; some very clearly derived, and many others which have been adapted. Whenever, in a workshop, I have wanted to talk about doing something in a particular way, back-up has come from quoting authors such as these. I have built on Goldberg's use of the image of compost and the necessity to have a rich source of 'things' constantly being poured or dripped into your mind. Cameron's edict of one step at a time, while not purely original to her, is clearly evidenced in her approach to building up to writing, and this echoes much of the advice I offer.

Contemporary academic writers on the visual arts, such as Alain de Botton, Simon Schama, Geoff Dyer and Caroline Evans, provide creative pieces of writing about art, design, photography and fashion that I often use in workshops as examples of good writing in one way or another – a clear structure, argument, a metaphor or a lively way of describing something.

Creative writers such as Jeanette Winterson write great fiction, but, in addition, she is very knowledgeable about art and its worlds. Her creative writing skills make her essays and newspaper columns very stimulating to read. These are, I feel, a really good way into any debate about art issues. The principle behind this book, of using creative writing techniques in art and design, is reinforced particularly by Winterson's works, as well as with those by Berger. Here is Winterson combining reading and art in an article, 'The secret life of us':

> When you take time to read a book or listen to music or look at a picture, the first thing you are doing is turning your attention inwards. The outside world, with all of its demands, has to wait. As you withdraw your energy from the world, the art work begins to reach you with energies of its own. The creativity and concentration put into the making of the artwork begin to cross-current into you. This is not simply about being recharged, as in a good night's sleep or a holiday, it is about being charged at a completely different voltage. (Winterson 2002: 10–11)

This illumination of the worlds within us, justifying the starting point to writing as lying at the heart of ourselves, as was seen with Cixous, and Winterson's making a verb out of 'cross-current' to give her own writing a vivacity, are fundamental features to the approaches I have taken.

The writer Penelope Lively has written novels for adults and children and several pieces which are non fiction, but which tell the stories of people and their times, often through the use of photographs and objects. Her A House Unlocked (2002) has passages about photography and its mores that inspired some of the creative exercises in writing from photography that I use.

The actress, Harriet Walter, in Other People's Shoes (2003) writes eloquently about the searching for character, the meanings of text, the subtext and the political gesture. Because of the theatrical nature of her approach to writing, I find it particularly relevant to my own response to text. Her one line: 'Plays tell stories through character in action' (Walter 2003: 115), is such a wonderful crystallization of what plays are about, and about the active nature of writing, and this reinforces my repetition of the fact that stories source so much of the writing activity. Reading this line was one of my 'Eureka' moments. Cut the waffle; say it as it is.

Eudora Welty was an American writer and photographer working in the Depression and beyond. Her experiences of being a writer are explored in One Writer's Beginnings (1995), and her encapsulation of the writing and photography 'moments' has given me many quotations, which are scattered throughout the book. In particular she has phrases about connections, about gesture, memory and story which are central to my themes.

There are many writers of manuals or guides to writing, some of whom have been influential to me before, and during, the writing of this book. Many books have been published to help with writing essays, improving writing skills and writing for college and university. Most of these are geared for subjects other than the creative arts. Therefore their advice is not always of great relevance to art and design practitioners. On the whole, in the arts, the emphasis is less on the form and the strict adherence to methods, and more on original and creative thought about people or schools of art and design, or about artefacts. There are some guides to writing which assume you are already confident in writing, and therefore can be heavy going. There are others which teach rules while the creative spirit withers.

I have mentioned some of the main creative writers who have influenced my writing. The following are the ones who are inspirational in their writing of guides for the area that this books covers because they do not neglect the creative spark.

Mike Sharples' book goes way beyond its title: *How we write: writing as creative design* (1999). It is about process and makes some wonderful analogies that help us see the process as paralleling the visual or active making of things. His analysis of Alfred Wainwright's drawings of maps for the Lake District led to my idea of viewpoints. His analysis of structure will be of use to many. It is a dense book, full of ideas and is exciting for someone who wants to deepen their explorations of design writing and process.

Paul Mills' *Writing in Action* (1996) is one of the very few books that looks to the creative arts to feed the writing itself. His use of examples is extensive and his approach to technical points is more useful than many books on grammar.

Carole Gray and Julian Malins' *Visualizing Research* (2004), geared towards postgraduate students, is also a very practically oriented book that goes into great depth while retaining an active and visual approach to writing. Their extensive use of visual metaphors justifies this approach at all levels of study.

John Wood, principally in articles such as 'The tetrahedron can encourage designers to formalize more responsible strategies' (2004) and 'An evolutionary purpose to Dyslexia' (2005), has done a lot to explode and explore the processes of writing, and in creating his models, will, for many people, completely revolutionize their ways into writing.

Wood is one of the founding motivators behind the Writing PAD community of practitioners, who are building the body of work in this area. Writing PAD is about writing Purposefully in Art and Design. Harriet Edwards' 'Design research by practice: modes of writing in a recent Ph.D. from the RCA' (Edwards and Woolf 2007), is a prime example of the realities of writing for specific purposes with imagination and visualization. Maziar Raein's *Where is the 'I'?* (2003) is an obvious source of inspiration for several of my exercises. The website for Writing PAD (for full details, see the Appendix) gives access to many articles and papers on specific writing experiments and researches. This will be invaluable for tutors, but also of interest to students who are becoming hooked on the processes of writing and alternative forms that are being explored at many institutions. Writing PAD has now launched The *Journal of Writing in Creative Practice* which has, and will, feature many ideas and inspirations for new forms of writing and experiments in extending the role of writing in the creative arts as a whole.

One of the writers on language I often fall back to is David Crystal. His vast range of works covers the academic, the anecdotal, the curious and the popular. His style changes for each publication. Changes, but yet does not migrate from his eternal passion about language and enthusiasms. It is impossible to read a book like *Words, Words, Words* (2007) and not laugh out loud and learn. It is this spirit that I hope to convey in the explorations that fill this book.

Fig. 3: Reading the writing.

28

THE PROCESS VISUAL

Introduction and background

This visualization of the writing process evolved from many attempts to *talk* about the stages of writing; trying to encourage a 'bit' approach rather than a mad rush for the 'final piece'. Whenever I talked about doing bits, many students expressed a relief. Writing did not need to be about 'start here, move to here, then here, then here, then end up there'. They felt they couldn't do that. My own experience is that, while I might have an overall picture in mind of what a final piece might be, I go about it in a variety of ways, and certainly not always methodically, start to finish, this leading to that and so on. So, if this is so for me, and I am confident about writing, why might this not be so for others?

When I did the first sketch for the process journey it was met with a *Eureka* moment from one scared writer – 'Oh I can do **bits**?! – Oh I **can** do that.' The relief was palpable. You can join up the bits later. You can re-work, re-adjust, later. Not necessarily earlier.

To an experienced writer this is a known, but there is something about the way writing has been taught (or not taught) that has left most people without confidence in creating their own processes.

Art and design students are being encouraged to find their own processes in their practical work and differences are celebrated. However, in their writing, this idea of process gets lost and they are either not introduced to possible ways of working, or are encouraged to think that the final logical structure of a written piece, read left to right, front to back, reflects the way it is *evolved*.

Not so. It does not have to be so.

Doodles of drawings or writings are part of the journey, and contribute to the final work, but are not necessarily seen as finished pieces in themselves.

So, while offering this visual process for writing, I am also not setting it in stone. It is meant to be liberating: different ways of doing different tasks for different people – but fluid, more instinctive, and always open to change.

While this process might look as if it is solely geared to essays, it is not meant to be so. In all areas of writing there are certain stages to go through. There is always the

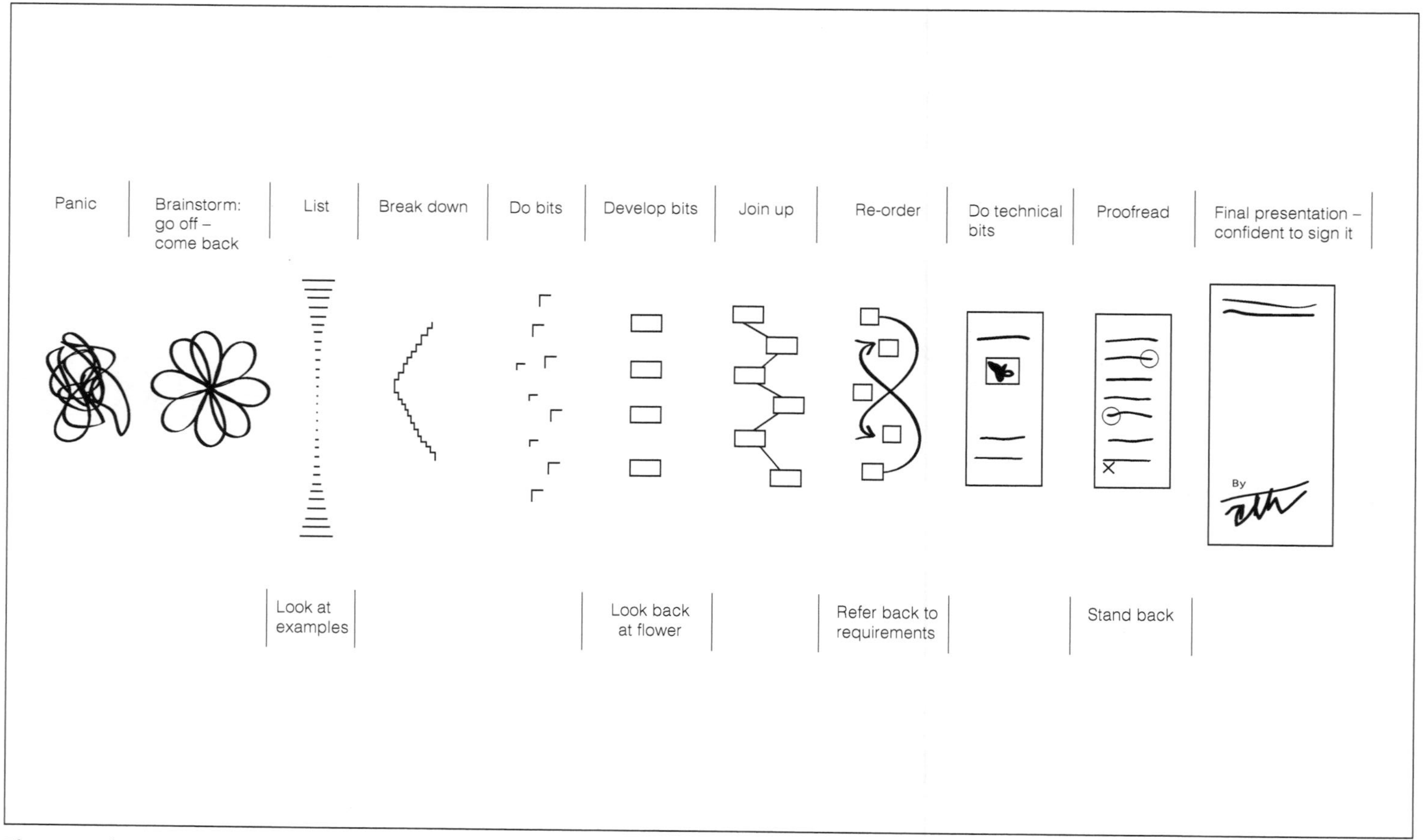

Fig. 4: Panic to production.

preparation, the doing, the altering and the final presentation; even if that is as big as a dissertation, or as small as a caption.

Re-work this visual to suit yourself.

Notes on the process (to accompany the visual)

For most people there is a sense of panic when first presented with a task. This is natural and is almost like the kick start of adrenalin to get the brain going.

Understand what is required – some pointers are needed, but total comprehension is not always practical. Some, if not most, revelations will come on the journey.

Initial thoughts, brainstorms, lists, mind maps ...

Understanding that this is an initial stocktake of ideas and what is known now.

Lists – and where they will lead and where they need to go.

Research – lots of different directions, lots of different types of research, but all linking back to a core. The writer needs to feel that *nothing is wasted*. Going off at a tangent is not a crime – it often leads to deeper understandings. Alternative viewpoints. There is also the serendipitous finding of something by accident; a vital lead coming up by chance.

Talking, listening, thinking – all these are vital research methods.

Breaking Down ideas.

Writing bits
Doodling thoughts
Writing from quotes – reactions, reflective and creative questioning.

Taking stock – standing back from material
Looking again at the task – what meant to be doing
Further research????

Writing bits – developing some of these. Beginning to select what to develop or what to leave.

Laying them out – looking at the bits.

Finding links between them and joining up the parts.
(For some tasks there needs to be a further stocktaking – where is further research needed? Doing it. Linking it in.)

Beginning to pull bits together, cutting up, pasting together.

Putting it together as a sequence – standing back, adjusting, deciding on the order.

Finding new links, finding new gaps.

Plugging gaps? – Maybe this will be through more research, quotes, visuals, evidence/ examples.

Draft, re-draft, constantly re-tuning
Link back to brief.

Doing the technical bits (having kept records throughout).

Final presentation:
  Reading through
  Proofreading
  Signing the copy – putting your name to your work.

Reflection on the Process Visual

While some of these points particularly relate to the academic essay, most parts relate also to *any* written pieces.

It is about process – not just the final product.

Therefore there is more emphasis on the elements of thinking, researching, doing bits, assessing, re-assessing, focusing, re-focusing, drafting, re-drafting, editing, proofreading.

It might seem tedious – there seems to be a lot of emphasis on do and re-do: constant 're-s'. But this is where it is adaptable. Some pieces require many stages of re-drafting and pruning. Others need perhaps only one. But apart from stream of consciousness writing, which is raw and unedited, all other tasks should involve at least one 're'.

Much decision making in writing can be summed up by reflect, resolve, re-do.

Maybe a key 're' word that sums up this process is **revision**, with its many layers of meaning, from revising for exams, to re-adjusting. It also crucially has the word **vision** in it. So maybe it is more about looking afresh, seeing anew. This brings the visual back into writing.

1

PRINCIPLES

Fig. 5: Beginning the journey.

Introduction

This section is about the principles behind this book, and explanations of the writing approach that I take, as my work involves one-to-one tutorials with students as well as running workshops for large groups.

So, firstly, there is a section of pieces under the heading of **Methods**. This details the background to the workshops where writing skills are developed, and the forms and formats of work, such as journals, which are mentioned throughout the book.

Secondly, there is a short section on **Reading**, and how this relates to writing.

The third section is about **Practice and Process**, which underlines the constant theme that practice in one area will help work in another area.

Finally there is a section entitled **The Writer: Self and Others**, with ideas about becoming aware of the process of being a writer, and finding your writing voice.

Methods

Workshops

This is just a broad outline to give the flavour of the workshops. These are referred to in many of the Practicals so I need to give the context.

I give writing workshops for Further and Higher Education students and also for tutors in subject areas such as fashion, design, jewellery, model making, illustration, graphics, photography and fine art.

Sometimes I only work with a group once. However, more often there might be a sequence of workshops – perhaps four or five spread over a period of time and paralleling particular activities: preparation for essays and dissertations; starting journals; writing summaries; statements for application to other courses, work experience or employment; and producing creative text for a personal project.

The point of the workshop is to generate ideas, give tips, or develop particular themes – so I try to make them fun. Many participants have a block about writing so I aim to present material in a non-threatening way.

One of the first things I say at the start of a workshop, and have repeated in this book, is that I present a range of materials and it is important for the participant, as with the reader, to 'do a pick and mix': select some activities, discard others, adapt some, develop some, and think about others. I encourage participants to keep an open mind and make connections, so that something which feels really simple has the potential to be complex in its development.

I usually start with quick warm-up activities: setting the mood, relaxing the brain, opening up ideas. Usually there is a lot of laughter here, and noise.

Then the specific activities are geared to what the students/tutors are doing at that time, or need to do.

A lot of material is prepared in advance, as is shown with some of the exercises in this book. Often a pack is given out, consisting of handouts and samples of papers and materials to write on or about. The workshop is planned carefully so that it runs smoothly and the atmosphere that has been created is not broken, with long gaps while things are handed out. Inevitably there is some of this, but it can be turned into a bit of a rest.

Some ideas *might* work instantly, or an hour later; that evening, next day, week, month; or it might be several years later when the light bulb comes on. Openness to those moments is all that can be asked.

I try to allow time during the workshop, and have encouraged it throughout this book, for reflection: the pause, the thought, the making of links, forming questions, the dwelling on, the sparking off, the going off at a tangent.

The vital key is to take what is offered and then make it your own.

Reflection and Reflective Writing

Donald Schon (1991) writes of reflection **in** action and reflection **on** action, and these threads are woven through the approach to reflective journals taken in this book.

Jennifer Moon has contributed a wide range of writings about journals and reflection, and although these were never originally focused on the arts subjects, much of her work does relate quite closely. Many writers and practitioners have used her work as a starting point, and this book is no exception. She created a diagram to visualize the stages of development in reflection (Moon 1999: 35), and later (2004) developed a series of pieces of writing to show stages in reflective writing. This is a very useful principle and can be adapted to the arts. These are particularly useful for tutors new to teaching reflective practice as they show the stages clearly, and this underpins a key principle of this book: that reflective writing is not instant and has to be given time to mature. It does not spring fully formed from the page.

Reflection while doing, and on how and what you are working on, helps the journey progress and encourages exploration of alternative routes that may be tried.

Reflection after action, explaining (to self and others) through writing, writing in different voices, and considering a range of perspectives and viewpoints are the key constituents of secondary reflection. This enables us to learn from the past and to develop skills and techniques that we call on in the future.

Writing as a way of crystallizing thoughts is the attempt to make physical the random flitting thoughts in our head. Practise in trying to capture these flutters is what helps us grow as people and practitioners.

However, reflective writing doesn't happen instantly.

For some people to whom writing comes relatively easily, exploration of thoughts will come naturally, although even some of these may need help with going deeper. But for most – it has to be developed slowly and incrementally.

Many of the exercises in this book help the early stages: moving from the initial:

> 'I like ...' 'I love ...', 'first thought is ...'
>
> to
>
> 'maybe ...', 'what is it about this?...'
>
> to
>
> 'what if?...', 'could it?...', 'can I?...', 'will I?...'
>
> and towards
>
> 'I will ...'
>
> and
>
> 'if I do ... what happens?...'

Writing Stages Schema

The reflective process detailed previously suggests the development of a possible basic schema for writing that can be split into three stages and summarized in key words:

first stage: explore, experiment, evaluate
second stage: define, develop, detail
third stage: personalize, professionalize, polish

This is not meant to be an exclusive or inflexible scheme – there is much more movement backwards and forwards. But perhaps this relates to the sorts of practical exercises suggested in this book, and which can be tried at particular points in a curriculum.

It must be emphasized that in addition to movement there are other constant strands:

Reinforce reflective)
) throughout all stages
Reinforce creative   )

Another feature is that all the words used in the stages are used as *verbs*, thus they are active.

Writing must be active and live.

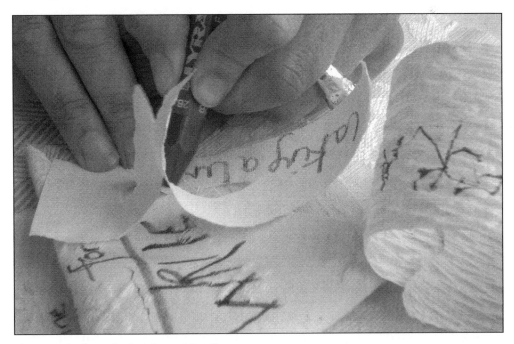

Fig. 6: Actively exploring the writing line.

The Reflective Journal

The reflective journal underpins most of the practical ideas offered in this book. It is an infinitely variable tool to help all writers. It is personal, even though some parts might be offered, at times, for public perusal.

Titles for journals change from one institution to another, but the following text will describe and evaluate the key characteristics and potentialities. As Moon (1999) revealed, journals have been a significant part of practice in subjects from social work and health, and science to education, but they have been less well documented and evaluated in arts subjects. This is changing, and this book also seeks to offer ideas for these developments.

The Rationale

The aim of the Reflective Learning Journal, as its name implies, is to aid students in their own learning development, and it can be geared towards their individual professional practice.

The purpose of the journal is that, from the early stages of the course, students are logging their thought processes, developing skills of analysis of these processes, and linking these to the range of influences and subjects to which they are introduced, and from this, developing the skills of contextualization. The journal encourages the practice of articulation through writing, starting from their feelings about the material they are researching, by exploring primary and secondary resources, and by responding to advice from tutors and peers.

There is no set pattern or model for the journal; however, it is primarily a written book or folder of writings. It is cross-referenced to the visual sketchbook in that it will attempt to analyse design sketches. It also will refer to research folders and explore concepts and theories from the range of reading undertaken. Visits to exhibitions, fashion shows, viewing of television programmes and attendance at lectures, both internal and external, will be written up – using descriptive writing in the first instance, but developing into analysis of what these events contribute to the student's own project work. In this respect, the journal is not *instantly* deep or analytical. The student has to progress from a recording and describing of events and will respond to questions initially set by tutors.

The journal is not being judged in language terms regarding grammar and structure. It is being considered for its content. However, another purpose of the journal is to provide practice in writing and therefore, as the journal progresses, improvements in vocabulary and structure should emerge.

The journal provides the chance to experiment with writing – therefore a student may decide, for example, to write a press release. Evidence of the preparation for this is the gathering of several press releases placed in research folders, and analyses of style, vocabulary and tone. A press release is then written, accompanied by a self evaluation of the work, showing the reflection on others' comments on the piece. This will prove invaluable practice for the work in the final stages of a course.

The journal's outward manifestation may vary from student to student, but it can be brought to a tutorial and will be a tool to aid communication for students to demonstrate at what stage their work is located. For instance it could include brainstorming or mind-mapping, flow charts, lists of intended explorations, links to bibliographies and breakdowns of research folders. Combined with these are analyses of outcomes from these activities, responses to feedback, and evidence of self-motivation. The journal could aid visiting tutors, clarifying the directions in which students are going, and enabling more specific advice on their work.

In terms of relating to a possible schema of writing:

- In the early stages, the journal will aid contextualization and a student's growing skills in communication and developing understanding.
- Secondly, it will display growing independence, skills of evaluation and locating work in terms of the structure of possible thoughts for future employment.
- In the final stage it will evidence the depth of learning and development and demonstrate how the student is evolving an individual professional practice.

The journal could act as a central spine to the student's experience of the course. In this, it can be closely linked to Personal Development Planning which, under a variety of names, now exists in all colleges.

Assessment of Journals

In the same way that the sketchbook is not always directly assessed and yet is a vital part of the process which leads to final work, so too the journal is not always assessed in that format. However it is the means by which goals are achieved and it is a vital component of overall work. In order to add a layer of deep reflective thought about theoretical research, interviews, market research, exhibitions, publication analysis, etc., a final report may be written about the progress of the project. This is reflective, analytical and proactive in terms of locating a student's work.

Therefore it is this Report or Summary, in its role as an evaluation, which is assessed, not the journal itself.

For assessment purposes, what will be seen is a development from early responses to later, more analytical and exploratory writing: the transition from passive to active. Assessment criteria will focus on evidence of improving vocabulary through writing, connections between theory and practice, development of ideas, growing independence of thought, generation of questions and setting of targets. The journal will display attempts to organize work, and reflections on the success of this and the strategies followed. Ability to determine and create an individual methodology should be evident in the journal.

The assessment criteria of that final report are more easily written and understood than criteria for a journal itself can ever be. Moon (2004: 151) confirms that in the setting of the assessment criteria it is vital that they match the aims of the *specific* project, or the course overall, and relate to growth and development. For the student it is important to see these criteria in two ways: the requirements of the unit or course overall, but also the personal journey and the decisions they have made.

Some Specific Forms of the Journal

Work Based Learning Journal

For a work placement, students might be asked to keep a range of records of work and experiences:

- a personal daily log in the form of the Reflective Learning Journal
- specific tasks undertaken in the placement
- an analytical account of what the work entailed, how it was approached and what elements of the tasks could be applied to college work
- analysis of the structure of the company and the range of work undertaken and a profile of the job titles
- personal approaches to work, time keeping, preparedness, etc.
- a short case study of the company attended
- conducting an interview, and then producing an article or report based on that interview
- CV with this work experience included
- any letters sent applying for the work, and any thank-you letters written after the experience, *with annotations* showing what is learnt from how to do the letters, and the responses given.

All these are to evidence the professional approach to the work.

Effectively this is a folder of written work. However it would *not* be in the form of essays or academic writing. It would more likely be in the form of a file.

This file could contain: letters, a series of reports, or analyses, a flow diagram explaining structures, etc. and also a file of examples of written instructions and notes. It would also contain the personal reflections on the experience, in whatever format is suited to the placement and the course. Essentially it is evidence of the work placement and evidence of what has been learnt and the changes to be made to personal working practice. A list of what is to be contained would be provided by staff, but if extra material is included, then this would be encouraged. Thus a minimum is set, but not a maximum. The key is that it is a tool for providing evidence. Therefore if it is long, rambling and disorganized, that would be seen as evidence of lack of objectivity. It is necessary to learn the skills of taking a step back from work, and understanding what is good evidence and what is extraneous to requirements.

A summary of the experience could be a useful task, even if not required, just as in other projects.

The visual nature of this work placement file could also link into other areas of work e.g. linking to the portfolio.

Reflective Research Journals

These could be folders of research material which are annotated and written about and should be encouraged with a range of projects. Although they can be strongly linked with essays and dissertations, they have enormous value in other projects where significant research is required, or where the skills of visual analysis are being encouraged.

The journal or folder is not just a collection of photocopies, as often happens, nor pages of a sketchbook, but a more organized accumulation of material. Some pages copied from sketchbooks, could be included. The emphasis is on the engagement with the research and reading: the reflective thoughts.

Brainstorms of initial ideas are useful to return to at stages in the essay/dissertation development. There may be strands which are discarded early on but come back into focus later.

Time lines are important ways of contextualizing ideas. Starting quite skeletally, they can be broadened and deepened as the research continues.

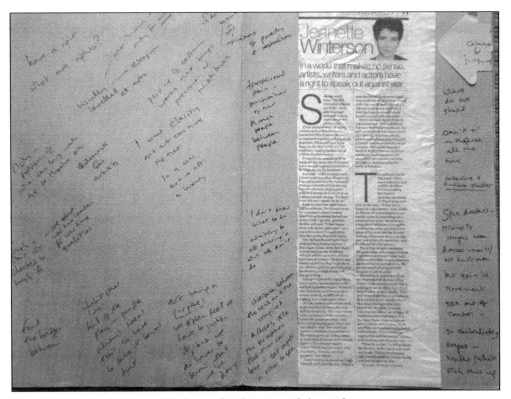

Fig. 7: Annotations on an article in a reflective research journal.

Book reviews (not on the lines of '8/10 – good read on the beach!') can begin the process of compiling literature reviews. Analysing the blurbs, the introductions and the conclusions and summarizing key themes could all be noted in the journal. Extracting possible key quotations and exploring these aids the writing of the final piece, but in the journal, writing can be free in style and personal.

Annotations on photocopies can lead to more extensive reflections and the linking with other pieces of work.

Reflective Research Journals may need, in form, to be loose-leafed, rather than bound, in order to aid organization of material. Some people may keep a folder that can be constantly added to and the order changed, but they can also keep a chronological log of reflection that mirrors the process of thoughts, researches and stages towards the final writing/work.

The Reflective Research Journal brings together the personal journey, and the more objective journeys, into research.

Dialogue Journals

A dialogue is created through the medium of the journal. This could be done informally between students or more formally between a student and a tutor (or tutors). The dialogue can extend thoughts and viewpoints, give insights, suggest new areas of work. It provides practice in writing that has to be clear to someone else. It is about talking/ writing and listening/reading – thoughtfully.

In a personal journal things are written down which the author can decipher or see the connections. Sometimes the writer has to clarify this if the journal has to be submitted, or a summary written. But with the dialogue journal the impetus of the ideas has to be captured, but written in such a way that someone else can follow the drift immediately. This does not mean it has to be formally written, with adherence to academic styles, but it has to be very clear.

For a more detailed evaluation of dialogue journals in practice, there is a useful article by Samantha Lawrie (2004), 'We have a lot to talk about: dialogue journals in graphic design education'. Erik Borg (2004), in 'Internally persuasive writing in Fine Arts Practice', while not calling the focus of his study a dialogue journal, also reveals the conversation of student and tutor through the medium of the journal.

In some ways, blogs might be seen to be a version of the dialogue journal. However it could be said that the blog is more of an equivalent to the diary. It is more personal, anecdotal, less focused, and some of the blogs on-line give a lot less than an objective response; in addition, frequently, it is not a dialogue between people who know each other. Some colleges are developing their blog activity, so more serious strands are emerging, where the contributors may know each other. There may be great benefits from working on these forms of writing.

Whether it is on paper or on-line, the principles of talk, write, listen and share are all very positive and productive areas of writing.

One of the best examples of the dialogue journal (but not called that) would be John Berger and John Christie's *I send you this Cadmium Red*. Berger and Christie are two artists/writers who exchanged writings about personal events, inspirations, thoughts and questions. They think out loud with each other, exploring theories or hypotheses and responding to the reactions and inspirations of each other. They use visuals – photos, postcards, blobs of paint, bits of metal, etc. – to show their reasons and then spark off from these into analysis, poetry, fantasy, fact, and everything in between. The letters are unedited, with all their spontaneous reactions clearly growing in front of the reader. There is the humour and liveliness that comes from a true dialogue of talking and listening and sharing.

Various forms of the dialogue journal could be useful or beneficial at various stages. Informal exchanges between students can extend and push ideas and develop listening skills. Between tutor(s) and students they can extend knowledge of context and help push ideas deeper. The importance of this form of journal is in the pace at which it develops – which is related to the people involved. It may be time consuming but the learning curves on both sides can be phenomenal.

Double Entry Journals

One of the purposes of this form of journal is to act as a reminder of thoughts in the past and is a means of deepening reflection.

Keeping a journal and writing on just the right hand page, and not on the left (or vice versa), may seem to be wasting paper. However, this space gives you the opportunity to go back on thoughts and re-think and add to your writing. Sometimes the writing on the one side might be raw reactions to events, thoughts and ideas. The writing on the other, done at a different time, will be reflective and analytical, and register new tones of thought.

This method will suit some people, but not all.

In my own writing journals I find this process very useful. On the train going home after giving a workshop, I might write about events: some reactions have been puzzling, some hilarious; the time that something took was surprising; the direction an activity took was completely unscheduled. I write about this and then I come back to it later, sometimes a lot later, often unplanned, and can then develop ideas, be reminded of thoughts and can analyse events more clearly because I now have perspective. This looking back later from changed perspectives is at the heart of reflection, and this format of journal encourages it. It is like a dialogue – it is your own dialogue with yourself.

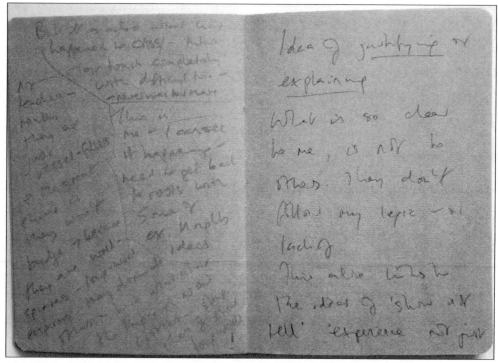

Fig. 8: An example of double entry from a journal – questions, worries, thoughts.

The Thought Book

One of the best ways into the discipline of keeping a journal is to keep a small book which just contains inspirations, odd thoughts, jottings, observations and overheard conversations.

The journal, *Creative Review* as a regular feature, printed extracts from a daily 'diary' kept by the Tate's Director of Media, Will Gompertz (2007). He had not kept a diary before, but detailed the ideas, links and inspirations encountered in his daily activities, and he specified that it was not a boring log of meetings and jobs.

Carrying the book around and noting ideas reinforces the value of regular writing. Getting into the habit of recording thoughts may come through this personal, small, private activity.

Finding a little book that appeals aesthetically and as a tactile object is also important.

The thought book is about logging: reflections on these thoughts come later.

Regular looking back on this potential treasure chest also helps build towards the keeping of a journal.

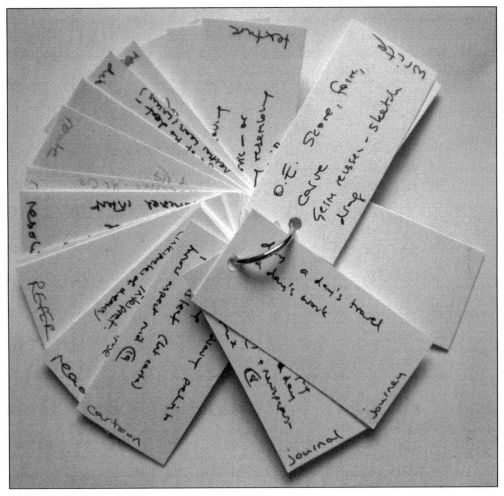

Fig. 9: Little book with big thoughts.

The Daily Detail

In preparation for a long project with illustration students, where they had to create their own text to illustrate, I set a two-week journaling task to help warm up to ideas and to stimulate potential subject matter.

Each day a page had to be written about the same activity. So, it could be washing up, walking the dog, journey to work, preparing food, etc. The activity had to be done each day, then written about. The activity might be the same and the initial writing might be quite descriptive, but, after a few days, as a writer you want to challenge yourself, to find something different. You look for detail; you start to see things in varying ways; you see as others see; you change perspective; you note detail in weather; subtle difference in moods; you consult a thesaurus, etc.

The writing, at first a chore, usually becomes an exploration, a creative journey.

This is invaluable warm up to a task and it acts as a focus: a moving from general to specific; a development of the writing muscles.

The two weeks, in this case, was the Easter holiday before the project began. But this principle can be adapted to form a preamble, a warm up, or an initial lead into a project.

An artist who has extended this concept into a fascinating body of work is Rob Pepper in *The Artist's Cut* (2006). This originated from his reaction to text-heavy blogs, and he called it his 'Daily Drawing Diary'. For a year he set himself to draw something without looking at the page as he drew and this was then posted on his website. He finally published a selection of the drawings together with his written reflections on the process.

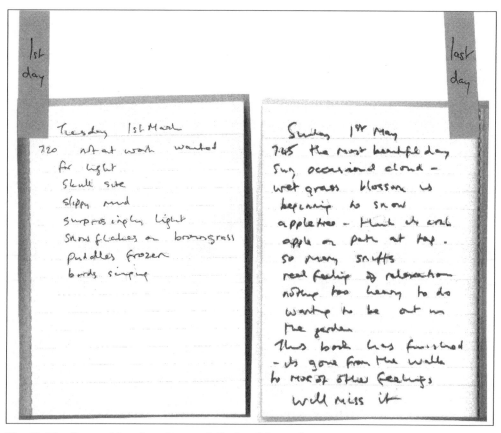

Fig. 10: The first and last days from a daily detail journal.

The Commonplace Book

This is a collection of writing, with perhaps some visuals, and with some annotations. It can be on a theme, or it can just be the ongoing collecting and noting throughout a life.

Some published ones give inspiration: Alec Guinness' *A Commonplace Book* (2001) is full of literary quotations, but often enhanced by a remark or a story that relates to his life, his work and his particular outlook as a character actor.

Joyce Grenfell's *My Kind of Magic: A Scrapbook* (2004) is a small volume, representing a fraction of her collection, and is also full of observations of characters, of mannerisms and human nature. She was a writer and a performer, creating characters based on her minute observation of people. These observations can be hilariously funny and achingly moving.

Both these published editions were compiled after their deaths, but Guinness was obviously intending publication. Grenfell intended to put one together but was so busy that she just collected and did not publish as they now appear.

This idea has many possibilities: as an ongoing sourcebook idea, and as a repository for observations, both verbal and visual.

So is it like the sketchbook or the journal?

In some ways it could be like either– perhaps more wordy than the sketchbook usually is, and perhaps more literary than the journal might be. The journal might have more of the reflective thought about processes, and the commonplace book more a reflection on specific pieces and occasions.

The form it takes is individual. In his introduction, Guinness writes of buying expensive books, which were lovely objects in themselves. He filled a few pages, then left them. After many years he changed tactics and bought cheap exercise books which he then filled and annotated easily. Is there a lesson here? The beautifully crafted paper calls for beautifully crafted writing and we do not do that instantly. Therefore the scrappy little book allows scrappy, lively writing. Maybe some people will fill the beautiful books with their crafted and honed pieces. But nearly all of us need the rough work book, which we can treat roughly and which does not frighten us. We run it; it does not run us.

One year I bought a big fat diary with a page per day – a beautifully bound book. But it was purchased half way through the year when the shop felt it was not going to sell as a diary, so I got it cheap. It was such a tactile, delicious book that I randomly opened pages and wrote in my favourite quotations or phrases that had just come up in my current reading. After a while, I forgot to put anything into it. I then discovered it a few months on and felt huge delight in reading the nuggets I'd laid down earlier. I added more. Then came another gap – and so this process will go on. It will keep me going for years and will always be an inspiration to get me going and also a record of changing influences and inspirations. There is space to write notes, ideas and thoughts after each entry, so this will, over time, also provide a useful, but more importantly, interesting collection of viewpoints as I get older.

Visual artists and designers might create their own version of the rather literary commonplace book. Graphic designer, and all round inspirer, Alan Fletcher, created books which are in this vein. *The Art of Looking Sideways* (2001) and *Picturing and Poeting* (2006) represent his particular melange of the found, the curious and the observed, and his work through serendipity and thoughtful juxtaposition. His own words, and those he chooses to use to complement his choices, reveal depths of reflection as well as great knowledge, and of fun and creativity, through a lightness of touch.

In *Inspirational Objects,* Alison Milner (2005) has created a book that is useful for the writing practice I advocate, as will be explained shortly, but it, too, is possibly a version of the commonplace book.

She has collected objects for years and, for her book, had them photographed. The photographs were taken in a consistent manner – all objects placed on a neutral background, and all in black and white. There is a small page number at the bottom of the page. Objects are juxtaposed against each other or classified with others, and that becomes a major part of the intention and effect of the book.

The second half of her book, on different coloured paper, has short writings about these objects and the page number can link the reader to the appropriate piece of writing. Some writing is pure description; some is about the historical significance of the object; some is about aesthetic qualities; some is about a specific memory that the object stimulates; some is factual and analytical; some is fictional and imaginative.

In terms of writing, this is a very stimulating collection. The variety of styles of writing is fascinating and inspires the idea of collections and writing: writing about your own collections of source material.

A fashion person might have a sample book – developing out from the swatch, but with words about colour, feel, weave, print, drape qualities and possible uses, and the memories of the garment the fabric came from or contributed to.

A product designer might photograph objects as Milner did and relate to shapes, forms, nature influencing design', etc.

There might be photographs of objects, or of scenes; of hands, of leaves, of driftwood or flotsam and jetsam, of dust …

All these sorts of ideas are constantly suggested by tutors to students in terms of keeping collections as inspirations. What I am suggesting is a slight extension of this – with some form of writing, for some, or all, of the visuals.

It is practice in writing, but in an enjoyable and personal way, and really helps with conquering the fear of never being able to articulate about your work and the inspirations behind it.

Scribbling about something helps form its own vocabularies.

Little Books

One way of engaging through writing is writing little bits, and one of the best ways into this is through the creation of little books.

These can take a myriad of forms – according to subject, stage of the course, and the inclinations of the writer.

A good way of engaging with new vocabulary is to keep a little vocabulary book – using perhaps the crammer books (used for revision at school) but which are also like flick books used in storyboarding and animation.

When you come across a difficult word, look it up – dictionary, thesaurus, word history, etc: get into the word – write it down on a page in your little book. Scribe some notes on meanings or bits of it that intrigue. Incorporate a visual device to help.

Keep adding to this book, keep the book on you, keep referring to it, and gradually the words begin to sink in.

The words that have blocked – the words you have to look up time and time again – are not embedding themselves in your memory, because simply looking up a word is not active enough. Writing it down, interpreting it, playing with it, and then referring to your own word book again and again will help you to log it into your own personal word bank.

Fabrics, papers, metals, colours, paints, dyes – all can have little books made about them: collections of material and the words generated around them – not in sentences, not in essays, but reflective, personal descriptive, creative words.

Starting writing is the hardest part, most people think. So starting from what you love, what you hoard, what inspires you – that is the point of encouraging the keeping of little books, in all their various formats. They may never be assessed but they are treasuries for the future.

It may be that you use a bought book, or it may be that you create or make a book (perhaps from the materials you collect), or you make your book adaptable so that it can be added to, or separated and then re-bound.

Little books that are active collections of words and things.

Folio of Writing

In the teaching of most art and design subjects students have to produce a portfolio of work: this nearly always represents the visual and practical areas of the work. An additional aspect of the portfolio could be a folio of writing.

The folio of writing could be accumulated throughout the course. This folio would include a wide range of writing 'exercises' or experimentations that could link to the professional world, but also be about the personal developmental journey that has been undertaken. It could also include extracts from any of the books kept – commonplace, dialogue, daily detail, etc.

Throughout his passionately written *Why We Make Art and why it is Taught*, Richard Hickman (2005) emphasizes the desirability of the 'learner centred' role in the development of wide-ranging work, and this is the impulse behind the idea of the folio of writing: compiled in exactly the same spirit – the individual voice of the artist's creating and writing.

Many students say about essays: 'Well I'll never have to write one of those again', and therefore, never look at them again. Later in the course, a dissertation may have to be written and this becomes a huge obstacle, rather than something that has been built towards. After it is written many people feel warmer towards it, but still may never feel they will show it to anyone else. What the folio of writing would encourage is the attempt at a wide range of pieces of writing that could be of personal relevance: a review of an exhibition attended, as if being written for one or more of such publications as *Time Out*, *The Guardian*, *Wonderland*, *Dazed and Confused*, *Art Review*, *Blueprint*, etc. (therefore using contrasting styles of language); a letter of application for a job; a set of instructions for an aspect of workshop practice (e.g. from a pattern cutter to machinist, or from an artist to print maker); a book review; a case study of a company; a comparison of brands; a visual and written analysis of a shopping complex; design plans for a new exhibition space; a consumer profile; an artist's interview: or, most importantly, creative writing (which is a major influence on the work of many artists and designers). Students and tutors could create ther own list from this and other lists.

Many pieces might be written early on in a course, but the Folio would encourage the revisiting of them and the opportunity for re-writing later. This is one of the best ways of learning about and improving your writing. It helps with editing, reflecting on styles, and encourages self criticism. These are skills that *can* be acquired, and this re-working means a constant evaluation of your own writing and ongoing reflection and practice.

In addition, this relates to the ideas of Reflective Learning Journals. They encompass the values to be nurtured in education: reflection; moving deeper in learning; becoming more independent; practising; stretching learning; not taking a surface approach; and creatively exploring ways of recording ideas in order to communicate effectively with a wide range of people – personally, educationally and professionally.

Reflectionnaires

Reflectionnaires is a new word combining reflection and questionnaires. And that is what they are:

- they are used to help start thinking of questions, to help think about things that haven't really been considered before
- they are a way in – not an end in themselves
- they stimulate active reflection – not just a mechanical answering of questions, as can happen with questionnaires
- they need thought; deeper exploration of the past; reasons for why things are as they are; why you think in certain ways, and do as you do; and then, how things can be used or changed for the future.

Where a questionnaire asks:

- What do YOU think/do?
- How do YOU work/learn?
- What are YOUR inspirations?

Reflectionnaires use 'I'.

So the questions are all questions you ask of yourself.

Just this personalization of the question helps ownership of the answers. You are less likely to lie or prevaricate or skirt the truth if 'I' is in the question and the answer.

Reflectionnaires are created for many of the workshops and are usually fairly short to get the brain and the imagination going.

They are also used to help prepare ideas for statements or summaries. The intention is that, while they are offered in workshops, they are a tool that can be adapted and used in all sorts of areas of work at other times.

Many people like them as it helps focus ideas.

It helps challenge the ways of working that have always been followed in the past.

Questions are asked that have not been thought of before.

Some people have called them quizzes – but not meaning that they are competitive – there are no rights and wrongs and they cannot be marked.

A few samples are given in Section 2, but they are infinitely adaptable to different subject areas, and occasions.

Postcards

Postcards are a theme throughout this book: used in their blank form to write on; examples collected in published books; used as starting points; copies of paintings from galleries; nostalgic reprints of bygone eras; old greeting cards; and early photographs printed and sent as personal letters.

Frequently, students are asked to write feedback at the end of a session on a postcard. I have never encountered negative reactions to this – the card is not too big and therefore they don't have to write too much if they can't think of anything much to say, although some run out of space and use the card as a writing journey in itself. Others take on the style of the holiday postcard in what they say and that in itself can be interesting and the styles of writing generated can be used as a starting point for discussion.

Even today, when fewer postcards are sent because of e-mail and mobile phone texts, the postcard is still received, and usually sent, with a sense of pleasure.

Ringo Starr's *Postcards from the Boys* (2004) reprints some of the postcards he collected over a period of years from the other Beatles. They were sent with a purpose, perhaps a quest for particular pictures and funny or cryptic or supportive messages. They represent a snapshot of the people, an era, and also show how this sort of writing can, or may, be a consistent means of communicating between people.

Beth Nelson's *Postcards from the Basque Country* (1999), is a mixture of personal writing and memories, creative ideas, research, drawings, painting, collage, photographs on one person's voyage/journey in search of roots and histories. The title calls on the idea of writing from one place as an invitation to come to another place, as in 'wish you were here'. This book could also constitute an example of an artist's journal.

Postcard fairs show another aspect of collecting and of a curiosity with their wealth of social information.

Artist Tom Phillips, who has collected a vast number of postcards on all subjects and styles, showed some of these in an exhibition in 2004, at the National Portrait Gallery entitled: 'We are the People'. Categorizing these anonymous postcards was an inspiring aspect in itself. Social history comes alive through these postcards. They reveal memories, social backgrounds and shared stories, all of which can be used to engage writing.

Postcards can stimulate:

- creative writing with imaginative stories
- questions to generate research
- reflection on personal histories and memories.

I also use a few photographic postcards that represent a process in the early years of the twentieth century when photographers had their own snapshots printed onto postcards and sent through the post. This always elicits a discussion, usually beginning with who owned such cameras and what sections of society are represented here. The stories that are revealed or hinted at in these postcards again stimulate writing and reflective thought and areas for research.

Postcards of paintings are useful in many ways, particularly as a means of generating writing about an art subject, with each person having a card that is easily passed round. The postcards can initiate a useful debate on the issue of galleries having to produce these artefacts to raise revenue. Visitors often spend more time choosing their postcard in the shop than they did standing in front of the original painting. They are collected as evidence of a visit, as a reminder of an experience – but what experience?

Yet, frequently, the reproductions on these postcards are appalling, with the colours totally wrong, and the regular postcard size gives no idea of the size of the original.

But talking can be stimulated, and that can lead to writing, which might be opinionated and quick and initially superficial, but it can lead to deeper thought, more research, and then on to reflections that transcend the original experience.

Postcards link to holidays – usually pleasurable. They are a brief note to people you know well, with a cliché such as 'wish you were here, weather fine, food good …' and often with a story attached – to be followed up on your return.

They are far removed from essay writing and therefore their format can be a non-threatening way into writing. Being asked to fill in a postcard does not seem to be a huge writing task, but is enough to get the brain and writing hand warmed up.

So within this simple format are ideas for great journeys into writing.

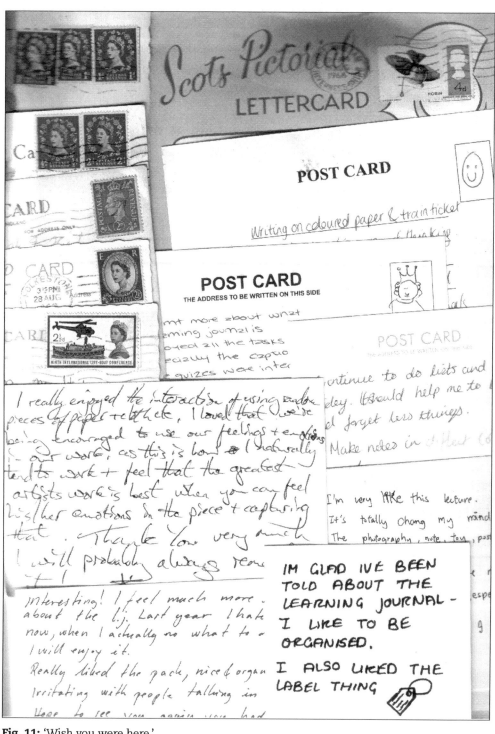

Fig. 11: 'Wish you were here.'

Visualizing Ideas through Metaphors and Analogies

Throughout this book, the idea of process is constantly emphasized and sometimes, in wanting to explain something, I invent, or expand my idea through use of a visual metaphor or analogy. Some of these are more successful than others: some are instantly comprehensible to the whole group; some work for a few students and leave others cold; some are not 'quite there' but in the presenting of them, an understanding is gained. The discussion itself can be valuable – this process of explanation is more engaging and more hands-on.

So some of the visual methods offered here are tried and tested. Some are difficult to present in a written form at a distance from the reader – therefore some have been illustrated.

But the spirit of metaphors is that everyone can invent their own or adapt others to suit the situation.

Metaphor can, as comparison with something other than the original, help us to see structures differently, or explore hidden implications and this can be particularly useful in understanding writing.

It is not about 'one size fits all'.

Take it off the peg and adapt to suit.

Fig. 12: The creative process according to Big Bird.

Big Bird and the Creative Process

Big Bird is a puppet, made from everyday items. She is used to explain and show the idea of incubation in the creative process.

When reading up on the creative process, the word incubation struck me as being the key to what students often struggle with in their design work, and also in writing.

In order to link the two areas and to try to make a point, not by just lecturing at, but by drawing in and also raising a laugh, I created and used Big Bird (see Fig. 12).

In my interpretation the Creative Process has four stages:

- The first is identifying the task, and researching and generating ideas.
- The second stage is a period of incubation when the work that you have done goes round and around in your head. It is important to let the brain make connections, and to absorb all of this material. Therefore you often find yourself sleeping on it, day dreaming, but also you often feel in a muddle. It is an odd time, with spurts of energy, troughs of inactivity, and feeling lost: a chaotic scary time.
- But then comes the third stage: after incubation of all the work, there can be a *Eureka* moment or a series of moments when it does all begin to come together and you can start to focus on the work itself. The egg has been laid and has hatched out.
- The final stage is of verification – testing, checking and fine tuning.

These stages are very broadly painted but the principles behind them are important. The research cannot come last, there has to be preparatory work, and there also has to be that 'muddly' time.

I introduce Big Bird pecking around, doing the research, picking up bits and pieces. Then she settles down, and her head droops and she sleeps. Then she wakes and lays an egg – the *Eureka* moment. Then she again checks and pecks around the 'work'.

It is a tenuous analogy – but the humour works. Everyone understands what I am getting at without me going into a lot of detail. Done in a workshop session on time management, research and reflecting on learning styles, this is often the most memorable part. Remember Big Bird? And everyone remembers the chaotic stage and the necessity for incubation.

For many people it is reassuring to have it affirmed that if you have done all the preparatory work, a period of chaos is natural. So often there is the response – 'no one ever told me that before'.

The use of a visual, and perhaps humorous, analogy allows discussion and dialogue about the creative process.

Context: the Metaphor

The visual metaphor that was devised to begin to explore the word 'context' or 'contextual' has raised much debate. This may be a metaphor that, only *through discussion*, opens up the layers of meanings.

On some courses the theory side of a subject is called *Contextual* Studies. But frequently, everyone has differing views of what this means. For most assessment requirements students are asked to contextualize their work but can flounder as to what that really implies and how important it is to understand the implications of their work. Some are frightened by the word and perhaps close down the potentialities of their work as a result. This word, more than many other words, also reveals the differing approaches that we can have to a word, and which also depends on the context in which we are using it, so it is a good word to use in a debate on the processes of writing. The process of writing is about the exploration of thoughts and ideas, through research, through differing styles of writing, in writing publicly and privately, promotionally and reflectively.

The visual metaphor of context is presented as a 'model' which is built up of layers of concentric shapes of differing coloured paper, fastened together in the middle by a paper fastener (see Fig. 13).

- the explanation starts in the middle with 'I' or 'you' represented by the paper fastener
- then thinking about *where* 'I' is located – at the desk, in a room
- and this also relates to *when* – now, at this point in the term, in this year
- the next layer out is where the room is located – the house, the street, the town
- the time is the university term, or the summer, or the run up to a General Election
- layers out from this could link to exhibitions that have been visited
- or books read
- or people seen and talked to
- then a piece of work that may have been influenced by the work of someone who lived 100 years ago
- investigation has located them in their time and space: the history, the social conditions, the politics, the literature, the art, the music, the housing, the factories, the materials available … etc., etc.

There is no single explanation or two dimensional way of explaining this. But the attempting of it, the making it into three or multi-dimensions sets off the thoughts that more clearly justify the contextualization of all work.

This model is used to underpin some of the processes that affect writing and which permeate this book. These include how text can be worked on, arrived at, and the thought and research behind it, and the considerations of time and period, of place of publication, or role within a project; but it may also help with other cultural and theoretical considerations. It also links back to Race's (2005) 'ripple in the pond' image for learning.

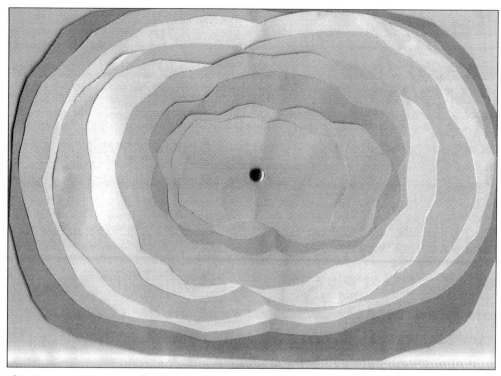

Fig. 13: A contour map of context.

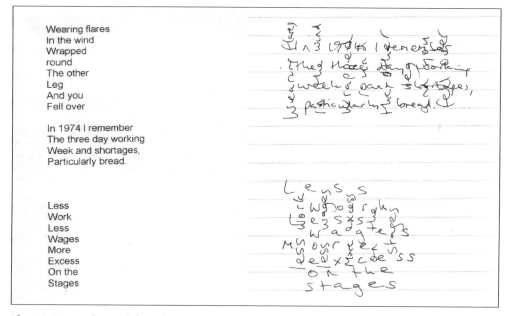

Wearing flares
In the wind
Wrapped
round
The other
Leg
And you
Fell over

In 1974 I remember
The three day working
Week and shortages,
Particularly bread.

Less
Work
Less
Wages
More
Excess
On the
Stages

Fig. 14: Memories and facts interwoven.

Context Linked to Writing Processes

The context of a word in a sentence gives some of its meaning. This also links to the context around an artefact or an advert or an expression and which gives it its meaning. There are often many interpretations that need to be considered.

Here are just two examples to amplify this.

Writing
I am writing this text – here and now, with a pencil.

When I put this text on the computer, it changes – the typeface gives it a different appearance to the handwritten scribble with its crossings-out. It has also changed in the sense of time: from the thinking-writing, writing in the present, to the copying of text and slight modifications and editing that occurs later.

When it appears on a page as part of a piece, it links in with other points and arguments. It has become a further step away from the writer.

When it appears in an article or book it becomes a small part of a big world.

In editing you have to think of the context: so telling a joke when you know who will read the text is different from telling the same joke to anonymous readers – where, often, it will not work.

We sometimes feel that a piece of writing has inspiring ideas locked away in its subject. And that links to the idea of text (and thus context). 'Text' comes from the Latin word *texere*, to weave – so that ideas are woven into the text – sometimes loosely, sometimes fixed (see Fig. 14).

Tear
She had a tear in her eye when she read the letter.

The tear in his jacket was evidence of the struggle.

'Tear' appears in both sentences but is pronounced differently in each and has different meanings. But other words in the sentence also are ambiguous.

So these sentences can become loaded and have other interpretations or words that the writer might need to work on in order to make the context clear.

e.g:

> 'the letter' could mean correspondence, or just one letter – as in L, which might have a particular significance in certain contexts.

or:

'struggle' could mean the physical – as in a fight; or that he had put on so much weight that the jacket wouldn't fit; or his struggle to look presentable, when really he preferred casual clothes.

This raises points about accidental or deliberate misunderstandings when the wording is not clear.

Even the word 'clear', in my handwriting, made the c and l come together and look more like a 'd'. So, **'clear'** becomes **'dear'**.

And **'tear,'** badly written, becomes **'fear'**.

Stories

Along with several other key themes in this book, stories permeate the whole.

Whenever we want to explain something difficult, we form it as a story.

Instinctively we try to explain the mysterious through story.

Story is not fiction, it is interpretation.

Whether as tellers of tales or listeners to lyrics, story infuses our existence.

I often tell stories to explore a point and metaphors have been given a whole section of their own, as I use them to communicate my thoughts and interpretations. Readers are encouraged to invent their own stories as mnemonics or as aids to understanding something more complex.

Robert McKee in *Story* (1999), writing principally about scriptwriting, makes some generalizations about them that are particularly apt for the principles of this book:

Story is about principles, not rules
I have tried not to be didactic about ways of doing things – not to set rules in stone, but to paint broader pictures and backgrounds.

Story is about eternal, universal forms, not formulas
A formula smacks of something neat and possibly shallow. Some of the points I make might seem simple, but they are not meant to be formulaic and prescribed. It is up to each reader to make ideas their own through adaptation, use and experimentation. Formulas are fixed; forms are not.

Story is about respect, not disdain for the audience
In the writing of this book I am aware of a possibly mixed readership, and therefore the tales, the parallels, the visual allusions, have to appeal to most, and not alienate anyone – at least not through disrespect. If anyone disagrees with points, and enters into debate, that is great: that is part of the dialogue.

Story is about originality, not duplication
Although copying is a word that crops up at times, it is not in the sense of fakery: it is more about copying in order to understand, so that you can then go on to make something your own, something original, having learnt from others. Originality is also to do with finding the personal voice, and that is a constant theme of this book.

There are stories behind inspirations; stories of objects and their owners; of photographs and what they tell us; and of writers and their struggles to tell us their tales.

And telling tales, here, is not telling lies.

Reading

Reading's Role in Writing

Reading good writing is part of the writing process.

It is not always about reading for the direct relevance of the content to the project which you are doing: the research, the background facts, the analysis of the artist's oeuvre. It might be about reading the rambles of the author, absorbing the anecdotes, immersing yourself in inspirational word art.

Reading good writers helps you aspire to transcribe your ideas in ways that might be non-traditional, unorthodox, rule breaking, but goal shifting – thus doing your words, and your work, justice.

Instead of always reading the set texts, the traditional readings about movements in art, definition of '-isms', etc., read the poetry, the stories, the reflections. Mix the standard essay, chapters, theses, etc., with the imaginative, the personal, the revelatory.

This is why there are so many creative writers quoted in this book, because their skill in writing can shed new perspectives on the subjects being studied. Many of these writers were also very knowledgeable about the visual or performing arts and their writings are energetic and stimulating.

It will not always be easy – but good writing makes you want to unknot the ideas and try to find the layers alluded to. Good writing can be transparent, translucent, dense, layered, fragile, deeply crafted, questioning, light or fleeting. Whatever it is, it always actively involves the reader in the process.

Some of us, when talking to others, unconsciously take on some of the speech mannerisms or regional accents of the person to whom we are speaking. It is neither copying nor criticism, but is a natural part of the dialogue. Reading can have similar effects. After reading one author, any writing that we do might have tones, or nuances of that writer. That is one way we learn. We absorb and then work on something and make it our own.

This need not be associated with plagiarism. If we read enough writers, think enough, practice our own writing, in all manner of ways, we will not be plagiarizing (in the sense of using and not acknowledging), but learning to craft our writing in the way of 'writers'.

The Reading Muscle

There is a reading muscle and this clearly links to physical exercise.

With physical exercise you start slowly and easily. You warm up. You gradually do exercises, and you learn how to do them properly. You start with a few particular, and simple, movements and then build up, as your stamina increases.

Then you extend your repertoire of exercises.

Different texts require different applications of the reading muscle. So although we can all read, we need to build our muscles to read different sorts of texts. This applies to style, length, vocabulary and conventions. Understanding these conventions is a major part of the technique of being able to do the exercise.

You don't start with the most difficult or complex, or ones which need more skill.

Sometimes you do need to plunge into something harder – and you don't understand it all, but it gives you something to work towards, to give you a sense of where you are trying to get.

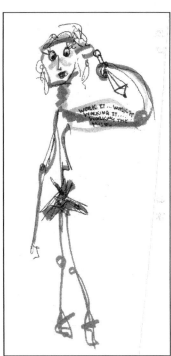

This is the direct analogy to physical exercise.

But if you do the harder exercise at the wrong time, it can be damaging – you strain something, or you get into the wrong habits.

Who builds the muscle? Only you. No one else can build your muscles.

Other people can help train you, guide you, but not do it for you.

In reading and writing we need to **break down** difficulties and then **build up** abilities and skills.

Fig. 15: Reading and writing biceps.

Disagree-able Reading

There is a great value in reading something that you disagree with, as well as that which you totally agree with, as the disagreeable makes you re-evaluate ideas and points of view and things we take for granted.

The following notes about one disagreeable reading show some of my reflections on this specific text. I describe the negative, and then try to find the positive values for my own work (these are in italics).

- He starts with the nearly finished written piece, works backwards and then skips over vital parts. *The parts of the process need identifying.*
- There is mention, but not really detailed about how or what that practice could be. *The aim of my book is to provide examples of this.*
- There are odd points about keeping a commonplace book – *which reminds me of the value of this and that I must write about it.*
- There are very detailed chapters on certain parts: e.g. on paragraphs and various grammatical aspects. These have been identified as needing attention, but they are so detailed that they would lose unconfident writers. *I do not want to do this.*
- Whole chunks of difficulty are dismissed in single lines: 'Just do ...' *But that is the tricky part and that clarifies for me what is being attempted in my book.*

Sometimes finding yourself disagreeing with something you are reading helps you to realize how much you know, or what your feelings or views are, and this then forces you into justifying them: you have to argue your case and that can help clarify your point. You have to find evidence to back up your ideas. It can help you to see what your particular viewpoint is.

So the moral of the tale is that if you read something, and then find you disagree with it – keep going: it may galvanize you into writing even more than does the piece you agree with and which seems to have said it all.

Fig. 16: Breaking through the pain barrier.

Practice and Process

The Practice of Regular Reflective Writing

One of the main benefits gained from writing reflections regularly (try saying that out loud, quickly!) is that it often gives you the spur for the next thing to do, as however fired up you are about a project or some other work you are undertaking, there are days that start with 'What shall I do – this or that?', and sometimes you can end up doing nothing.

One of the values of writing about feelings and thoughts at the beginning of the day is that it can inspire the direction to take. Alternatively, or as well as, summing up or reflecting at the end of the day, may well give the clue as to what to do the next day. I have often found, when I am in the middle of a writing project, that deciding what I am going to do the next day, means that I wake up, knowing what I've got to do and so get going more easily. If I wake up and, in those waking moments, there are too many voices going in many different directions, the temptation is to stay in bed a bit longer, to prevaricate, and the energy of the day drifts away.

These are my ways, and sharing these, and being open to how others write or talk about what they do, is often a way into finding out how you can do something.

The novelist John Steinbeck, when writing *East of Eden*, kept a journal (2001). He used this journal as a warm-up to writing. In it he wrote letters to his editor about the progress of the work in which he discussed his thoughts about character and plot development. He logged the blocks, and the dilemmas he was having. But he did not send these letters; he hadn't meant to when he started writing them. They were a device to help him practice and warm up to the creative process of writing the book. Later he did show them to his editor. But visualizing who he was writing to had helped him work on this internal dialogue: it made him express his thoughts. He needed that debate and could create the environment for himself. That was his way.

Acknowledging that this regularity is a slog is also part of it. Creativity sparks within the routine, the smog, the mundane, or even just in the trying.

How many meanings are there to 'trying'? This is not a rhetorical question: the attempting, as well as the frustration, are actually fundamental parts of the practice, along with the creativity.

Practice and Inspiration

The whole issue of creativity and inspiration makes for a fruitful discussion. The processes of creativity (written about elsewhere under 'Big Bird') involve a collecting and sifting and sorting of information, both at first and second hand, using both primary and secondary research. But research can also be about practice – therefore often what is being encouraged is the active experimentation and practice of work: researching how a line varies, how colours collide or collude, and this may then lead to research into artists who explored in similar ways, and might also include a study of *their* writings about these journeys.

Linked to the keeping of the reflective journal is the issue of reading. Writing is improved by reading, if that reading is active. The dialogue with the text – the annotating, the extracting and working on specific points of the writing encourages further reading. It emphasizes that reading is not instant, nor is the full comprehension of the layers of meaning in a text. Annotating a text for yourself, graffitiing it if you need to, questioning it, celebrating it, leads to excitement and confidence with text.

Annotating your own copy is fine but we all have experience of borrowing a library book and finding other people's annotations which divert you from the text itself. This will frequently happen when a tutor has recommended something to a whole class and the text is too long to economically photocopy, or there are few copies of the text available. As a reader, you find yourself disagreeing or being alienated from the text because of their comments. You read the text with annoyance and diversion. This is destructive when this is your first reading of the original text. Later you might enter into a dialogue/response with the other reader, but initially you need to read it for yourself, by yourself. The dialogue is with yourself and the writer/author.

Reflection is also about considering what your own inspirations and triggers are, and how, as individuals, we vary in this according to a whole range of differing circumstances. When filling in a personal statement when applying for a job, or for a place at university, you often have to write about what inspires you. I have found that this question causes much soul searching with the initial answer, 'Well I really don't know – what do they mean, what do they want to hear?'

One way of unlocking some self knowledge, and also giving ideas for further development, is to read other people's writings or comments. Artists' statements frequently begin with what inspired either this work or their work in general, therefore an understanding of what lies at the root of your own work is important.

These roots can also be one of the key ways to unblock creativity. If you are able to identify that a particular activity such as walking in a wood, or sitting at a pavement café, or going to an exhibition, reading comics or watching rubbish on the television, is an effective route to galvanize your own creative juices, then it is crucial to pursue this for those many times when the block occurs.

Practice and Blocks: Finding the Right Words

A block to writing, and a feature that also comes with age, is the endless searching for the right word. Just as you come to it, the word flies away – you can almost see it going, but what it was is a mystery. The harder we search, the more we concentrate, the less likely it is that the word will come.

In a way, this is where some of the writing exercises come in – they loosen up, they also encourage the carrying on of writing, even when you can't get that word. The important thing is not to stop. Some of this is also to do with vocabulary: writing and then pushing yourself to find a good word, or an adequate word, is sometimes the spur to deepening vocabulary. Talking can sometimes have the same benefit – as conversation creates a joint fund of words.

But mostly it is about practice. With designing or drawing, if you cannot find a 'solution' you keep working on it till you do – so, isn't writing the same?

In a way the *trying* to do something is also part of the way. *Wanting* to do it, *wanting* to find the expression. There is no cure-all. There is no one answer to finding the right word. But it's about practising the strategies to finding the words.

> I cannot write any more, and indeed I cannot: ... But how it rolls into a tight ball the muscles in my brain! (Woolf 1987: 167)

Virginia Woolf here emphasizes the physical and mental hard work: and many other writers say the same. Some of it is about stamina; some of it is about perseverance; and then some of it is about the reward of it all coming together. But we have to build the *want* to find answers/solutions.

Reflective writing emphasizes feelings: this can be in the form of a dialogue with the self, which can help with blocks, and inspirations, because it is trying to find form, expression, etc. So stream-of-consciousness writing can be a help with this.

We have to go with instincts. Woolf again:

> ... I've just typed out my morning's work; and can't feel altogether sure. There is *something* there (as I felt about Mrs Dalloway) but I can't get at it, squarely (Woolf 1987: 147)

And a little later she writes words that resonate with us all:

> Yesterday I had conviction; it has gone today.

But you keep going. One of the main reasons for writing this book is to offer some of the things that might help you find the practical hints, or exercises that will help you keep going.

Instant or Real

Writing is not instant: not in the learning of the skill, nor in its practice and its outcome.

The faster our lives go, the speed with which we develop labour-saving devices, and demand leisure-filling pursuits, the more the mechanics of doing something are refined, the greater the wish for everything to be instant. We want instant results/effects, for minimum input.

Instead of garbage in, garbage out (gigo), perhaps it should be 'minimum effort, minimum effect' – but we ask for minimum effort, *maximum* effect. Not for nothing is this acronym 'me me'.

While most people accept the need to work at, and practice, some skills relating to their subject, in the area of writing they want, and expect, instant results and, what is more, successful results.

I liken this to coffee or wine. Coffee can be made from instant granules, but is it really coffee? Or coffee flavoured, manipulated, hot water. Water that drips through the coffee grounds, through a filter, or in a cafetière does not produce instant coffee: the water has taken time to extract the essence of the coffee. It is water no longer. It is real coffee.

So, you want a coffee? You can have one instantly (the flavoured), or you can wait for a real one.

So, too, with wine: you can have grape juice or you can wait for wine.

This analogy may be slightly flawed but the principle is true.

Supermarkets have encouraged the availability of instant food, and we have become ignorant of origins, growth and timescales.

Many people want supermarket writing: pay your pound and receive instant iterations.

But writing has stages: odd thoughts; ideas; jottings; brainstorms; lists; associations; research; rough drafts; playing around with words, with the order; re-structuring; cropping; pruning; editing; polishing; and the arriving at a final draft which is eventually handed in. Looking at it later, you could tweak it again or pinch and prod.

In fact the process may never end, although you often have to call a halt, sometimes because of a deadline, but often it is that you move on: on to another piece.

The more you produce, the more eloquent, the more controlled, the more expansive, the more crystallized the work can become.

The writing encouraged in this book develops over time – it may be rough and quick and instant in the early stages, but then it is pored over and matured.

Writing is about a journey from the first draft to the last.

The Writer: Self and Others

Talk Write

Many times in this book I will refer to something leading to discussion, or that a word or idea will stimulate a debate and questioning.

I think that one of the best ways into writing is through talking. If ideas are generated and talked about in a stimulating way, then writing can be encouraged to grow out of this. It is therefore important that writing does follow such conversations. This reiterates my point about having something to write about. It might be that some of the writing is quick, is in bullet points, is part in note form – but the point is that writing occurs and later you may want to go back through notes and write on them more reflectively, more deeply, or after research.

The writing of personal statements is really hard, so the best way into this is through talking about yourself to someone who feeds certain questions and shows an interest in the answers. You do not always realize that you have a strength in a particular area, or that a personal interest is worthy of putting in a statement. The talking to someone, which is a form of interview, is a good device to lead into writing, and often proves to be a way that you can use in future to get writing going.

The idea of interviewing has many other applications. I often interview myself, sometimes out loud, while walking my dog. The questions and the attempts at answers reveal layers of ideas that were previously subconscious.

Interviewing is an art and John Tusa's book, *On Creativity* (2003), has a wonderful section on the act of interviewing. He reveals the amount of research and the level of preparation he undertakes before he interviews an artist. But he then talks of the fact that all this background allows him to follow in whatever ways the artist might lead. It is a dialogue and the discoveries that the artists make when they articulate ideas in a particular way can be as valuable to them as to the interviewer.

> Hearing them deviate from (the questions) is joy – the element of surprise, the opening of real dialogues, the opportunity for discovery. Something new has surfaced, something that I did not know might be said, something that my interviewee may only have thought of in response to my questions. There are the moments when the interview becomes such a rich experience. For talking face to face, person to person, is a very intimate activity. Both partners in the dialogue offer something of themselves. It is part courtship, part self-examination, part jousting, part self-justification, part self-revelation. (Tusa 2003: 267)

Analysing and Transcribing

An interview is usually a spoken dialogue, which can be taped and then transcribed. It will probably not be transcribed absolutely verbatim – with all the 'ums' and 'ers' – and it may have to be turned into proper sentences, as we often do not talk in proper sentences. So here there is a chance for practising the art of forming written material and acknowledging the differences between the spoken and the written.

The understanding of these differences in styles is most valuably done in an exercise in transcription. Analysis of different styles of interviews and their transcription and then practice in doing this, thus making a feature of the differences, is perhaps the most valuable way of understanding the variances and the appropriateness of styles for different occasions.

Talking leads to writing: even if the talking is out loud, just to yourself.

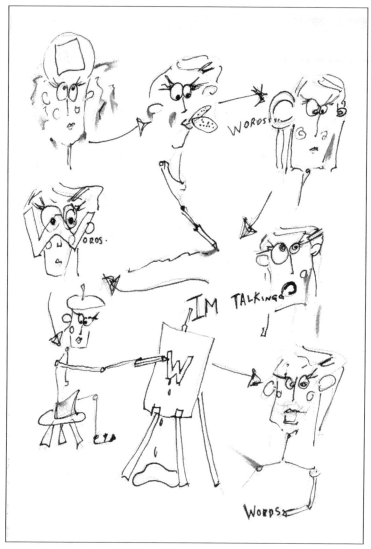

Fig. 17: Ummmm and errrrrrr.

Environment as Inspiration and Workplace

A common theme in the writing by, and about, writers, artists and designers is the importance of their working environment. *The Guardian* on Saturdays runs a feature called 'Writer's Rooms' in which a different author each week talks about the room in which they write, shown in a photograph.

Dan Crowe's *How I Write: the secret lives of authors* (2007) details the writing obsessions, places and habits of many writers.

- Will Self notes and jots ideas on Post-its, which he puts on the wall and then arranges and re-arranges them into sections – classifying them according to what he is writing.
- A.L. Kennedy has a different notebook for each book written. The notebooks are small enough to go in a pocket and are treated roughly – sometimes hurled across the room when frustration strikes.
- Isabel Young has photographs of strangers, around whom she invents stories.
- Tash Aw makes endless cups of tea: the process of making reflecting the stages of creation.
- William Fiennes doesn't have a desk of his own, but he has a cypress cone – and that travels everywhere with him.
- Nicholson Baker buys vast packs of ear plugs in order to seal out extraneous noise.
- A.M. Homes cannot write without the view of a tree.

A wonderful, eclectic list.

Inspired: how creative people think, work and find inspiration, edited by Nielsen and Hartmann (2005) has a similar survey of artists and designers, which looks at their studios and their processes of work.

Virginia Woolf's famous essay *A Room of One's Own* ([1929]1990) signified the importance of women having the chance to write in a space of their own. This does not have to always be a distinct room, but it needs to be a respected place.

What these examples show is that:

- *some employ devices and rituals to 'get them going'*
- *others de-clutter before embarking on a new project*
- *a few re-organize their collections as a warm up*
- *others gather together their sources of inspirations*
- *some play music: some play one piece over and over again*
- *others prefer silence.*
- *some hoard; some minimize*
- *some expand; some contract.*

Whatever the size of their space, they mould it to aid their creative process. Knowing what you need, and why, helps counteract THE BLOCK.

Feeding the mind is common, in some way, to all. Natalie Goldberg (1986) writes about composting – feeding the mind with all sorts of material – squirrelling it away, so that it can come out when mined/needed. So the environment is both a place and the space within you and it demands constant attention.

Finding a Voice

For some tasks, a neutral and passive voice is required; for others the core 'I' is paramount. In a world of 'me, me, me' the true 'I' is not easily found. Writing is perhaps one of the means by which it can be located and developed.

The reflective writing that is advocated so highly in this book is the nurturing of a sense of self; a questioning; a listening; a reflecting upon; a moving forward from one standpoint to another. The writing could, and should, reflect the movement of the journey and is the vehicle that enables the writer to cogitate on the process of that journey.

Some of the exercises that tap into memory are the means by which roots can be explored; seeking the formations of identity. The use of words to reflect emotions, the attempts at forming opinions and ideas, all contribute to the formation of the writer's voice.

Writing is always about communication: between 'I' and 'I'; between 'I' and 'you'; between you and others; between individuals and individuals; between officers of the state and the people. This latter example is a mass of 'I's but who are often not treated as 'I's, just as a 'they' or 'them'. In the deliberate tautology of these last two sentences are the contradictions encountered in the finding of an 'I': the acknowledgement that the 'I' has a responsibility; that the 'I' who communicates has as many responsibilities in what they do as the 'I' who listens. (Note: there are four 'I's in responsibilities.)

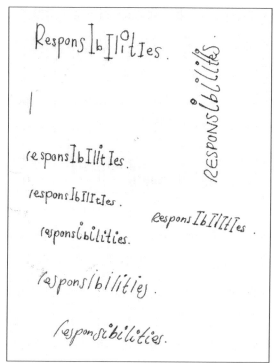

Fig. 18: Finding the I in responsibilities.

Gesture

Dictionary definition:

> Gesture: a movement of a limb or the body as an expression of thought or feeling, or an action to evoke a response or convey intention. From Latin *gerere gest* (meaning: to wield).

Writing is the gesture of the writer's thoughts and of their very being.

Writing – in the sense of what is written, but also in the manner of the doing: the handwriting (as in the hand writing) can be an important part of the finding of the thought.

When I am spinning ideas, when I am on a roll, my writing is large, flowing, free and full of spaces, with some letters flourishing and expanding. I actually gesture with my hand as I pause to find the right word. I speak out loud to find the emphasis, and the marks on the page can end up with indications of the energy.

With the advent of computers, this visceral, physical nature of writing can be lost and that may not only stultify the writing and its content, but also remove the connection of thought to action: gesture to deed; gest as self.

Early warm-up exercises in experimenting with pens, pencils, charcoals, pastels, and varying sorts of paper, are fundamental to a loosening up of attitudes to what writing is. Many students and staff have an inbuilt fear of writing. Writing is what you are forced to do – on lined paper with a biro, neatly and legibly and evenly, and there appear to be lots of rights and wrongs in the style to be used.

Playing with implements and surfaces, forgetting the 'outcomes' of a written task, can free up writing muscles.

In workshops, I may introduce/show/talk about my favourite implements and for what tasks, and how this can affect my writing. I then encourage participants to think and write about these themselves. This can sometimes reveal blocks from the past or give explanations for difficulties or surprises about what works. Thinking about the process is useful and it also gives something to write about, which is an un-blocker for thoughts, and writing about thoughts and feelings.

So what I mean by gesture is the movement of the writer: the energy, the attitude, the direction, the thought, and the essence of the person.

One of the ways of finding these gestures of the self, the tone of voice, the character of the writing, is by exploring words, and therefore a lot of the exercises I offer start with this. This means either sharing understandings of words, which leads to greater curiosity about meanings and roots, or an appreciation of the differing effects words can have on listeners or readers. It would also include the looking up of words in a variety of sources; encouraging the use of reference sources and usually *not* the Internet. There is nothing like browsing through a book – finding what you were initially looking for, and then being distracted by first one thing, then another, and taking a circuitous and enormously pleasurable diversion through and around the word, and including impressions of the journey through that book. (That was deliberately a long sentence showing the routes and changes a journey such as that could take.)

So, even the understanding and exploring the use of the sentence, and the aids provided by punctuation, can be another way into generating a love for writing.

Just as gesture and voice are different with us all, so with the ways some people use lots of 'ums' and 'errs', and some have staccato speech and others drift, so this is also shown to exist in writing.

Therefore we can encourage the looking at:

- the asides that some writers use
- the caustic comments
- the excitement of following the line
- the pleasure in analogy
- the crispness and the precise phrase
- the typography, font, etc.
- the use of the dash – often indicating speed of thought, twists and turns
- the use of the brackets (...) more information, or a remark or comment
- the existence and proliferation of exclamation marks!!!!!
- the question mark – is it a genuine query? Or a rhetorical statement
- the lists that writers use to make their point.

The aim in these observations of writing gestures is to teach style through style.

> Making pictures of people in all sorts of situations, I learned that every feeling waits upon its gesture (Welty 1995: 85)

Fig. 19: Gestures of writing.

Viewpoint and Knowledge

It is important, as a writer, to remember our own particular perspectives, which are based on our knowledge and experiences and, therefore, inform where our writing voice is coming from.

We always have to remember the context in which something happened, and this is important in the writing and the understanding of viewpoints. In much writing that we see today, in magazines and newspapers, and also in many essays, there are huge generalizations about issues, which usually come from a lack of research or understanding of the context of a time.

However – you don't always know that you don't know something.

So perhaps the best way into this is to always assume you know nothing. That will lead to questions. So, for example, what was life like before mobile phones were so prolific, and when were they invented? We are now becoming very used to technology, and we forget just how recent some of it is. And the impact it had, and the implications of it.

I often recount a child's comment on looking at a black and white photograph: 'Was it all black and white then? Was life in black and white?'

We laugh – but actually that is not dissimilar to forgetting to take account of the time before colour reproduction and the time before photography.

Many of the practical pieces in this book are about exploring viewpoints through using visual materials, objects, time lines, talking and listening. It is not about being told there are differences, but experiencing and exploring them.

Virginia Woolf writes reflectively in her diary, relating to this idea of changing perspectives in the sense of visual perspective:

Proportions changed

That in the evening or on colourless days, the proportions of the landscape change suddenly. I saw people playing stool-ball in the meadow; they appeared sunk far down on a flat board; and the downs raised high up and mountainous round them. Detail was smoothed out. This was an extremely beautiful effect: the colours of the women's dresses also showing very bright and pure in the almost untinted surroundings. I knew, also, that the proportions were abnormal – as if I were looking between my legs (at Rodmell 1926) (Woolf 1987: 99).

Penelope Lively in A House Unlocked (2002) reflects on the differences in the way life was lived and the social history revealed through a study of old photographs:

In all these photographs the family is defined by dress. What they wear and how and where they are wearing it tells you who they are: upper class. They may be on holiday, in an isolated spot, engaged in strenuous country pursuits, but they cannot be without their badges of identity. The girls must have their matching coats and skirts, their hats, the men their tweed jackets, their collars and ties. Looking at family parties in summer Somerset today, I note that everyone is again clad very much alike – in jeans, leggings, chinos, T-shirts, trainers. But nothing tells me where the wearers fit into the social system – they are classless, anonymous. Until they open their mouths, and even then distinctions are blurred. Back in 1900 that family's dress and utterance set them apart instantly. Anyone seeing and hearing them could have told you what sort of home they occupied and their manner of living (Lively 2002: 5).

So, often it is through *reflective* writing, that these viewpoints can be considered. These ruminations lead to discovering histories, developments and changes.

But the starting point is you and your own experiences.

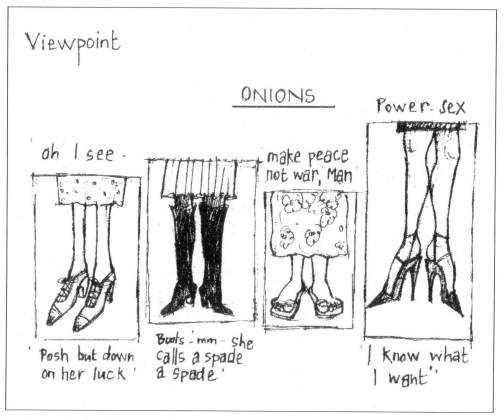

Fig. 20: 'Who shall I be today?'

Properly Informed Onions

The requirement in dissertations and essays is not for opinions about the subject, but evidence, facts, interpretations, comparisons between other writers. No hand-on-hips 'I think ... I believe ... I feel ...'

In other pieces of work, the writer's opinion is paramount: it *is* the work.

Perhaps an important point in writing is that there should be a distinction between *ill informed* and *properly informed* opinion.

Hence:

O(**pi**)nion
    properly informed

Take out the 'pi' standing for 'properly informed', and what you have is an onion which has layers and layers. It is not two dimensional or shallow, but is complex in structure.

What is being sought is a variety of sources being brought together and presented, with passion perhaps, but also an objectivity: a seeing of other sides, a balancing of views. It is about peeling back the layers.

Maybe there is not a balance. With some issues it is very hard to see balance. But there is always another viewpoint.

Some of the practical exercises look at viewpoints in a number of different ways that may give some ideas to try.

Beryl Reid, the comedy actress, famously said that she could only really find her character when she had the right shoes. Sometimes it is finding what it is like in someone else's shoes. It is about *feeling* the viewpoint: feeling and peeling back the layers (see Fig. 20).

Some other aspects of viewpoint are more cerebral, some geographical, some historical, political, etc.

Some are to do with seeing or hearing or touching.

Some are to do with differing senses of humour.

So my title for this will have amused some, irritated others, to some, drew a blank. But if you've read this far, I hope the point has been made.

2

PRACTICALS

Fig. 21: Destinations unknown.

Introduction

This is the largest section of this book and is at the core of it because it is about practice, not theory or background.

What I hope to do in here is to inspire experimentation with writing, using warm-ups and fun ideas, but giving practical ideas as to how activities could be extended and developed.

The sections are:

■ Keeping a Journal
■ Warm-ups and preparations
■ Generating ideas
■ Developing ideas
■ Starting pieces of work
■ Working towards essays, etc.
■ Structuring
■ Viewpoints
■ Final points in the writing process
■ Specific pieces of writing.

There is a logic to this order, but you can dip in as you wish. The logic relates to the process of writing that underpins this book. There may be some titles that seem related to what you are doing at the moment and need help with. There may be other titles which intrigue you.

The tone of writing in this section is quite personal. I have tried to write it almost as if I was doing a workshop – so it has asides, and attempts at humour, and personal anecdote to help some of the material seem less daunting.

A reflectionnaire is a reflective questionnaire which is meant to help you think about things that influence the way you work, what inspires you, and may give ideas of alternative things to try. The reflectionnaire has proved very helpful to many people in developing a vocabulary of questions to ask when they are asked to reflect on themselves and their work.

Give something a go. Try to put aside doubts until you have tried something.

Develop ideas in any way you wish, and do not feel you have to do exactly as I say if you are coming up with something else. The aim of all these ideas is to generate writing.

At the bottom of some of the sections is a short comment under the heading **Reflection**. This is a note which also includes any thoughts relevant to anyone running a workshop, including how something works or how it needs to be organized, or unseen benefits, etc.

Keeping a Journal

Why keep a journal?
The first point to emphasize is that a journal can be a memory aid and is a log of everything you do. Vast amounts of information are introduced and this means you cannot keep it all in your head – so this acts as a record. In order to fully take on and deepen your knowledge, you need to develop the skills of reflection on research, activities, visits, lectures, tutorials, etc. The process of keeping the reflective log leads you to assess the material you are gathering.

The journal is evidence of all the work you are doing and helps you find connections between areas. This evidence can also help you enable others to understand what you are doing and is a very useful starting point for discussion and dialogue.

The journal is a valuable tool in that it introduces the regular practice of writing in a range of styles. This skill is an essential part of your course.

What the journal is and what it is not
It is:

- personal, and can be formatted in any way that meets the criteria set by your project brief, and suits your own learning style
- about your work and how your ideas relate to the material that is presented to you on the course, and the research that you undertake
- self-initiated – you may get advice on areas to research and look at, but the motivation for keeping it and extending it comes from you
- about the reflective thoughts you have on your work, the progress of the work and how this fits into your subject area
- about initiating questions and dilemmas, and showing attempts to answer these questions.

But:

- it is not a daily log with mundane entries
- it is not purely a diary, listing events
- it is not simply descriptive about what happened to you
- it is not just visual with some basic descriptive captions to the visuals.

Practically, the journal can consist of:

- a folder of research and annotations
- a diary with reflective writing – kept regularly
- a range of little books varying from reflective writing, to analyses of texts or visual source books

- fabric books or swatches with annotations of description, technical properties and reflective thoughts on uses and possibilities
- own reviews of exhibitions visited, articles read, TV programmes and films watched
- a thought book – rough ideas, inspirations, a treasury of serendipity.

How can the journal be used as a communication tool?

The creation of the journal is for you to use to develop your work. However it has another function in that it can be used to show/demonstrate and evidence what you are doing. It might well be valuable to summarize every now and then what you have discovered and what new areas you are following, and what dilemmas you have come across. This might mean writing a one-page summary every month. You can use the contents of the journal as the material on which you can reflect. This summary will aid the tutors' understanding of your work and progress, and would contribute greatly to the final report – in a way it gives you all the groundwork for that final piece of work, which is the summation of your project.

The final report/summary/evaluation

The final report is impossible to write if you have not accumulated the stages of reflective analysis as you have progressed throughout the year(s). The evidence in your journal, the decision-making, and the contextualization of your work, contributes to the depth and range of the final report and ensures that your work shows originality and rigour and meets the needs of the world outside education, as well as your own aspirations.

The future?

Whatever format you develop, this journal could form a backbone to your future work: it gives you the means to record all the experiences you have, and it has developed in you the reflective tools of analysis and judgement, so that you can use that knowledge fully and sensitively. You are active in pursuit of innovation, not passive. You will have gained the skills of lateral thinking and are not narrow or restricted in your ideas and their implementation. It will be a valuable communication tool with other professionals and could provide the evidence of your originality and creativity; this could tip the balance in future work.

For practical ideas on what to write about in your journals, the exercises in the following sections provide many places to start.

Pick and mix
      dip in
           try out
               and then extend the ones that suit you most.

Warm Ups and Preparations

Ways of Writing: a Reflectionnaire

Have a go at doing this reflectionnaire, thinking about the way you write, how you write, what blocks you have, etc. It is NOT a test. Do as much as you can, but perhaps come back to it at another time. Often we do not think about HOW we do something, but it can be really useful to us to do so.

- What are my favourite implements to use for writing?
- What are my favourite surfaces and textures and colours to write on?
- Do I prefer lined or unlined paper for writing?
- Do I write longhand?
- And only go on the computer when it is ready?
- Or do I write straight onto the computer?
- Do I love word play/do I play with words?
- Do I work rough and fast or neat and slow?
- Is my writing small, large, tight, loose?...
- Is writing laborious or a pleasure?
- Do I write too much and go too wide and have difficulties in focusing my writing?
- Do I plan first and then write?
- Do I just write and sort it out later – or not?
- Which of these styles of writing do I enjoy or not enjoy writing: academic essays, articles, reports, fiction, poetry, abstract, personal ...?
- Which styles of writing do I like to read?
- Which writers do I like/admire?

Reflection: Doing this reflectionnaire at the beginning, or near the beginning, of a writing workshop helps focus us about the processes involved in writing. Everyone writes in different ways and there are no rights and wrongs. Exchanges of ideas and methods can help, and we all find it fascinating to discover how someone else works, and, in observing or discussing this, we might encounter ideas that we can try.

Reflectionnaire on the Thought Book

This reflectionnaire was given out after students had kept a Thought Book for a month. This was early on in Level 1. It acts as a prompt to thinking about self and ways of working, and helps focus on features that can be carried forward. It tries to move thoughts beyond 'I like it', 'I don't like it', into encouraging the asking of 'Why and why not?' Instead of it just being about the keeping of the Thought Book, it also gives questions to help with early reflection on keeping a journal.

- Did I write in my thought book?
- How often did I write?
- What sorts of things did I write about?
- Did I start and then forget?
- If so, why was this?
- Did I find it difficult to remember to do it?
- Was I not sure what to write about?

If I wrote regularly:

- Did I enjoy doing this?
- Did it get easier?
- Did I find myself looking forward to writing?
- Have I looked back over what I wrote earlier?
- What ideas has this writing given me for my work?
- Will I carry on (or if I have to, how am I going to change/adapt my ways of working)?

Reflectionnaire on the First Few Weeks of my Course

This worked as a focusing exercise at the end of a 10-week project but is a useful tool at about the end of the first semester, or half way through the first year. Some reflective writing could emerge from these prompts.

The PMI referred to in the last question is from de Bono (1996):

■ What have been the highs so far?
■ What have been the lows?
■ What did I **feel** when I started the course?
■ What do I feel now?

Strengths:

■ Identify the strengths I have found in myself in coping on the course.
■ Identify the areas I need to strengthen.

Structures:

■ The areas of the course that have I enjoyed the most – theory lectures, workshops, learning new skills, location work, research ...
■ What sorts of classes do I feel most comfortable/confident in – lectures, workshops, tutorials?...
■ How do I cope with speaking up in a group?

Time:

■ How have I managed my time so far?
■ Is there anything I need to change in the future (in regards to time management)?

Following up queries:

■ What questions do I need to ask the tutors – and which tutors should I approach?
■ If I have missed something, what have I done to catch up/find out?
■ Did this work, or do I need to do something else in the future?

Inspirations:

■ Which new practitioners (*this is where the subject can be specific*) have I found?
■ Why do I like their work?
■ Which new techniques have I discovered or learnt?

Reflective Journal:

■ What are the pluses, minuses and interesting (PMI) aspects to keeping my journal?

Reflectionnaire on Time

This is an appropriate early reflectionnaire when considering learning styles, planning and organization of work. It also relates to how and when writing is carried out, or can be related to this.

- At what times of the day do I work best?
- When do I find it hardest to work?

- Am I a **POT** (arrive in plenty of time)?

or

- A **JIT** (arrive just in time)?

or

- An **OOT** (arrive late: out of time)?

- Why is this?

- Do I like having lots of projects on the go at the same time?
- Do I have problems juggling lots of things at the same time?

- Do I have a diary or calendar to mark up project dates, etc?
- Do I put off starting things?
- How do I plan a project?

- Do I break a task or project down into different parts?
- Do I write lists?
- Do I plan my work by using brainstorms?
- Do I use colour to help me organize work?
- Do I use other methods of creative thinking to help with my work?

- What do I need to change in the way I work and how could I do this?

Write on Anything

This is a warm-up activity which is useful just to get the writing brain and hand going – it is fun and can last as long as you want.

Collect a range of materials that you can use at different times:

- different sorts of paper – craft and more traditional; lined, squared, graph, music manuscript, coloured, different shapes and sizes and textures
- fabrics – principally whites and creams and not particularly patterned: cotton, silk, linen, muslin – creased and smooth, open weaves, man-made and natural
- wood – lolly sticks (craft sticks)
- tickets – train, bus, tube, entry to theatre, concerts, galleries and the like
- newsprint
- packaging – particularly differing textures
- any other material that relates to your subject area.

Have a variety of pens, pencils, charcoal, pastels, etc. that you can try out. Use your favourite implements but also unfamiliar ones that you might not normally use for writing.

Initially take one implement and one surface and write your name (full or part – it does not matter). Then write your name in different ways as suggested below. Use these as starting points for themes. Occasionally change implements – explore how these writing tools work: blot, spread, resist, scratch, etc.

Write your name as if you were:

- *really angry*
- *signing a love letter*
- *old*
- *cold*
- *drunk*
- *nervous*
- *frightened*
- *tired*
- *very young*
- *excited*
- *a celebrity*
- …

Then swap hands. Use your non-writing hand and try all those emotions or states.

By using just your name, you do not have to think about the content of the writing, but subjects to write about might occur later. These might include writing about what something **feels** like as you write on it: 'I thought this would be smooth and easy, but it isn't, it resists. It's blotting. This is frustrating.'

After experimenting and playing with materials and implements, write reflectively on what happened – what you liked/disliked, what effects you could get; any artists you are reminded of; how you could use these techniques. Link this activity to your own practical work.

Look back to the reflectionnaire on **Ways of writing**, and think about how you, and also other people, write: in rough draft, then on the computer, or directly onto the computer. What happens when writing roughly?

Reflection: This can be a long or short activity and can be done again and again for different purposes and on a number of occasions – as a warm-up, as fun, and also to stimulate discussion. It is useful to explore the physicality of writing and expand the sorts of implements and surfaces we like or dislike and that might inspire or inhibit our writing.

In a workshop, different materials could be provided or participants could be encouraged to bring in materials themselves, so that they start to look out for varying surfaces. They could then try writing on these themselves, or share with others.

Fig. 22: The right to write.

Envelopes

There is an excitement in receiving an envelope, either through the post or by hand – not knowing what is in it. This links to receiving a letter – not an official one which might be a summons, a bill, or a statement, but the personal missive, the *billet doux*, the invitation … A sense of intrigue starts to work: the imagination is tickled; memories are jogged.

This envelope could be full of odd things – bits of paper, some fabric, a train or bus ticket, parking permit, car park ticket, a raffle ticket, a lolly stick and so on.

Take each item and write, using the list below as prompts – but expand away from this when you are ready or if a thought strikes you

Write just odd words or whole sentences, and don't worry about grammar or spelling.

- *Papers: what is this like to write on, what sort of message could this paper be used for, or what would it be more suitable for?*
- *Fabrics: could this be used to write a poem on, a book, an advert? What effects are found with different implements?*
- *Train or bus ticket – write about the journey to work/college and about the routes taken or the people seen.*
- *Relate it to a journey made by train or bus in the past.*
- *Car park ticket – what occasion could this have been?*
- *What was the car park like – its atmosphere and setting?*
- *Fines received or got away with …*
- *Raffle ticket – the dream ticket: what would you do if you won a big prize?*
- *Shopping receipt – what could you do with the items listed on it? Who bought them? (If you, invent someone else.) Where do the items come from? Of what journeys do they tell?*

Don't worry about reasons for why you are writing: experiment first, ask questions later. Then stand back, pause and reflect on what you have got.

Could you take any ideas off in different directions for any of your project work?

Reflection: in a workshop, discussions can be generated about:

- The art of letters and letter writing and the modern equivalents – text message, e-mail etiquette …
- Surprise about what is in the envelope and what part surprise plays in idea generation; experimentation and attitudes towards this in writing as visual activity.
- The material that often appears in journals, tickets, etc. – are they used for style or content, and are there issues from this in terms of aesthetics or meanings?
- Ideas of evidence – often tickets are stuck in as 'evidence' of going somewhere – which is not always so. Therefore, what is evidence?

Generating Excitement – Something has to Happen for Writing to Happen

Sometimes you read a line, see a slogan, glance at a title and internally you punch the sky and say YESSS!!!

Sometimes, too, on reading *around* that line, there is disappointment – the rest of the article, the development of the idea, does not follow through with what you initially thought.

Sometimes it does, and you are off …

But whatever happens, your own idea chain has been launched. Metaphors fly in and out, red herrings turn blue, thoughts are trapped like flies in amber. Words escape …

Trying to encourage this scenario is what I aim to do in the workshops I run.

It is vital to generate excitement in order for personal feelings to be stirred and fear dissolved and writing to happen. Writing can be born when this energy erupts.

Writing cannot flow, for those who fear it, when they are faced with a blank page and no idea what to write.

But using an idea, a sensation, a memory, a surprise – writing will follow.

That is what writing can be:

writing is about some thing
something that happened
is happening now
or will happen

So it is necessary to have things around you so that when you sit down to write, whatever the task, you have something that will energize you. Whether it is the bits you collect, the papers, the fabrics, the words – it doesn't matter.

Whatever the writing you have to do, there are going to be times when you just cannot get the task started.

In creative writing books, devices such as 'free writing' or 'stream-of-consciousness' styles of writing are encouraged. Some authors recommend a five minute free-write, or fill three pages. Maybe you need to set yourself some specific goal like this, maybe not. But always have the material available so that you can forget the work you have got to do, and concentrate on something more pleasurable.

Things to do, or to collect or to prepare, in advance, for those times:

- *prepare an envelope when you have materials to hand – leave it, and then pick it up when you are stuck*
- *tear out bits from adverts*
- *collect slogans that remind you of your childhood*
- *keep a box of objects that have memories and when your mind feels blocked, take out one and write on it*
- *collect photographs to use as inspirations*
- *use the exercises in this book as starting points – not ends in themselves.*

Reflection: As a warm-up activity in a workshop, have a number of objects, sayings, words or memory joggers to use. Use the fact that we all have different associations with the same objects, or words, and let something happen.

Many of the practicals in this book give the starting points. But as with so many other areas, it can also be the discussion raised in a workshop situation that can be utilized to fire up more writing and further research.

Fig. 23: Finding Inspiration.

Paper Plates

The purpose of this exercise is to generate ideas for writing through thoughts about how we spend our time. The plate represents a clock face.

You need a clean paper plate and pens/pencils in differing colours.

Draw lines to divide the plate into 24 wedge shapes.

This represents the 24 hours in a day.

Write in, or over, the segments to indicate how the hours of the day are used.

Take an average college day as your model.

Do not go absolutely by the clock, e.g. 8 o'clock to 9 o'clock, but express the filling of time as 'two hours food', 'three hours travelling' – more like a pie chart – and you can invent visual codes or use colours to represent activities.

Although you may find this a bit of a childish activity, keep going because, as you enter into this more deeply, you might find you haven't got enough time in the day, or more frighteningly, cannot account for three hours each day.

If I was running a session on time management, I would be talking about using travelling time as thinking or reading time, or waiting around times that happen at college as being ideal times to access the library, find research, or keep up to date with journals, thus giving ideas about filling time more productively. It is an old wives' tale that as you grow older you use your time more wisely. Some people do, some don't. But as you get older, time seems to go faster, and you regret the wasting of time.

In terms of writing, this activity could be followed by a few minutes writing about your ideas of time that have been spurred by filling in the plate. What might be your first thoughts? 'Oh this is like Blue Peter' might be followed by your second thoughts about your use of time and your reflections and conclusions. So this is personal writing about the self and use of time. This is certainly an occasion where writing can reveal underlying problems or strategies and the written thoughts might even lead to actions and resolutions.

Another point can be the reflections on this as a metaphor – the use of the paper plate.

- *Would a circle divided into 24 sections suffice?*
- *What does the paper plate add to or detract from the activity?*
- *What is the importance of the clock face as a depiction of times?*
- *Why do we call it a clock **face**?*

Here there is the potential for a wide range of investigation.

For example:

Films, where the clock plays a role itself

- as in the films of Harold Lloyd, a early silent film comedian, who perilously hung from the hands of a clock face way above a city street
- or the use of Big Ben to symbolize London
- or the adventure film *The Thirty Nine Steps*
- the ticking clock in *High Noon,* and film time and action time unite.

Literature

- Orwell's 1984, where the clock strikes 13
- in popular detective fiction, such as Agatha Christie, there is the altering of times and the significance of clock faces to the deductions
- in poetry there is the reading of the W.H. Auden poem 'Stop all the Clocks' in the film *Four Weddings and a Funeral.*

Painting

- Dali's liquid watches.

> **Reflection:** What this exercise demonstrates is that you can follow a practical, hands-on and fun exercise with deeper thoughts, personal reflections, symbols or metaphors and potential for research. By opening up the possibilities of this journey, we can encourage the expanding of the ideas that arise. An initial idea can be very simple, basic, shallow, common, and seemingly overused – but it can be deepened and made valuable in many ways. It is the reflection on the exercise that is possibly the most valuable contribution to writing.

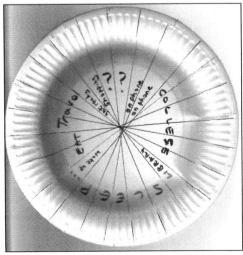

Fig. 24: 'What happens in those two missing hours?'

Spiral

As with many of my metaphors, this one comes out of a phrase that I hear frequently from distressed students:

'I feel as if I am going round and round in circles.'

It is always used in the sense of being lost, being in despair, feeling rudderless, out of control.

To introduce my take on this, I pick up a paper plate and a pair of scissors.

I ask 'Does anyone feel that sometimes they are going round and round in circles?' Usually (alright, always), there is a resounding 'yes'.

'Well I feel that that way, madness lies' (my Shakespearean expression often elicits a hollow laugh).

Then, as I am talking, I cut the plate into a spiral.

My theatre background taught me that there is nothing more fascinating than watching someone working or doing something. As I cut, the spiral emerges.

I say: 'I don't believe that we do go round and round in circles. I think it is more of a spiral. Yes, we can go down, but we can always slide up again, we can jump between layers. (I demonstrate the relationship of the layers.) We can go up and down. It moves. It is not that endless dispiriting idea of always returning to one point. With the spiral there is movement. We can see up and down. We can slide or leap'.

Sometimes there are laughs or expressions of 'YES' (a metaphorical punch in the air of agreement). There might also be suggestions that the spiral can be hung either way up, which is obviously an aesthetic response, engaging with the idea.

Versions of the spiral can be hung in the studio to represent the process, to remind everyone of the *movement* that *will* take place: a sense of the positive, when you are feeling down.

Perhaps this links to your individual optimism or pessimism. I am certainly of the more positive persuasion and the spiral is my attempt to try to encourage positive thinking even when you feel downwards bound.

It is our inward journey that leads us through time – forward or back, seldom in a straight line, most often spiraling. Each of us is moving, changing, with respect to others. As we discover, we remember; remembering, we discover; and most intensely do we experience this when our separate journeys converge. Our living experience at those meeting points is one of the charged dramatic fields of fiction (Welty 1995: 102).

The Plait

The plait is a metaphor here for entwining: of parts of a project; of ideas; and for the strands of the process of work.

Visualize, or make a plait, with three differing strands of material – wool, cotton, ribbon, paper, wire, etc. Each strand can also consist of a number of threads.

- begin the plait in the normal way – outside right to middle, outside left to middle ...
- then change the tension – plait tightly, then plait loosely
- then make a deliberate mistake: this is not easy – but try to create an error in the plaiting
- then go back to the correct way
- carry on until you finish your plait
- take a few moments to write down your reflections on this and how it relates to you.

Look at the final result.

You have varying tensions – loose, tight, neat and rough.

There is a mistake – this might have given rise to an unusual design pattern (depending on the materials), or is a beautiful visual, or it might look dreadful.

That does not matter. What this plait represents is the way of working, which could be writing or design or life. Sometimes we go in a regular way, and everything falls into place at exactly the right moment. Other times it is more fragile and loosely connected. Sometimes something goes wrong and it has to be got back on track, or the mistake leads to other ideas and new thoughts.

The strands could represent: practical work, research and writing, or could represent sketchbook, research and samples.

What is being shown here is the constant interplay and inter-reactions of work and processes.

The plait represents how different parts come together to make up the whole.

Fig. 25: 'Everything comes together in the end – somehow.'

Generating Ideas

Brainstorms – Thought showers
There follow several different ways to generate ideas that might be called brainstorming; mind-mapping; thought chains ...

They all help your brain to make connections with what it already knows or has stored.

But it is not always about listing facts, as is encouraged with most brainstorming exercises. It can be about making associations between fact and imagination, unearthing memories, recalling sensations and utilizing feelings.

These all have the potential to deepen writing – whether that is fiction, fact, interpretation, analysis, theory or fantasy.

Brainstorms are useful to re-visit during a project in progress. Sometimes, points that were missed at first become more important. Other threads emerge. Some ideas reveal that they can be deepened.

Brainstorms have a role in journals. Often dashed off on pieces of paper, they should be kept in the journals as evidence of the journey, as reminders, and also as ways into re-stimulating your ideas when you feel jaded.

go out, come back, go out again: always returning to the central point

Fig. 26: Flowers flourish – flow out and follow back.

The Flower

The flower is a metaphor for wide-ranging research and brainstorming.

While listening to a student, who was bothered that she was constantly going off at a tangent and getting off the point, I doodled a response to her fears (see Fig. 26).

The shape I drew was a flower, and as I drew it, I explained the concepts behind it.

You have an idea – that is the centre of the flower.

Then you go off and research, think, draw and follow ideas; then you come back to your main starting point. That is one petal.

Then you go off in another direction and then you come back. That is another petal.

You might do this several times and finally create all the petals of a flower. It could be a multi-coloured flower – each time you go off you add more colour, more depth.

So you have one main project/idea/point that you are doing. Then you go off all around the subject – but keep returning.

But the point is that you do come back.

So instead of feeling that what you are doing is bad/a mistake or something, and that you are evading doing the project, try to feel that it is a positive thing. You are adding to your idea. Then you can stand back from it and select which bit(s) you want to follow in more detail.

The art is in *selecting* which ideas to follow on this particular occasion.

We have to be honest with ourselves – sometimes we are genuinely following up on lots of ideas; all, or some, of which will help with the project.

Sometimes, however, we *are* procrastinating.

Senses

There are not just five senses. We often talk of a sense of humour – so maybe that is a sixth. Others might talk of extrasensory perception as the sixth.

Maybe there are more, or maybe some branch out into other areas.

But using at least the five, plus humour, can expand any form of idea generation.

Visual: In art and design it is obvious to use this as a starting point: colours, tones, shape, size, aesthetics, patterns, illusions, visual memories of events, perceptions. You remember something from what it looked like, not necessarily anything else. Use this visual strength as a way into exploring the memories further.

Hearing: Make links to music, poetry and the power of words – spoken by yourself, or by actors or politicians. Think of advertising jingles, song lyrics. Rhythms, speeds of speaking. Noise, peace.

Touch: Call on this sense to help with ideas for the tactile qualities, the reassurance of some surfaces, the danger in others. These might also link to sounds that are created by materials.

Smell: Memories are frequently triggered by smell, and this is possibly the remnant of an ancient sense to help with finding food, or sensing danger. It can help jog detail about an event or place.

Taste: Maybe less obvious in brainstorming – but very personal and can help with description and the effect of something on us.

Humour: Can this be used to find more words or ideas about something? Perhaps word play discovers more aspects to an idea than almost anything else.

There is a line of John Donne's poetry, so often quoted in isolation:

'No man is an island/ entire of it self'

But no word, no idea, is an island completely independent of others.

No sense is ever employed on its own; they usually come together.

The contributions that the senses can make lie behind much good writing.

> Children like animals, use all their senses to discover the world. Then artists come along and discover it the same way, all over again. Here and there, it's the same world. Or now and then we'll hear from an artist who's never lost it (Welty 1995: 10).

Senses Plus – and Links to Writing

We don't know what someone else sees.

Do they have the same impression of colours and what, for them, stands out in the foreground while other things are backgrounded? Can they see shapes in clouds or puddles or leaf shadows? And do they see a cacophony of tones, forms, movements in a crowd of people?

We use the word 'see' not only to apply to the visual, but also to how we perceive something – and that is usually applicable to the other senses.

And this is why, in our writing for some, though not all, purposes, we often have to clarify our meanings more clearly. If we are talking to someone, the differences in our interpretations of an object or scene can emerge and create more dialogue.

At times, our writing, if we are not present at the reading, needs transparency. There may be other times when we deliberately want confusion or diffusion of views – but only when we want it and write deliberately so.

Hearing and sight share similar characteristics regarding selectivity. If someone is losing their hearing, they might pick up selected sounds, specific words and not others, and their interpretation of a conversation might be very different from the other speaker or a third party who is observing. When we talk to someone about something we both saw, we find they picked out different things from us, sometimes according to interests and associations.

And hearing and sight share other qualities, particularly in how we describe our sensations. If we cannot hear everything, we pick up visual clues – and there is a deliberate use of the word 'cacophony' (a mass of sounds) in the above description of the visual qualities of a scene.

In the arts, the possible reason for some artists working as they did has been pondered over, and proposals made for their differing powers and senses from most other people. Monet's diminishing eyesight is a classic example.

Beethoven lost his hearing and felt the vibrations of his music, and the word 'felt' also links his music to emotion. His work very clearly derives from, and speaks to, individuals and their lives and experiences. But each person listening will relate differently, according to their life story.

Reading and writing are activities which require all the senses, in varying quantities, to make the work truly alive.

Try describing a piece of music – using just words that describe sounds, then words that are descriptive of visuals, then tactile, and then humour.

For example:

- the music was resonant, percussive, harmonic
- the music was thunder-black and vibrant red and mellowed to hues of grey
- the music pulsated, reverberated,
- instruments argued and niggled, then giggled and made up.

Take other subjects:

Materials – from velvets to plastics:

these may be primarily tactile, but could spread into sounds and visuals and smells (dyes have varying scents, which also sometimes give a strong sense of taste in the mouth).

Media – from charcoal to watercolour:

principally tactile and visual, they can be juxtaposed in humorous ways and make sounds on the surfaces they are applied to.

Films – early silent and sound films, black and white and technicolour:

humour as used to underpin or undermine the contrasts in what is seen and what is heard.

Your favourite book:

the feel of the cover, the smell of the paper and ink, the sound of the paper turning as well as the visuals used and the sounds of the words.

If you are stuck, just look around you and take something and write to the obvious sense, and then move to the less obvious.

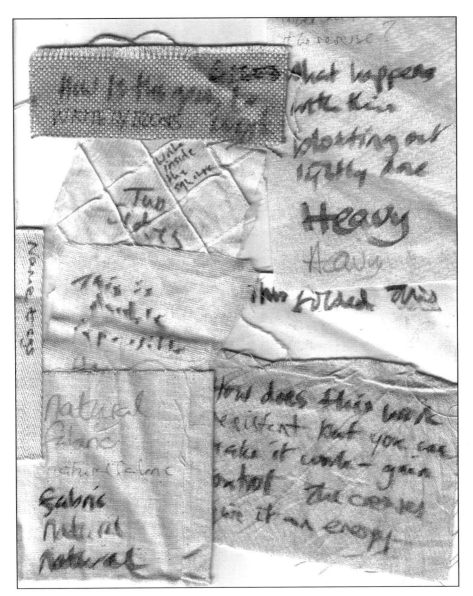

Fig. 27: Inspired by textures.

Addictive Alphabets

This is a good way of generating ideas, and also helps develop vocabulary, as often you want to look up words or need to consult a thesaurus.

It is similar to lists.

Try to think of a word for every letter of the alphabet on the subject given below. You are allowed to cheat for the very difficult letters – but be creative in your cheating. The letter could be within the word, or it sounds like it, or you can make it a visual connection. It is not being marked, so if you can't do one letter – don't lose sleep over it.

Create an alphabet for:

- food
- animals (wild or domestic)
- colours – shades and tones (this might lead to looking at paint charts)
- weather
- names – male and female
- emotions
- domestic products
- fashion garments
- authors
- films
- music
- mechanical processes.

An extension to alphabets is then to use the device of alliteration.

This is where two or more words share the same sound/letter. Rules can be bent and twisted creatively in this.

So you might have:

active ant
busy bee
curvaceous cat
dotty dog

Or, for fashion:

mousy moccasins
neglected necklace
outsize overlocking
prissy pinafore

These exercises might help with any sort of promotional writing – for example fashion journalism is full of alliterative description and slogans. Marketing products might require experiments with sounds to create catchphrases to attract customers. In creative writing for illustration, visual ideas can be created from the humorous alliterative associations of the alphabets.

Lists

A way of limbering up, and helping develop associations, is to make lists.

We often have to make lists of things that we have to do, so that we remember what we have to do, and this is always a good way of releasing the brain from having to try to remember some things. Putting it down in some physical and/or visual way, helps us to log it.

But creative list making can act as a wonderful idea-generator.

As a warm up, do one of these lists:

- *all the roads you have to walk down to get to college, to the shops, etc.*
- *all the shops you pass*
- *all the shops you have visited in the last week*
- *all the colours you can see from where you are sitting now*
- *take a colour and list all things that could be of that colour*
- *all the house numbers of houses you have ever lived in*
- *all the places or rooms that you have been in today*
- *write one word on how those rooms influence you*
- *everything you did since waking up*
- *the sights, sounds, smells and textures of your favourite places*
- *all your favourite music – past and present*
- *your favourite artists*
- *your favourite films*
- *your favourite .... whatever (your particular interests)*
- *thumbnail sketches – words or doodles of your family*
- *thumbnail sketches of people you know*
- *your life – key moments*
- *words that you enjoy*
- *animals you like*
- *same as above but instead of animals do colours or shapes, or food ...*
- *people you know – just first names*
- *obsessions – the big ones (politics, animal welfare ...)*
- *and the little ones (use this pen not that, wear something pink)*
- *likes and dislikes (initially try five of each – but then see where they go).*

All these ideas are warm-ups, but each could be taken and developed into other areas. For example, when writing personal statements, your favourite artists are relevant. When trying to think up ideas for a new project, your obsessions, likes and dislikes are good starting points, so that you never have to leave your page blank.

So lists can often spark visual ideas for practical tasks, but they can also inspire more academic work.

In terms of developing an essay idea where you are writing about an artist, list:

- *what seem to be the colours they always use*
- *the media they use*
- *the exhibitions they have had*
- *the books they have written*
- *the books they have appeared in.*

Or if it is about a design movement – then list:

- *all the sorts of work they did*
- *the sorts of products they produced*
- *their colour range.*

This may seem mundane, but it is a starting point that might reveal interesting aspects that might not show up otherwise. You could discover that an artist only uses a particular palette, and that had not been obvious before, or only certain colours at certain periods of their work, or that a design group never made particular items – why not?

You might need to do some research for some areas – but get down what you know, and then list the research you could do. This might just mean skimming an index (another list) in the first place, before going on to do more in-depth research.

Your lists do not need to be columns of words – as a shopping list implies:

- *they could be on different Post-its*
- *they could be in bubbles on a bubble diagram*
- *they could look like links on a family tree (a complex list of your predecessors or ancestors)*
- *you might make a list and then colour it in different ways in order to develop it or categorize it.*

> **Reflection:** The work of Georges Perec (1997) may be inspirational in the compiling of lists and developing this sometimes obsessive activity into creative writing. Some people prefer to do lists rather than create brainstorms that are more like mind maps or spider diagrams. The point is to do something with the lists – not just tick off jobs to do, but make links and connections, juxtapose and invert, and make sense of others' lists.

Developing Ideas

Colour Pairs

This is like a game, but is surprisingly adaptable and, potentially, can be a good activity to prepare for writing. It seems unlike work because it is rooted in memory and association, and is very personal.

Use a number of pieces of varying coloured papers; cut or tear the papers in half. Two people are each given the same colour.

Without discussing them, jot down as many memories or associations as you can think of for this colour:

- *reminds you of curtains in your bedroom as a child*
- *the colour of packaging of favourite food*
- *the colours of the sea where you lived*
- *the dress you hated, etc.*

Then talk to the other person; each can talk about what is written down, and then you discuss any differences or similarities. This is one of the simplest things to do, but gives ideas about what lies behind our view of colours and how associations and memories play such a part in our perceptions and behaviours.

Discussion could be on:

- *the paint catalogue and the fanciful names given to colours, and how they are geared to marketing*
- *how fashion uses and drops colours season by season*
- *how we can be swayed by the colour of something in packaging*
- *how we are all different in our personal responses to colours.*

This is a real example of talk write. After talking to someone, jot down and perhaps expand one or two of the thoughts. It will be subjective, reflective writing, but can easily be the foundations for a deeper analysis or discussion or discovery. It might lead to research, or exploration of the work of different artists or designers – some of whom may have been suggested by the other person.

Instead of paper, you could use: fabrics; parts of adverts; paints; dyes; plastics, etc.

- *What difference does the material make?*
- *What part does texture or age play ?*
- *Does the other person's reaction affect you: does it spoil, hinder, add to, provoke, excite, etc?*

Reflection: This is a warm-up exercise, but a good way into ideas, and absorbing viewpoints of others and a questioning of how we are manipulated and how we operate in our own work and styles. In a workshop, it is probably more effective if participants are given the colours, so they are all reacting anew to what is offered to them.

Objects

The principles outlined in this activity have many purposes and uses.

They can act as a warm-up to writing – just jotting down words, not worrying about putting ideas into sentences.

The points help build up description, which is a good first step to analysis.

The hands-on nature of this suits writing that is more 'real', rather than abstract, i.e. one where an object is imagined, not felt.

Vocabulary is stretched and a thesaurus is usually needed.

This also acts as a brainstorming or idea-generating activity, which is fun and useful.

This can be done anywhere, anytime – so is good to fill in a few minutes, or as a diversion when there is a block in writing, and will probably help give ways back into the task you should be doing.

In workshops, I have a bag or box of small objects varying in age, materials, functions, etc. These are handed out, or hands are dipped in like a lucky dip. However you can use or find your own objects. They do not have to be small, though for workshop purposes they always are (but this is mainly for portability).

Jot down words to describe:

■ *the colour or colours – give details – e.g. what sort of red*
■ *the material or materials it is made of (even if you don't know, have a guess and this might lead to following this up in some way – expanding vocabulary of materials)*
■ *the texture it has – rough, smooth, etc.*
■ *its weight – heavy for its size, etc.*
■ *what it smells like (this might depend on the object)*
■ *whether it has a sound – either that it makes itself, or when tapped, stroked, rubbed against something else, etc.*

Note: these are all related to senses, which deepen the approach to writing.

Then extending the thoughts about what it is:

■ *its function (again if you do not know, guess, and then follow up with research at another time)*
■ *imaginatively, what it could be used for – be as wild as you like*
■ *who owns it – not literally, but who could either own it now – invent this, or who in the past – a factory worker, craftsperson, a particular class of person, etc.*
■ *fun or functional – or if these could be interchangeable*

- *what context there might be*
- *what it was used for – and why*
- *who used it and how they fit into the society of the time*
- *whether it has changed its purpose now*
- *what it tells you of its time*
- *what research you could do around it*
- *what thoughts/memories it sparks off – whether it reminds you of something else, makes you want to explore, etc. – so this could be both personal and work related.*

These are just some of the questions. The more you do of this, the more questions arise naturally.

Some of these questions do not relate to every object; some need more depth, so these are just starting points

Objects I use include:

small replica toys of older toys – eg wooden spinning tops, yo yos

small wooden toys where you push your thumb underneath and the figure above, which is threaded on elastic, bends and contorts

optical spinning discs

Jacob's ladders.

Darning mushrooms made of bakelite or wood. The function of this often needs explanation. In the times before throw-away socks, when a hole appeared in the heel, the sock would be stretched over the dome of the mushroom and the hole would be darned and mended. In some mushrooms the top unscrews to reveal a container for the darning wool and needle. The materials that these mushrooms are made of are also of interest and include early plastics, carved wood, etc.

Another object I use is *an egg timer* – which was made from a yarn spindle. This spins off ideas about how British industries have provided artefacts which are now adapted as items that are sold as mementoes and tourist curios. There are so many questions that could arise from this in terms of context:

- *What was the function of the object?*
- *Who used these objects?*
- *How did the industry decline, and why?*
- *Why and how are the items salvaged?*
- *Who adapts them, and where?*
- *Who buys them, and why do they do so?*

■ Do they end up as decoration or ornaments, yet have blood on them from the workers who originally used them?

Using objects in this way is writing through experience; writing from life. So this could be said to be life writing – just like life drawing.

> Reflection: What this exercise develops is a greater skill in the describing and analysing and questioning of objects. But this more intellectual investigation starts with a kinaesthetic, hands-on investigation of the object itself; drawing on the innate skills of the artist or designer.

> Too often we are expected to write about things that are depicted in a book and have no real atmosphere, history or patina of use by people. Milner's book *Inspirational Objects* (2005) is another good source of reference as her writing is in a range of differing styles according to the object she is writing about.

Materials – Fabrics, Wood, Plastics, Paints, Papers, etc.

This is just like the section on objects – the purpose is to explore, physically, personally and intuitively, using your chosen material as a starting point to writing. Description comes first, then analysis and development can follow.

These are just some of the questions to ask, if you are stuck:

■ *colours and shades and tones – whether they have been given a name or you can name them*
■ *natural or man made – and to what extent*
■ *patterns – natural or created*
■ *feel – texture and tactile qualities: sensuous or alienating*
■ *sounds – the sound of the material, and then its sound with or against other surfaces*
■ *shapes – symmetrical, practical*
■ *weight, bulk, density, fragility*
■ *warm or cold to touch – and whether it changes in your hands*
■ *whether it is conducive to touching more and playing or experimenting with.*

What it is used for:

■ *What could it be used for – realistically, and the uses it probably would not have – but why not?*
■ *The issue of recyclability (this might be a particularly relevant contemporary question to explore).*
■ *Which artists or designers use it and how?*
■ *How is it made or how does it evolve?*
■ *What is its history, its geography, its social place?*

Personal links:

■ *What memories does it evoke in you – what do you associate it with, who do you associate it with?*
■ *Is it a material you would use in your own work – if yes why, and if no, why not?*
■ *What research could you do on it?*

Extending the writing:
Think of metaphors or similes that would help you describe the materials:

Paper which is soft as fine silk (a comparison to help give the feel, but perhaps not a usual one).

Wood which is steeped in ancient traditions (steeped here means that it is soaked in the traditions, completely infused with its role in society, thus in using the word 'steep' you are giving layers of meaning to the reader, extending their range of responses).

Metal which is like freezing water (the simile uses 'like' – so again a comparison which gives the idea of its cold, unfriendly, dangerous properties).

Museum Object Analysis

The following is an example of a handout used for a specific exhibition in order to give practice in the early stages of object analysis. It can be adapted for a range of purposes.

'The Golden Age of Couture' at the V&A 22 September 2007–6 January 2008

Select a piece from the exhibition and write an object analysis of it.

The questions below give you the broad ideas to follow, and act as a starting point, but some will not be appropriate to your object. Do a 'pick and mix' of the ones that are of use, and extend them where possible into further research. Remember that analysis is about asking questions and researching and thinking about the reasons behind why something is as it is.

When handing in your written object analysis include a visual (photograph or drawing) of the object chosen.

Description

- *designer*
- *what the object is described as (e.g. suit, evening dress ...)*
- *the colour or colours – give details – e.g. the sort of red*
- *the material or materials it is made of*
- *the texture– rough, smooth, etc.*
- *the weight*
- *whether it is decorated, how, and with what*
- *shapes*
- *construction*
- *date it was produced and where and for what purpose*
- *who it was made for*
- *who owned it*
- *what it cost – to make and to buy*
- *any personal impressions you had of it in the exhibition*
- *how it was displayed*
- *importance/prominence attached to it*
- *your feelings about it.*

Construction – in more detail

- *how was it made and by whom*
- *the conditions there were in the place where it was made*
- *what were the hierarchies of people involved in the making of the garment*
- *how long it took to make.*

Context 1:
Where did any visuals of the garment appear, e.g. place of publication or newsreel, and how were they presented?

Context 2:

- *social – who the garment was made for – their social position*
- *social event it was made for – how it fitted in with the society of the day*
- *historical – what was happening at the time*
- *politics*
- *films*
- *music*
- *aesthetics – how it fitted in with or compared to other designs of the day.*

Title of your object
This can lead to interesting thoughts and discussions about the importance of the title and how this is used and manipulated by the designer or the media.

Does the title influence the way we look at the garment?

Stories
Are there any stories or myths associated with your object and why did these develop?

Today
Reactions to your object today:

- *reviews*
- *observations you have made from watching viewers looking at it in the exhibition.*

How this object is viewed today:

- *important in the history of design*
- *iconic*
- *symbolic of a period*
- *influential on a designer.*

Using Language Devices as Idea Generators

There are a number of parts of language that can be helpful in writing, as they are very visual, or tactile, or inspire associations that might be helpful to your project work. They can be used as warm-up activities, or in brainstorming for ideas, and when writing something up. They can sometimes be useful when describing something, or setting a scene or background.

A **metaphor** is when one thing is said to be another. This does not literally mean it **is** that other thing, but the comparison or analogy gives an insight, an added dimension to it.

We are all familiar with 'all the world's a stage,' a Shakespearean line. People are acting parts throughout their life and life could be considered to be a performance. All these ideas have a greater flavour, but the world is not actually a stage.

We also use the word 'theatre' to mean more than just the building where plays are performed. It comes from the ancient Greek *theaomai* meaning 'behold or look'. This links clearly to the lecture theatre or operating theatre. But for theatre of war it really means scene or field of action.

Thus it is not only about looking, but being involved, which, in the best theatre, you are – if not physically, you should be mentally.

All these subtleties of meaning and usage enhance our writing, and when a writer uses all these layers of words, we are opened up to new understandings.

Similes compare one thing with another and often say something is 'like' or 'as' something else.

E.g. 'She/he is very graceful and glides like a swan': this is a more evocative expression of the way he or she moves.

But some similes have become overused and **clichés** result, as for example, 'at the end of the day': a politician's favourite, meaning 'finally', or as a consequence – and usually preceded by 'but'. This is their way of saying 'well after all that talk, finally, nothing is going to happen – but I don't want you to think it wasn't worth listening to me, and I certainly am not responsible for nothing changing'.

Some of the following activities explore these aspects of language, so that your writing can be enriched.

Using Metaphors and Analogies to Find Out About/Create a Character

This Reflectionnaire has possible uses in profiling consumers. It is also fun and not meant to be a serious psychological profile of you or of someone you might make up. It could be very useful in creative writing and illustration.

It asks questions to reveal subtleties of character, or behaviour. The way to phrase the questions is:

> If you were .... what would you be? (Write not what you *like*, but what you would be, e.g: If I were a *coffee* I would be strong, but with milk and sugar, and if I were a *cheese* I would be crumbly and mature.)

For the first three, I have given some options.

■ *coffee: instant; filter; cafetière; latte;*................................
■ *tea: bag; loose-leaf; herbal;*....................................
■ *cheese: cream; mild; mature; crumbly; blue veined; smelly;*............
■ *bread*
■ *transport*
■ *pet*
■ *pattern*
■ *type of TV programme*
■ *wild animal*
■ *film type (genre)*
■ *book type*
■ *piece of jewellery*
■ *colour*
■ *piece of clothing.*

(add some categories of your own)

Are you the sort of person who considers life to be like a glass that is half full or half empty?

> **Reflection:** This is a fun exercise which can lead to thinking in different ways about other people, how characters are created or how marketing can be targeted. It is a starting point, not a finished thing in itself.

One Thing in the Style of Another

This is based on a popular idea in the radio spoof quiz game 'I'm Sorry I Haven't a Clue' and is also a mainstay of creative writing practice.

This exercise is funny, but is also good practice at thinking about different styles and language and vocabulary that you have to use at different times.

Take one item from the list and then write about it in the style of something else on the list. Select at random and don't think too much before you try it.

You can also make up your own categories.

- *Map directions*
- *Look book*
- *Alphabet*
- *Thesaurus*
- *Poem*
- *Blog*
- *Review*
- *Poem*
- *Song lyric*
- *Limerick*
- *Haiku*
- *Murder mystery plot*
- *Riddle*
- *Monologue*
- *Obituary*
- *Biography*
- *Diary*
- *Scientific experiment write-up*
- *Cookery book*
- *Stage directions*
- *Famous painting caption*
- *Lonely hearts advert*
- *Newspaper headline*
- *'Dear John' letter (dumping your girl/boyfriend)*
- *Melodrama.*

Thus you might get:

- *map directions in the form of a lonely hearts ad*
- *a riddle in the form of stage directions*
- *an obituary in the form of an alphabet.*

Do it for as long as you want.

Do it in whatever way you want.

But think of its more serious applications and how different styles of writing have to be.

What specific things make them different?

> **Reflection**: An inspiring example of one thing in the style of another, taken a great distance, is Matt Madden's 99 Ways to Tell a Story: Exercises in Style (2006) which is one visual story told in 99 different ways. It is based on Raymond Queneau's Exercises in Style, ([1947] 1981). This latter book is a literary exploration, which is now a little dated, but is nevertheless an example of how far you can go to practice and to explore the creative potential of one idea.
>
> In all areas of visual and performing arts, this is a well-used method of working. Extending this into writing styles is both fun and also pushes ideas further. It is good practice in preparing for the number of pieces that you might have to turn your writing hand to (see example in Fig. 28).

Practicals

If you were here
You would turn first right
Take the narrow lane
    under the trees.
You will see the viaduct
    on your left and the
ruined cottages in the
        foreground.
After a mile you climb steeply
alongside the remains of the
    conveyor belt.
At the summit
    you can survey
mine shafts, quarry bottoms
and waste tips now
    covered in heather.
The silence and the
clean air
    return.

POSTCARD

THE ADDRESS TO BE WRITTEN ON THIS SIDE

Fig. 28: Postcard home in the form of a guide book description – but with underlying social comments in the form of poetry.

Analysing Magazines: Some Headings to Use

This is an example of a handout that is a useful starting point in showing how to begin the specific questions for an analysis of a magazine.

Cover – balance of words and images
How clear are dates, price, ISSN, barcode, etc?
Headlines promoting features?

Price (is subscription a possibility?)
Frequency
Availability – where sold

Size of magazine – size of paper, as well as thickness
Binding – glued/stitched, etc.
Number of pages: then work out the balance of contents

Contents page – how it is arranged
In page order regardless of subject
Or subjects in sections – page numbers all over the place
Or magazine itself is in separate sections

Page numbers – are they clear, or, in parts, non existent?

Editor's letter – length and detail – how does it address the reader?

Readership

Paper
Texture/gloss/matt/varied throughout magazine/smell …
How does the paper affect the pictures – pixels, clarity, bleed, etc?
How does the paper affect the text?

Fonts and typography
Legibility and variety

Colour(s)

Use and Balance of Visuals: Illustrations Photos Diagrams

Photos
Where are the captions and credits – are they on the photo, or separate?
Are there double page photos (how do these fit into the magazine – do they disappear into the binding?) or single pages?
What is the relationship to the article?
How do they relate to the adverts – same styles as the photographs?

Adverts

Proportion of adverts to the rest of magazine

Sorts of adverts and length/display of these adverts

Who is advertising (and what this tells you about the readership).

Starting points for an article/feature analysis

- title and subtitle
- rough length (words/pages)
- any visuals and types (illustrations, photographs, diagrams, etc.)
- author – name (any details/biography given of them)
- style(s) of writing
- vocabulary used
- subject –
  - ☐ serious – thought provoking
  - ☐ researched
  - ☐ sensational
  - ☐ gossip
  - ☐ interview
  - ☐ controversial
  - ☐ funny
  - ☐ information
  - ☐ ideas
  - ☐ …
- aim of the magazine – and how article/feature fits into this.

Reflection: This gives the bare bones for starting an analysis. The writing that is generated may start by being just key words, but gradually the detail is added to the bones and fleshed out. Getting into the structures and really looking at something under the microscope can stimulate questions and, then, reflective thoughts and responses. In spotlighting magazines, the stuff of the everyday, prejudices and pre-conceptions can be challenged, and many surprises emerge – for example, just how many adverts there are in some magazines, and how little text, or how invasive captions or editorial comments are. This handout is not spoon feeding, but guidance in the detail required.

Proverbs and Sayings

Some proverbs or sayings are very old and the original meaning has disappeared, or the reasoning behind it is now unknown.

An example of this might be: 'A stitch in time saves nine'. This means that one stitch to mend the tear now will save having to do nine stitches later, when the tear has become too big. This is almost out of date now in the throw-away society that exists, but alludes to a time when something was cared for as it couldn't easily be replaced and was felt to still have a lot of life left in it.

Chinese proverbs are very philosophical, and also quite beautiful:

You cannot help shoots grow by pulling them up

Flowers look different to different eyes

These are like metaphors in that they set off a range of thoughts in your mind, going beyond just the obvious interpretation.

Fig. 29: Written in stone?

Proverbs and sayings are a useful area to think about in writing, as you could use them a lot. However, not all your readers will understand what you are meaning. You have to think of your readers. If English is not your native language, or that of your readers, the words may not be familiar, and if you take them literally, you might become very confused.

Sayings can be very useful in creative writing to indicate a character – but in academic writing they might divert attention from what you really mean. However, they might be vivid if used in a project statement, to encourage your reader and viewer to look at your work in a more imaginative way.

Quickly draw or sketch ideas on proverbs or sayings that you find.

Do them *literally*, exactly as they appear to you.

Then *interpret* them, and try to illustrate the *meaning* of the phrase.

Turn Things on their Head

Turn things on their head – literally take the opposite of an idea and work on it.

Take a phrase or title and change the words around – so, *Little Red Riding Hood* becomes *Big Blue Bovver Boots*. Draw or sketch these ideas. This might make you think more laterally about a design idea, and might give other ideas for writing.

This is related to Edward de Bono's ideas in *Lateral Thinking* (1970), and this is used in many aspects of creative thinking.

Homophones are words that are pronounced in the same way, but differ in meaning and/or spelling. This can also turn ideas around or upside down:

manner/manor; where/wear; etc.

Key ones for this book are **write/right/rite/wright**

write – make a mark on a surface with symbols or letters, etc.

right – correct; or the opposite to 'left'

rite – religious or solemn observance or act (ritual event – as in a rite of passage)

wright – a maker or builder: as in wheelwright, wainwright, playwright, shipwright

And **wrote/rote**

wrote – this is the past tense of write (as above)

rote – mechanical repetition: usually used about gaining learning – doing your times tables, for example, by going over and over them, drumming them in.

With all these devices, if you are unsure about them, draw them. That might help you remember which to use, or give you ideas about when you can deliberately use them for effect.

This drawing on a round paper plate gave the idea for looking at things in different ways, and inspired more thoughts about going round in circles, looking inside yourself to see what is already there, etc.

Fig. 30: 'Topsy turvy'.

Alliteration, Blunders and Slang

The most usual version of **alliteration** is when all the words begin with the same sound – this is usually the same letter, but as this is an aural device, the sound is the important criteria:

all ants anticipate applying antique alabaster

or

the right royal ran the wrong race

Alternatively alliteration could apply to the internal sounds of words which are repeated:

ensuring your drawing is enduring not boring

(repeated 'or' sound)

In journalism this is a common device – sometimes just pairs of alliteration, or sometimes, as in headlines, longer stretches.

For press releases and statements you might want to use this effect to draw attention to something:

This collection combines whispering white windswept worlds of woven wool with granite grey gabardine.

Whenever you are doodling, do a few of these – it is also a good way of extending vocabulary, but in a fun way, as you often have to use a thesaurus or dictionary to extend your repertoire.

Blunders and misprints: these can often be very funny and get attention and set off different thoughts. Usually they have occurred accidentally, but you might want to use them deliberately. Look out for them in newspapers and on notices.

That last line could have read *'look out for them in new papers and novices,'* which has a different meaning.

Another one is: *'He fell in love with the heroin'* which should be *'heroine'*. This is one of the commonest mistakes in student essays today, but with very different connotations: drugs or the girl?

Again draw or doodle these to inspire ideas, and also become aware of ones that you might fall victim to.

Slang – particularly **rhyming slang,** is a good inspiration. Many words or phrases are very visual which may give ideas.

Most people know *'up the apples and pears'* as *'stairs'* but what about the following (the answers appear after the main list):

1. city tote
2. penny locket
3. curry and rice
4. night and day
5. New York nippers
6. ideal home
7. box of toys
8. don't make a fuss
9. watercress
10. fish and tank
11. fly by nights
12. tomfoolery
13. tomato sauce (tomato sauces)
14. rabbit
15. rats and mice
16. John Wayne
17. Gloria Gaynors
18. glorious sinner
19. pot of glue
20. jellied eels.

Meanings
1. *coat*
2. *pocket*
3. *a price*
4. *grey/a play*
5. *kippers*
6. *a comb*
7. *noise*
8. *a bus*
9. *a dress*
10. *a bank*
11. *tights*
12. *jewellery*
13. *a horse (the horses – i.e. horse-races)*
14. *talk (from rabbit and pork = talk)*
15. *a game of dice*
16. *a train*

17. *trainers*
18. *dinner*
19. *a queue*
20. *transport (jellied eels = wheels).*

Some of these could be used in press releases or statements to draw attention, but this is also an area to think about your audience. Do they understand rhyming slang and therefore would be able to have a go at deciphering what you mean, or is this completely alien to them?

However, even if you don't use these forms in your writing, they are good warm-ups to idea generation.

Mnemonics

A mnemonic is a device to help the memory. At school we were often given a mnemonic to help us remember sequences of kings and queens, mathematical formulae, chemicals, etc.

For some people they are very helpful, for others not at all. But if you do find them fun or addictive, then they can help with ideas and vocabulary.

To remember the spelling of the word 'because', each letter of the word is used to form a silly sentence. This is memorable – as often it is very visual, and that means that when you come to have to spell the word, you remember the sentence, and then you have got the correct sequence of letters.

Various versions of 'because' exist. A visual one is:

big elephants can always understand small elephants

As a warm up try your own name and write it down, vertically, on the page

P
A
T
R
I
C
I
A

Then create a sentence:

Patricia
Always
Teaches
Really
Interesting
Creative
Intelligent
Artists

OK, I do know how to spell my name and you, yours, but this is just a warm-up.

Take any word that you have problems in spelling and try to invent a mnemonic to help you in the future. Particularly useful might be designers or artists that you often have to write about, but always get wrong.

In fashion, Jean Paul Gaultier is often mis-spelt; so, how about:

Gaultier
Always
Uses
Lycra
To
Inspire
Every
Ruche

Some letters are very difficult to use as there are not many words for them, and other letters you find yourself repeating, over and over again, but it doesn't matter; the point is to try to create something memorable, even if it is surreal. Look at how I have played with some of these in the following examples. Use a dictionary. Some letters soon cease to be major problems.

Throughout this book you will often find me playing with this device to emphasize a word or a sequence of actions. Here are some mnemonics that particularly relate to education, and the choices of words for some letters emphasizes the qualities of the original word. You will also see that I often begin the sequence with the word itself, to further aid the memory.

Evaluation
values
all
learning's   (alternative)
understandings;   unlocking
attentive   all
twists   turns,
in   inspiring
original   other
nuances   notes

Assessment
seems
seditious
except
sometimes
softly
meanings
emerge   (alternatives)
neatly   newly
turned   transitioned / together / transformed

Procrastination
relies
on
creatively
retreating
and
sidestepping
the
inevitable
new
achievable
task,
instead
of
(k)nuckling down (this is a bit of a cheat, but it sounds right)

Creating Words

The purpose of this exercise is to explore and create new words and vocabulary, to play with words, and think about different meanings in different contexts.

Write down several inspirations for your work – just key words.

This may need some prompts:

- *the visual inspirations behind your project*
- *the influences on your creative process*
- *weather, food, colours, fabrics, moods, etc.*

(If you are feeling particularly stumped by this, it might be a good idea to do a reflectionnaire which has generated thoughts about the influences and inspirations behind someone's work.)

When you have got a few words down:

- *select two or three*
- *and then combine the words in some way – playing with combinations*
- *push these words – really manipulate them*
- *look at letter patterns that are common to both words.*

(favourite activities)   (the combinations)
swimming   swimoodling
eating   museating
sleeping   doodlewatch
doodling   telesleep
listening to music
watching telly

(ideas behind the design)
red
cactus   (the combinations)
plastics   placticus
silks   plastisilks
parrots   paredots

Then write down your reasons for some of the combinations and which worked for you and which didn't, or reflect on this as a strategy for the future: did any surprises emerge? This is just as notes – it is not an essay. Further development could be to work with someone else and get them to look at your words and see how they respond to them – do they get it? Do they see what you see?

Reflection: In a workshop, this activity can be started with individuals working alone, then moving into working in pairs, and then in small groups. This encourages working with others' understanding of words and building awareness of cultural and language differences in perception and meanings of words. These devices can be useful in liberating writers from always following the rules. In breaking rules, or by creating alternative rules, more awareness can be developed of syntax and correct usage.

Practicals

A Handout for Analysing some Aspects of Writing Techniques

Puns – e.g. the bottom line (a phrase which could mean 'basically' – or the shape of the body's bottom).

Alliteration – a number of words begin with the same letter or same sound
e.g. horrendous hemp hemlines hang heavily.

Homophones – words that sound the same but are spelt differently, and have differing meanings – e.g. waste (rubbish) and waist (above the tummy) – and wasted (can also be 'wrecked' – as in drunk, or as in eating disorder – wasting away) and waisted (a garment narrowed or fitted at the waist).

Rhyme – e.g.	Models on the catwalk
	Primp and preen and stalk
Slang terms – e.g.	strides = trousers
	heel = petty criminal
	pants = rubbish
	do-rag = scarf used to bind up recently straightened hair
Quotes –	famous ones that everyone knows,
	or from people being written about
Lists – e.g.	alphabets of fashion items
	or lots and lots of details to add colour to a description

Metaphors – something is compared to something else – e.g. the fashion exhibition, 'Spectres', used the extended metaphor of a peepshow and magic and illusion. Another famous one is: 'All the world is a stage.'

Many trends use versions of metaphors – e.g. nautical, preppy.

Implied metaphors – e.g. 'shopping heaven' or 'Westwood is the Queen of fashion and McQueen is the Bad Boy of fashion'.

Similes – like metaphors – but usually they use the word 'like' e.g. 'roared like a lion' 'floated like a cloud'.

Clichés – overused sayings – e.g. 'x is the new black' or 'y is the must have' or 'at the end of the day'.

Onomatopoeia – words can sound like the noise they are implying – e.g. mewed, roared, slithers.

Sayings and proverbs as in 'Too many cooks spoil the broth' or 'Too many chiefs and not enough Indians'.

Mnemonics – this is where you take each of the letters in a word and make up a silly sentence or phrase, e.g. Design: Design Enhances Someone's Instincts – Greatly Needed.

Direct speech to reader – using speech idioms – eg 'don't be shy' 'you are walking along minding your own business, when ...'

Use of do's and don'ts – e.g. 'Do wear this ...' or 'Don't be seen in ...'

Description:
Adjectives which are paired – e.g. cool and calm.

Words which are linked with hyphens – e.g. pencil-slim.

Adverbs – usually end in 'ly' e.g. simply, casually, provocatively.

*(**Adjectives** describe nouns and add colour, detail and, if over the top, they might be signs of selling or persuading.*

***Adverbs** describe verbs, which are the doing words, and these help to paint the picture and give a sense of mood or movement.)*

Headlines
e.g. Catwalk Catfight!
They have to be catchy and sometimes have humour to attract attention. They can be clever and appropriate, or sensational. They can give a sense of the article which follows, or could mislead the reader.
They often use particular devices – such as alliteration or metaphors or puns.

Word Play
This can be made up words – perhaps combinations of words: known words put together to make up another new word
e.g. grey + blazer = grazer
or woolly + pullovers = woolovers (this could also imply wool lovers = another meaning).

Double meanings – as in wasted and waisted (see above)
And several of the other devices already described.

Word Play often draws special attention to something, makes people laugh and then remember the point.

Reflection: This handout principally covers journalistic writing styles and techniques, but is a useful starting point for looking at the elements that are involved and can encourage greater use of the devices in the creation of writing, not just in the analysis of it. As with other examples I have given, a pick and mix approach needs to be taken in applying it to chosen material.

Pushing ...

I came across a tea cloth in the Crafts Council shop. In the centre of it was printed a vast spiral of words – all inspired by the phrase 'wash up'. There then followed hundreds (it seems like that and I am not going to count them) of phrases with '... up'. For example: *roll up, shake up, turn up, show up, blow up, het up, parcel up, hurry up;* you get the drift.

This was taking an idea and pushing it as far as possible. You don't even need to go as far as possible – just somewhere beyond the normal.

These are good warm-ups:

■ *take any sort of phrase that we use a lot and push it; or take one word from it and extend it – as with wash up*
■ *take any simple word such as 'down' or 'round' or 'through' and push it for a while.*

You could set yourself a time limit, or you could do it until you are fed up.

You can use reference books: this is a good time to get familiar with some of the inspirational reference tools (some are listed in the bibliography).

Help yourself think with the sorts of paper or implements you use:

■ *so, if you take the phrase 'go round and round in circles' – use a circular piece of paper and spiral in with phrases*
■ *if you use 'in and out' – write on fabric which has woven threads weaving in and out.*

The reason I have called this little section 'pushing' is that this is often what we need to do to ideas. We often just sit and stare at something, passively – it is there, we are over here. But everything can be pushed, extended, worked on. And in the process, energy is galvanized and ideas begin to flow. The brain loves to do this sort of thing – it is a muscle waiting to be exercised and pushed. Maybe this could be called 'brain gym' (but I am aware that that is already the trade name for a programme of brain training).

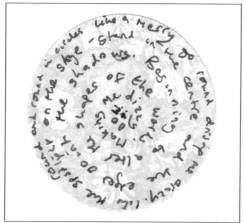

Fig. 31: Pushing the line to write.

Repetition

This is another 'game' – useful to do to generate ideas, build vocabulary and creatively manipulate language.

Take a word from something that you are doing or working on at the moment.

Do any of the following:

- *repeat – change one letter at a time*
    seek, seen, seed, need, nerd, herd, here, mere, mete, mite, mine
- *repeat part of it*

research	released	realize	re-charges
re-suss	relief	re-changes	re-new
re-surge	resurrect	resource	

- *play with the prefix/suffix*

de-search	re-search	re-seek		
pre-search	re-surge			
searching	searched	searches	searches	see search

- *alliteration*
    revealing   research   realizes and   releases results
- *rhyme*
    research   lurch   birch   besmirch   perch   church
- *sounds: the words need to be said out loud and played with*

sty	style	stylus
	stile	stiletto

    steal
    stole
    stiff   stilettos   steal style
    style   bile   file   mile
    styles   sighs
    style   smiles
    styles   smile
    word   work
    world   whorled   whirl   worse   worth
    weird   wired

- *homophones*
    style   stile   serge surge   root route

And finally *word play*, which is partly some of these, and all of these, but just fun, curiosity, similarity and anything else that strikes you:

   word stories, or word histories, or word stones (words are or aren't set in stone)

When you have generated some of these word lists, look at them for inspirational ideas, silly connections. No more, no less – but often, something springs …

Word (hi)stories

Many words have highly interesting or headily inter-related stories.

Souvenir is a word that often comes up with some of the objects or materials I use to stimulate writing. For a project with Illustration students, three words were offered as starting points: **souvenir, inventory** and **journey**

Most immediately veered towards journey – it setting off a range of images and ideas. The other two were actually perceived of as being limited and boring.

However, when the word (hi)story was shown, layers of meanings and ideas were revealed. This is something I do naturally, as I am curious about words and enjoy them. See if you are surprised in the roots of words, which may then spark off other ideas that you might never have thought of.

All these words can be nouns or verbs, and although they may change in form, the ideas behind them are what is important.

JOURNEY

This is a noun and a verb. It can mean the act of going from one place to another, or the distance travelled in a specified time, or the travelling of a vehicle along a route at a stated time.

It comes from the word *journeyer* which is Middle English from the Old French *journée* – day, day's work or travel, and ultimately from the Latin *diurnus* – daily.

INVENTORY

This is a noun and a verb. It can mean a complete list of goods in stock or house contents, etc., or you can make an inventory of something. If you had taken an inventory you would have 'inventoried' the items. This sounds like inventing stories.

It comes from the Middle English via Medieval Latin – *inventorium* – from the late Latin *inventarium* (as invent). Therefore there are layers of meaning to a word which on the surface might seem rather prosaic or dull.

SOUVENIR

This is a noun and a verb. It means a memento of an occasion, or a place, etc., but also in slang can mean that you pilfer or steal – as we might understand in the phrase 'take a souvenir'. 'To souvenir' is 'to pilfer'.

It is from the French for remember, from the Latin *subvenire*, 'occur to the mind' (as *sub* – before, and *venire* – come). Again this reveals the layers of meaning attached to a frequently debased word.

Their use in *proverbs, in clichés, in sayings,* is another fruitful source.

Brewer's Dictionary of Phrase and Fable is a must-have book for idea generation. It is a mine of folk lore, sayings, facts, associations and many other possibilities.

Another stimulator is searching for *quotations* that use the word.

There is a vast range of dictionaries of quotations, including novelty or coffee table publications – which raises questions about why so many of these exist and how superficial some are and how inspirational others are.

Words Whirl (nouns and verbs)

1. One version of this can be 'played' with someone else.
2. But you can also develop a version on your own.

1. Each person folds a piece of paper in half. On the left hand side, write six **nouns**.

Choose from one of these categories:

a. *all occupations: e.g. tailor, writer*
b. *things in your house: e.g. bookcase, table*
c. *abstract nouns: e.g. happiness, anger.*

Fold this list back so that your partner doesn't see it. Then swap papers.

Now write six **verbs**.

Use any of these categories:

d. *to do with occupations: e.g. sews, drafts*
e. *any physically active verbs e.g. runs, hops*
f. *verbs to do with the weather e.g. drizzles, melts.*

Now open up the sheet. You should have pairs of nouns and verbs. Some will work, some will be crazy. Mix and match: pair with opposites; or then the first with the last; second with the fourth, etc.

2. The version by yourself could be worked by having several pieces of paper and then mixing them up so that you may get a match, but probably not. Even list some on one day, and do the rest the next day.

The imagery generated can be very funny, which might give ideas for practical work. In terms of writing it makes you think of clichés – how we often say the same old things; and this might encourage exploration of alternatives.

For example, we usually say that rain pours or drizzles, but *rain meanders* gives a very different and evocative description.

And

bookcases are often very solidly placed in rooms; but a bookcase which *strides* across a room gives it a very dominant impact to the interior.

This can show how important the verbs are for creating a mood, or defining a pace or movement.

In the theatre, actors are often encouraged to highlight the verbs in their text, and this can give insight to their character, but also ascertains the energy of a speech or the underlying tensions and subtext.

What this exercise can also help with is comprehension of some parts of speech. In a workshop I can explain more about these words, other than just the definitions.

The exercise can be expanded beyond nouns and verbs:

Add an **adjective** before the noun (adjectives describe the noun).

Add an **adverb** to the verb (usually ending in 'ly' they give detail to the verb).

So, for example *tidy tailor sews slowly*

or (if it had got mixed up) *grumpy tailor kneads mincingly*.

Sometimes text needs this elaboration and expansion of detail. At other times it has to be sparse with no descriptive words. It could be equated to a black and white or a colour version. However, often black and white and tones of grey give more subtlety to the description than colour, particularly in some colour printing processes: e.g. the garish colour prints of the 1960s and 70s.

It could be the objective, factual version or the subjective, emotional variation.

Thinking about the way you describe things encourages you to consider how other writers do this and how advertisers can manipulate consumers.

Think of the Marks and Spencer's food adverts on television:

'This is not ordinary food, this is M&S food.'

M and S is used here as an adjective that equates with excellence and the sentence is spoken with a soft, sexy voice.

'These are not just strawberries.

These are farm-fresh, hand-picked, succulently-juicy strawberries.'

Fashion journalism goes in for similar excess: pencil-thin, rain-cloud grey, long-legged, bell-bottomed trousers. (Note the use here of the hyphen joining the multiple adjectives: a particular device of this branch of journalism.)

Creative writing courses try to get their writers to expand their vocabulary and ways of expression, so **Nouns and verbs** is a good warm up exercise.

But for all areas of writing this is a, sometimes funny, sometimes absurd, way of expanding descriptions and actions.

Examples to help as prompts:

nouns

- *Clothes: trousers, shirt, corset*
- *Utensils: pan, sieve, grater*
- *Tools: chisel, knife, saw*
- *Writing/painting implements: pencil, charcoal, brush*
- *Types of book/film: romance, adventure, saga.*

verbs

- *Person's movements: hops, meanders, mooches*
- *Weather: pours, drips, swirls*
- *Mechanical things: roars, spurts, splutters*
- *Sport: sprints, dives, thwacks*
- *Occupations: kneads, saws, twirls.*

Another variation is to look at the **tense** of the verb (past, present, future).

Make the verbs active and in the present tense, third person singular:

> so it would not be: I dive
> but: he/she/it dives
> and not: 'dived', which is in the past

When pairing the words, adjustments can be made: for example trousers (you don't usually have one trouser, although there are trouser-suits).

However, you could deliberately change the tense for some exercises and see what a difference this might make.

Painter exploded

(this makes you want to write: the angry painter exploded into a creative maelstrom of colour, hurling pots of paint at the giant canvas)

Shirt dripped

(this, instead of dripped with sweat, could be: the shirt dripped layers of silk embellishments which merged into the velvet skirt)

Fig. 32: Words whirling.

Adverts

This can be a hilarious activity for two people, and is also a good warm-up for thinking about writing that has to persuade or sell. (It could be argued that all writing has to persuade in some way, so the exercise does have layers of application.)

In a workshop, I give out adverts which have been torn from a range of magazines, with products ranging from foods to white goods, cosmetics to cars, jewellery to jumpers.

One person has to sell this product to the other. However the potential customer is very reluctant and does not want to buy. The salesperson has to be very persuasive, in words – no physical coercion is allowed.

Even if the salesperson doesn't like or know the product it is quite possible to have a go.

After a short while, choose another advert and swap roles.

The salesperson has to employ a range of persuasive tactics and the other has to assume a range of excuses and negative responses. The reluctant consumer might be so bowled over by the rhetoric of the other that there is a decision to buy.

After each has had a go at each role, talk about this.

Then write reflectively about it:

- *What sorts of language did you use: jargon, clever sounding, but empty?*
- *Did you keep going with no pauses for interruptions?*
- *Did you use any particular words or simple, easily understood vocabulary?*
- *Did you use alliteration or rhyme or rhythm – or could you have done so to help?*
- *In order to build up to something, did you present points logically, did you list reasons that something would be good?*

Full frontal offensive rarely works, unless incredibly clever; but a subtle, slowly building, reasoned approach might win the target round.

This is meant to be fun and I do not endorse the methods of salesmanship. But it gets you thinking about the language and devices of promotional writing – from both points of view.

You could take this further: away from random adverts, into exhibition advertising, fashion show promotion, etc.

As with many other exercises this is a starting point – not an end in itself.

Drawing the Journey

The purpose of this is to reflect on the process or journey of the project, the writing or whatever else it is that you are undertaking. The point about it is that it is sometimes easier to visualize this process before you verbalize it. You could use it as a point of reflection during and at the end of a project. The regular reflective writing in a journal will also help.

Draw the journey of the project you are doing (or have completed) (see Fig. 33 overleaf):

- *It might look like a map, or a heart monitor, a shape, a flowing line, spiky line …*
- *Start simply, then add more detail in as you wish.*
- *The idea is to chart the ups and the downs, the turns and twists, the highs and lows, the going by byways, the returns, then drifting off, etc.*
- *A nosedive can show a rapid decline in the focus of the project.*

(Note that in these instructions, various visuals are suggested, but you will find your own.)

When you are ready, maybe you can add in odd words, or build detail with lists. Do not compare yourself with anyone else – the point of this is to make this personal to you. This is optional, but the words can really help if you have to write a summary or evaluation.

You might find this drawing enormously useful as a summary of *what* happened, and this can lead more easily to thinking about *why* something happened and what you *did/think* about it. This too is excellent preparation for the writing of summaries and evaluations. The detail should be found in the journals – so this reinforces the idea of keeping thoughts and reactions and reflections.

The other useful aspect of this visualzation is that it communicates very quickly to the 'author' (you), but also to others what has happened, or is happening.

An inspiration for this comes from Alfred Wainwright (1992) who carefully drew and annotated maps for walks in the fells of the Lake District. His drawings are a combination of a map in terms of directions and paths to take, but they also incorporate views of the landscape and silhouettes of the terrain: the shapes of hills and valleys and the relationship of the skyline and the mountains that you might see ahead of you as you walk. The combined viewpoints are useful in terms of understanding what reflection is about and also as a visual means of seeing where you are on your own journey.

> **Reflection:** This can be a very useful shorthand way for tutors to see where students feel they are, during a project. A quick viewing might most clearly identify those who are spiralling down and need some positive input to help them back on track. These people might have been hiding this, but the visual will reveal it.

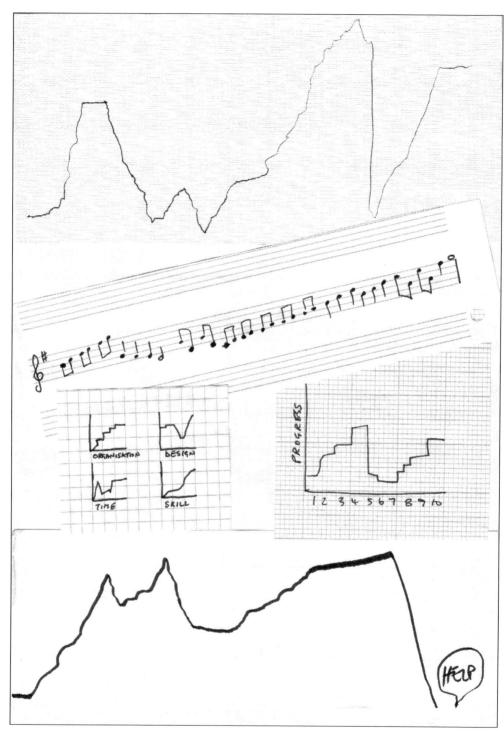

Fig. 33: All journeys are different.

Mistakes

A message that we all can encounter at different points in our lives and education is that mistakes are bad. Memories abound of our writing being rejected or returned with red lines all over it, highlighting our mistakes. We know the feeling that we have failed, and mistakes are identified with failure.

In creative studio work mistakes are a vital part of the process. It is what we *do* with the mistakes that is important. They are not an end in themselves.

We need to unlearn our associations with mistakes and come to feel that a mistake is just an opportunity on the journey. Mistakes can lead to greater, broader, more fruitful ideas. When we come across our mistakes, we might have other ideas as a result. If it was perfect first time, we might not have got round to exploring other byways. Even the repetition of the word 'mistake' in this paragraph could prompt questioning of the word itself, and this leads to play – so we might get 'miss-take' or 'mist-ache'.

These approaches are vital in the area of writing. Sometimes a mis-spelling or the inappropriate use of a word can lead to deeper or alternative thoughts and writing.

What I try to encourage in workshops, and with anyone I am working with, is the openness to make mistakes: allow them. Edit and correct later. Not now.

- *write – get it all down*
- *if you can't think of a word, leave a line of dots, or write the nearest word, but underline it so that you know you want to work on it*
- *but get things down*
- *do not edit as you go along (that is an unfortunate legacy of exam-led education).*

Remember these mnemonics for the words: edit, rough and final:

rough	edit –	final
outpouring	do	is
until	it	now
got	tomorrow	attempted
heaps		last

The mnemonic for **mistakes** is vital, as mistakes are full of positive 'e's

mistakes
initially
seem
terrible,
although
key
experimentations/**e**xcellences/**e**xpressions/**e**xtras/**e**fforts and so on
surface

Starting Pieces of Work

One step at a time
A few mnemonics to remind you to start small and not try to do the whole at once.

often
needing
explanation

start
tiny –
expanding
purposefully

at
times

a

thought
is
my
escape

taking
a
kindly
initiative –
not
groaning

pausing
awhile,
until
several
experiments
start

                                   another
                            after
                    step
               one
           bottom
        the
    at
> start

Can't Do All – Start with One

This is not an exercise, more of an approach to work.

The title of this reveals one of the main solutions to writer's block, creative block, banging your head against a brick wall, and so on *ad infinitum* …

When you are overwhelmed with the amount you have to do, or when you do not know where to start, but are pressurizing yourself to make a start, but just cannot, the answer is to start something. It doesn't matter if it's not the right thing (that may emerge once you have started). The bit you do may be short-lived, but it gets you going.

> "I do know some stories I think a lot of people would enjoy … maybe I should start them."

> "Don't start them. Start one of them."

> "That's all?"

> "That's all it ever takes." (Cameron, 1998: 191–2)

This relates to pieces I have mentioned about practice and warming up, limbering up, etc. Once the writing hand is flowing, once the brain is relaxed, then ideas flow; energy is energized.

You can't do it all, particularly all at once, but you can make a little start.

This is one of the most valuable pieces of advice to a reluctant writer, or to anyone who is blocking or panicking.

All the time your hand or your brain are saying 'I can't do it… don't know where to start, don't know where it's going to go,' nothing WILL happen. But make a start HERE. It is not set in stone, you may not use it, but you start doing something, then the ice is broken, and the first step taken.

The route of the journey can never be known in advance: in the creative arts, as in life. So we need to encourage an open mind, an 'openness' to what might happen – the creative mistake, the sudden inspirations, the contradictions, the making of new links/ connections – in the practical subjects. So, for all the planning, there is still an openness to what will happen.

This justifies the starting anywhere – as long as it is starting.

- brainstorming, making a list, getting odd words down, is the first step
- then choosing one word, one idea and going with that gets the process going

- take any word: don't think too hard
- don't look at all the pros and cons of starting with that word: just see where it goes
- if it leads up a blind alley – leave it
- take another word.

The energy to write is being galvanized and before long it will make sense of the ideas and the writing.

False starts are never failures. Never, ever, a waste of time.

In our past education there has not been much time for false starts, for blind alleys, for cul-de-sacs. We are often encouraged to just go for the straight main roads, the motorways: fast, but boring, predictable and uncreative.

I can give my own example of this. I had been humming and haahing with this book for a long time. I was telling myself that I'd got to make a start. I'd got lots of ideas. Odd lists, odd thoughts, but I was continually skirting round the book.

'I've got to write a BOOK. It's huge – so big, I can't start.'

One day my inner voice made itself heard: 'Do what you always tell others to do – remember Cameron. You can't write a book – you can write one *bit* of the book.'

And that was all it took.

It seemed a *random bit* that I started on. Very probably that bit of writing won't appear in the final piece – it might be too raw and too unformed, but no matter, it got me scribbling. I filled a page; the energy was tapped; I'd started, and I've not stopped.

Sometimes it takes someone else to suggest a tiny nugget that could be the starting point, to help us make the leap, There is a little bit in us that feels that if someone else says what the starting point could be, and that if it turns out not to be, then it's not our fault. That becomes a safety valve. But even if it is the *wrong* (really there is no such concept in this area) starting point, it will have got the writing going.

One Step:
one
nudge
excites

steps
to
encourage
process/progress

Working Towards Essays, etc.

Making the Start on Formal Pieces of Writing

If you have got to do an essay or dissertation, the first stage is probably to make some sort of plan and a loose structure.

Some people do need to start at the beginning and work through. Some think they do – but may never have tried anything else. Some follow the advice of leaving the introduction to last and therefore start with chapter one or the first section. Some may need to do bullet points for the early parts, even if they don't write them in full.

It doesn't matter – whatever gets you going. It may be that you have tried all sorts of things, and nothing has ever worked before. See if there is anything new, here in this book, that might be worth a try. Give other things another go, but with new energy. Often what is needed is one trigger – one key idea that will make the move.

Are there any *visuals*? Could that be the starting point? An analysis of that – which will include why it is in the essay – will probably lead to the need for justification, explanation, links to history or theory or linking to a person. Maybe the writing of this might seem to be backwards:

- *one visual – this then needs an explanation:*
- *but firstly it needs a description,*
- *but before that it needs introducing.*

This can all be sorted out later. This is so important to emphasize. The writing is not final: it can be cut and pasted – manually or on the computer: LATER.

Rather than a visual, it might be a *quotation*. In all your reading and research I would encourage you to keep quotations: one or two lines that you react to with 'yes, I really agree, that's intriguing, that shows something up'.

Maybe take that quotation:

- *Introduce it – linking to what you are saying.*
- *Who said it, when, in what context?*
- *What does it refer to?*
- *How do certain words work?*
- *Does it sum up the main thoughts that seem to be driving the essay?*
- *What does it link to? – move the quotation on to another level.*

Or you may have done quite a comprehensive *brainstorm*:

- *Maybe you have already made a lot of links.*
- *Can you see a structure or grouping of ideas from this?*
- *Take just one bit.*
- *Set yourself to write a paragraph on that.*
- *If it really doesn't work, try another one, in the same section.*
- *If you are still blocking go to another section.*

Keep doing this until something does start to flow.

I really don't think the blocking will go on for ever. If it does, there is evidently not enough research, because if writing is not flowing, there isn't enough back up, or connections haven't been formed properly. And that will give you something to do.

If writing a paragraph is too daunting:

- *bullet point the brainstorms*
- *if brainstorms are single words – then do bullet points that are several words.*

This is starting with a small unit and building on it. Bullet points can be moved around, given different orders and sequences, and can be expanded. And that is encouraging.

One word *leads to a*
bullet point of eight or more words *which*
turns into a sentence of twenty words.

Suddenly a start has been made on the 2000 word essay and the essay is on its way.

Reading and Noting Techniques

There are three different ways of reading.

- *Read **every** word, carefully (think of a centipede reading with each of its 100 feet – plodding carefully through the text).*
- **Skim** *through – looking for the main points, and 'skimming' over some of the text, where it is not so important (think of a duck floating over the water – skimming over the text).*
- *Scan through – just looking for certain <u>key</u> words: much as you would do if you were looking for someone's name in a phone directory or index. (Think of a butterfly – flitting from flower to flower to find where the nectar is – only stopping where there is the right sort of nectar – stopping only when you find the key words.)*

It is worth thinking about which technique you need to use when using written material. Skimming and scanning do take some practice and it is worth working on this – to make the best use of your time, and to find what you want from a text.

Do not read every word, if you do not need to. You do not have the time. Be selective.

Notes can be taken in the same way:

- *word for word – this could be used as a quotation*
- *skim-notes – the main points*
- *scan-notes – key words only.*

Highlighter pens can also be used in this way, and also using different colours:

- *the whole passage highlighted*
- *one sentence or a phrase highlighted*
- *one word (every now and then) highlighted.*

Fig. 34: Buried in a book.

Using Postcards to Inspire Writing

Painting Postcards
For this exercise you can use postcards from galleries (there are also some books of postcards available). If you do this exercise with someone else, then you will be able to use material not familiar to you.

- do not turn the postcard over to reveal the written side
- don't spend ages choosing a card – just take any one
- look at the picture
- then write on a piece of paper using the following questions as stimuli
- you can jot words down or use full sentences – it doesn't matter.

Just write:

- *what it makes you feel*
- *whether you like it or not*
- *what it is about*
- *what its title could be*
- *how colours are used*
- *what forms, shapes, patterns are there*
- *if there is a narrative*
- *what medium/media have been used.*

When you feel you have exhausted ideas, turn it over and look at who did it, what it is, etc.

The reason for the questions being quite personalized is that this should be writing that is not inhibited by art history. If we know something is by Picasso we approach it differently. Sometimes, even if we only know a little bit, it can 'colour' our view.

The aim is to encourage looking and questioning and feeling.

Now you know who and what, write a bit more:

- *How does your impression of the work differ?*
- *Is the title very different from what you had written?*
- *Can you see why it was called what it was?*

Are you surprised at:

- *who the artist was*
- *the medium used*
- *the date*
- *the size, etc.*

Further areas of questioning:

Pure description of the image

■ *Colour, medium, figures, abstract, representation, detail, narrative.*

The point of building up descriptive writing is that this is the main way into analysis: it aids real looking, it brings a logic into the process that can then be built on in an analysis. Detailed description requires close viewing and questioning.

Title
This can lead to interesting thoughts and discussions about the importance of the title and how this is used and manipulated by the artist. This, in turn, can go on to how people look at the title *before* they really look at the work, and why this is. This might be particularly relevant if you have to create a title for your own work.

Stories
This is more appropriate for some subjects than others but is always productive for developing writing.

■ *What is going on?*
■ *Who are they?*
■ *What are the relationships that can be surmised?*

This sort of exercise, when unhindered by knowing what something actually is, can help build confidence in developing analytical skills. There is no absolute right or wrong; it is about interpretation and observation.

It is a completely different task to writing about something with labels already attached – 'from x's late period when he was experimenting with ...'

We are very quick today to give labels to everything or to categorize, and that can inhibit ideas and also the writing.

Other areas of postcards that might be useful for differing writing styles and ideas.

Nostalgia postcards
These are usually reprints of old postcards, frequently rather whimsical or nostalgic and are good to start thinking about the growth of these in contemporary design and society generally.

Look at the image and write notes about:

■ *the styles, colours, subjects, graphics*

- *if they remind you of anything contemporary*
- *whether these have been copied in design today*
- *if such copying is critical of or cynical about the original, or respectful, etc.*
- *think about nostalgia and vintage and the meanings of these words.*

Greetings postcards
These might include postcard birthday cards which were particularly popular in the first half of the twentieth century (see Fig. 35).

Firstly just look at the front, commenting on:

- *the graphics, the colours, the embossing, the sentimentality of the words.*

Then turn over and read the handwritten message:

- *put this in context – in a period where there were no phones in general use, this might be the only message received*
- *the link with the films of the period: overblown language, glamour, etc.*
- *or a card sent during a time of war when the sender and receiver might not see each other again.*

The date is often evident from a postmark; if not, what could be the date? This can lead to questions about how we date items such as this.

This can lead on to writing:

- *creatively – the possible story*
- *research – into the period and relationships and what was going on at the time – e.g. war, The Depression*
- *comparative – how similar messages are transmitted or given today*
- *what sentiment is and how and why notions of this have changed over different periods.*

Photographic postcards
These were popular in the early years of the twentieth century when people would have their **own** photographs printed as postcards to send to family and friends (see Fig. 35).

Just looking at the image, write about:

- *what it is about – a pose, or a snapshot*
- *who is in it*
- *what occasion it might have been*
- *whether the subjects are relaxed/happy/formal*
- *and who the photographer could be.*

Then turn over and read if there is a message on the reverse:

- *write about the public nature of this – how many people could read the message (going through the postal system, etc.)*
- *think about this convention of sending oneself through the post*
- *think about whether there is an equivalent today*
- *and if this is like the growth of the Internet's MySpace pages, etc.*

Further subjects to research in order to back up writing:

Costume:

- *what we can tell from this*
- *how it is possible to date items*
- *what has to be taken into account – e.g. class, money, best clothes lasting for years and therefore not always indicative of the date of first appearance.*

Photography:

- *the sorts of cameras and who owned them*
- *albums and how photographs are kept and displayed and how this is changing today.*

Relationships:

- *in the family*
- *who takes the photographs*
- *then and now.*

I have suggested just a *few* of the possible writing ideas from postcards – but this is the sort of activity that once started could go off in lots of different directions depending on interests, subjects, etc.

> **Reflection:** This is a particularly useful exercise to present in a workshop as the leader can choose the postcard and often use material not familiar to others. It is important to emphasize not turning over the postcard to look at the written material. Judge when to suggest turning over, depending on how writing is flowing. Explain why this approach is taken – starting from the writer's perspective, not the art history one. The 'feeling' aspect might not always be a traditional approach, but this is a way into helping writers acknowledge the part their feelings play in perceptions of work and how they can start to articulate their responses. Get participants to bring in their own postcards and swap with each other. Walter Benjamin's (2007) reference to the contribution of postcards in the building of his Archive might be fruitful. His writings on their social value to his project could stimulate much discussion.

Fig. 35: 'I am here …'

Quote Circles

For many pieces of work, both practical and written, quotations from other sources are encouraged. 'Quote Circles' gives practice in integrating them into your own writing. It is visual, and this often generates greater connections than words alone might suggest.

When reading for an essay or with a specific task in mind, you often come across a few lines that you instinctively feel are going to have to appear in the finished piece. But how do you integrate these and not just plonk them in?

In the centre of a piece of paper write out the quotation and surround it with a rough circle. This is like a giant speech bubble, which puts it in the context of words which are said or written (see layout overleaf).

Branching out from this circle, make five legs.

Now there are five questions to act as starting points to writing about the quotation.

For some tasks, other questions might replace these, but these will act as starting points if stuck.

- *Is there any link to the **ideas** (however vaguely, and in either agreement, or a disagreement with the points in the quote) of any other person who has been researched or encountered?*
- *What is the **context** of quote – who said it, when, why, where?*
- *Can you **link** it to your argument/title, again however vaguely to start with?*
- ***Key word or words**: unpack these – look up, find deeper definitions and decide which words are the keys – the important ones.*
- ***Instinct** – why did you have a gut feeling about this – what was special, what was so good or so well expressed?*

Circles may connect or intersect and visually this might help develop the ideas. It might end up looking a little like a spider diagram, which might lead to other ideas.

Each of the five original questions could lead to others:

- *What is the subtext?*
- *Are there paradoxes in it (contradictions – says one thing but means another; says one thing – but did another)?*
- *Does the context, for example, lead to many different areas of enquiry about the time it was written, why it was written, reactions to it?*
- *Is it controversial now – or was that only so when written?*
- *Are there differences in point of view then and now?*
- *Who wrote it and are they famous for any one thing or one action?*
- *Are they an expert, or is this ill informed opinion?*

With some of these areas you might only write one or two sentences, others might expand into whole paragraphs.

Context of
quote

Link to
own argument

link to ideas
of someone else

Xxxxxxxxxxxxxxxxxxxxxxxxxxxxxxx
Xxxxxxxxxx The Quotation xxxxxxxxxxxxxxxxxxx
Xxxxxxxxxxxxxxxxxxxxxxxxxxxxxx

gut feeling or
instinct about the
quote and its
possibilities

key word(s)

meanings   double meanings

Other ideas for brainstorming the quotation: it provides evidence
it caused controversy
it gives an explanation
it inspires your work
it has a metaphor which is particularly apt

Quotations Consequences

This is based on the game of consequences and needs to be done with two or three people. Even just working with one other person will give some ideas.

A quotation is written at the bottom of an A4 piece of paper.

- **1st stage:** *the first person reads it and makes notes about it at the top of the paper: reactions, agree/disagree, comments, reminds of... etc.*
- **2nd stage:** *when they are done they fold the paper over to cover their writing – but leaving the quotation clearly showing at the bottom*
- **3rd stage:** *hand to the next person, who reads and writes underneath the first person's work, but not having seen what they wrote*
- **4th stage:** *they then fold the paper over so their writing is hidden and pass to a third.*

When everyone has had a go, or there are a number of comments on the quotation, the paper is unfolded and you can read other views on it.

Sometimes everyone will agree but usually there are differences of opinion, or different interpretations.

This can be really useful in thinking about potential quotations for an essay.

- Looking at something from a number of points of view is very valuable.
- Understanding differences in interpretation and why this happens broadens and deepens an essay.
- If the quotation is anonymous, everyone is coming from a similar position – not knowing who said it or when.
- If the quotation is attributed and some people know something of the author and others do not, there can be various interpretations that might influence how something is understood.
- Context, in terms of when something was said or written, is another aspect that contributes to varying reactions and is essential to essay writing.

Even if the reactions to the quotation are not very deep, discussion can direct your ideas to encourage you to delve in a more detailed manner. If three people do this, three quotations are used and then a lot of debate is to be had.

This is 'talk write': talking, discussing, disagreeing and listening, before writing, and all these contribute to deeper writing. It would be useful, after the playing of the consequences, to spend a few minutes writing about thoughts from the discussion and differing reactions.

It might seem that this game calls for instant responses and at other times I am saying that instant is not good: there has to be time and work in order to develop thoughts more deeply. However this game alerts and activates questions about instant responses, about knowledge of context and others' views – so it stimulates further work.

Variations:

- *attributed quotation*
- *non-attributed words*
- *subject specific*
- *related to topic being studied*
- *notes on other people's views – so also analysing responses: this would be good practice for essays in particular.*

> **Reflection:** This exercise is obviously more geared to a workshop situation where someone else had found the quotation and all participants are coming from the same position of being introduced to the quotation at the same moment.
>
> A variation of this could be that each person brings a quotation that they respond to, and present it to others – so one person has the advantage of having thought in more depth, and is not having to 'instantly' respond, and may also, in discussion, be able to lead a more detailed debate.

Example of how the paper is laid out:

First response to quote

Fold the paper over

Second response to quote

Fold the paper over

Third response to quote

'Quotation is laid out at the bottom of the piece of paper'

Visual Analysis – Some Points to Help

The questions in this section are not all applicable each time you want to analyse a visual. You need to do a 'pick and mix' and adapt some of the questions to suit the subject. They are meant to *stimulate* questioning, not be an end in themselves. Your first question might be: is more research needed on the image, or can an immediate analysis be made, or is it a combination of the two? Make a list of what needs research.

Form:

■ *description*
■ *colour*
■ *form*
■ *size*
■ *medium.*

Aesthetics:

■ *What role do all the above ideas play in the piece?*

Content:

■ *What is it about?*
■ *What does it say?*
■ *Has it got a purpose to sell something?*
■ *Does it portray someone or something?*
■ *Is it meant to entertain the viewer?*
■ *Does it educate the viewer?*
■ *Has it a decorative function?*

Aims:

■ *What does the 'artist' aim to achieve (or you **think** they are trying to achieve)?*
■ *Has this worked? And why it did or didn't.*

Audience:

■ *Who is it aimed at? Be quite specific about this if you can.*
■ *Was it praised or criticized by people who were not the target audience?*
■ *What impact did it have? Did it cause controversy?*
■ *Caused outrage?*
■ *Did it win prizes?*
■ *Was it copied, or has it been copied since or plagiarized?*

Context 1:

■ *Where is the visual placed (i.e. place of publication)?*
■ *What is it placed next to?*

Context 2:

■ *Social, historical, political, aesthetic, theoretical …?*
■ *Where does it fit into all these categories?*
■ *What are the beliefs, customs, etc. of the time the piece was created?*
■ *How do these relate to today?…*
■ *How contemporary is it – or what is its relation to the past?*

References:

■ *What does the visual allude to (refer to or imply)?*
■ *Does it rely on the audience knowing something to get the message?*
■ *Parallels – what sort of work is it like or similar to?*

Is it **original** in style – or is it like others, a copy, part of a school or movement …

Manipulation:

■ *Is the image changed or edited?*
■ *Is the audience manipulated in their reactions?*

Editing and selecting:

■ *What is in the visual and what is not, and who selected this and why?*
■ *What is the 'picture frame': where does the visual begin and end? (This links to references, and also to contemporary society, and also to words.)*

Do the pairs of words below need to be explored in relation to the image and how?

Viewer and Viewed   Subject and Object   Viewer and Spectator

■ *Who is in the picture?*
■ *Where is the author or photographer or artist?*
■ *What relationship do they have to the subject of the image?*
■ *Does the subject of the picture collude with the author in the message put over by the image (the subject knows what they are doing and is willing to be used/manipulated by the creator of the image – or not)?*

Words:

- *What is the relationship to words (and who creates the words)?*
- *Is there a caption, or are the words inside the image?*
- *Or are there no words at all?*
- *Does it need an audience to add words?*
- *Does it make reference to some other subject or idea?*
- *Is there use of jargon or the use of familiar sayings?*
- *Does it ask questions or make statements?*
- *Is there a 'clever' relationship of words to image?*
- *Does it need both words and image?*

Sub text – hidden meanings:

- *Do you see that there is another message going on, or do you get a sense there may be even if you don't understand it?*

Humour:

- *What sort of humour is there: verbal, visual?*
- *Does it mock, is it physical humour, is it cynical …?*
- *Is it humour by juxtaposition – one thing next to another, but in an unusual or different context – so it is surprising?*

Time Lines or Lines of Time or Lines in Time

The time line is a rough working out of contexts. It helps formulate questions, deepens ideas, and adds to knowledge. It is useful, and is also a fun way of engaging with potential research, and can link to, and with, many areas of work.

- *draw a horizontal line*
- *on the left hand end, write your date of birth*
- *on the right hand end, write the current date*
- *mark on key dates or years where you have specific memories of events.*

This can then be followed by adding in national or international events.

Above the line, can be the personal events.

Below the line: the national events.

Then spread back from your own era to earlier times. Use parents' or grandparents' dates as starting points. There maybe many gaps in events for them, but the national and international events will coincide with when they were twenty or fifty etc. This personalizes history – gives a key to relating cause and effect; explains some of the 'whys'; asks some of the 'what ifs'.

In many pieces of work, the initial sketching of such a time line will help build an understanding of context – the choice of events to be put on the time line can vary for differing requirements.

It can be largely visual, with examples of inventions, or events. Or it can be a mixture of biographical with portraits, and pictures of events these people were linked to.

Labelling of eras becomes a line of enquiry that will give rise to ideas for writing.

Generalizations about eras can be recognized, but can also lead to thoughts about what we write with the benefit of hindsight; about nostalgia, with rose-tinted spectacles; about personal knowledge and involvement with events.

If a time line is done on a strip of paper it can be built up at various times and in various ways to produce a multi-layered visual which creates links and connections that can lead to other lines of enquiry and further research potential.

Another related visual form of research-gathering might be the family tree. Links and connections and legacies and, again, cause and effect, can be visualized by creating the general principle of the family tree. How one designer was influenced by x, y and z, and how two people coming together amalgamate their backgrounds in differing subjects, in order to create new ideas. This is a useful way of visualizing how things happen. It can help us explain sources of inspiration for work that we do.

This was used to great effect in the 'Spectres' exhibition at the Victoria and Albert Museum in 2004. The relationship between designers, movements, trends, and influences was inspiringly conceived as a giant family tree/brainstorm.

The process of creating a time line is not instant. One memory leads to another; dates have to be calculated, verified, adjusted. Links create further links and connections and 'aha' moments evolve.

Finding your place in the scheme of things is both salutary and reassuring.

Expanding the Visual Time Line from a personal focus into wider projects can be done individually or in a group. Use a large roll of paper – a roll of wallpaper is ideal. To build up to this, thinner strips of paper can also be used: for example, till rolls. Post-its, and/ or coloured tape are also good.

Develop a time line for the particular period for your project. If this is a large period in time, maybe work with other people on a decade. Alternatively you could each decide to look at specific areas such as films of a period, music, fashion, politics, etc.

As material is built up, a complex visual time line is created. Decisions can be made on how you display this material – but the idea is not to have masses of written material on the time line itself. This can be collected to be a resource which is referenced *from* the time line. The time line itself should be full of visuals, key words, and key dates. It could link a fashion with a political event, or a film with an invention.

There are many books which have such time lines in them and these can be used for source material, but it is important to create your own.

This should be about primary research and primary source material, not second-hand or ready-made. So it might be that objects or items are attached to the time line: objects might have belonged to, or have a significance of some sort with someone placed on the time line.

Starting points could be:

- *taking the **key dates in a designer's life** – such as in Crafts magazine where they have a profile on someone and then a column with key dates down the side: these dates could then be researched under a number of key headings which you would decide on*
- *research into **contemporary journals and magazines** as the key source: not reference books – just contemporary material*
- *taking as inspiration, the dates of the **releases or openings**: of films, of music, or buildings, or inventions, or the covers of fashion magazines, or the launch of magazines: these act as the keys or leads to finding out about the events of that specific date or year*
- *taking **quotations** from a period – thus using more words than suggested above, but presented in a more visual way – with perhaps the speakers depicted in photographs, illustrations or caricatures, or through typography in a range of styles and experimentations.*

Making Links, Connections and Threads through Key Words

One of the common problems in writing is making connections that the reader can follow. Often the writer is very clear about the links and knows what they mean, but frequently forgets to stand back and see if the connections are clearly there for others.

A title may be made, even a clever one with some word play, but if the writer forgets to use those particular words in the written piece, the reader can become confused.

So a writer has to be able to read their own work, step outside their own field of vision and see with others' eyes.

To help do this, use **Key Words**:

- *make a list of the key words for the piece you are about to write*
- *continually review them*
- *add to the list*
- *relate the list to the piece of writing*
- *when you are stuck, look at the list*
- *when you come to edit, this list will be a guide.*

So, for example, at least one word from the list may appear at least once in every paragraph.

This is something I often use if I am struggling to see what someone's writing is about, or what their structure is (or more likely isn't). I write down the key word that sums up each paragraph. If there are no paragraphs, I try to find the one, two or three key words for each page. The resulting list of words can be very revealing: it shows the backwards and forwards, the repetitions, the building of an argument, or the lack of one.

A fun way to think about key words is to think about Hollywood Cherokee. This is referring to Hollywood Cowboy and Indian films. The cowboys spoke garrulously and floridly. The Indians spoke monosyllabically and to the point.

They would not say: 'Well the battle's over now and it lasted a long time. So long, in fact, that we didn't manage to eat or drink – so we're absolutely starving. Let's hope the little women have got a good meal on back at the ranch ...'

What the Indians would say is: 'Battle over. Home. Food.'

In their stereotyping, the film-makers have actually given us a wonderful way of demonstrating the nuggets in a sentence:

- *What is the core question?*
- *What do we need to know?*
- *What order does it need to be in?*

When reading other texts that we might be researching, finding the key words is useful to help with note taking.

Key words can also link to your research: when discovering an article in an academic journal, consider the Abstract and key words. If these relate to your own key words, this might be a very useful article to read. If nothing connects, then it goes on the 'maybe' pile.

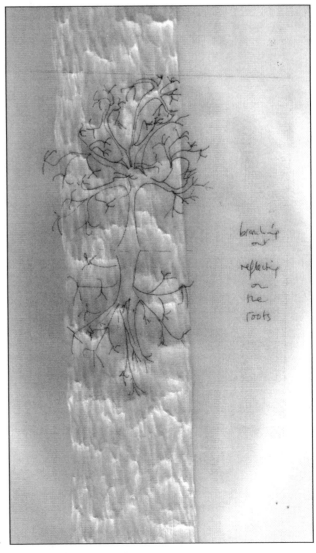

Fig. 36: Roots routes.

L:S:D:
This is not a promotion of hallucinatory drugs, but L:S:D: here, is a mnemonic.

It stands for:

Look back through your work
Select
Deepen

It is a strategy to use when stuck: when you have gone off at all sorts of tangents and then don't know what to do.

It is when crunch time happens – you've got to make a decision about which idea to follow; when you know you have got to focus down on something rather than carrying on, forever broadening.

First of all you need to stop and take stock:

- *organize material in some way: perhaps put it in chronological order of how you evolved the ideas*
- *or you might want to clump it into sections so that you can see the number of areas you did cover – like the petals of the flower.*

Look back through your work.

- *allow time for this, don't rush it*
- *immerse yourself in what you did – look at all the little entries, the odd words, the doodles: you are immersing in it but you are also now at a slight distance from it and your brain begins to filter some things in and some things out*
- *some ideas no longer make the sense they did*
- *others have more potential in them.*

Select: this is the key.

- *when you have looked through everything, make notes*
- *or build a heap of the ideas, the bits, the keys that are resonating*
- *use your instinct – not necessarily your intellect*
- *listen to your gut feeling that one idea has more possibilities than another.*

If necessary, do this select/sort/sieve process a number of times:

a first sort
then a sort through that selection
until you have a manageable amount.

Then **D**eepen some of these selections:

- *decide on more research – what you need to find out*
- *whether you need more drawing or visualizing of the idea*
- *more writing around, amplifying quotes*
- *developing a metaphor, linking one idea with another*
- *relating one writer's views with another.*

At this stage of deepening, the work will become more focused. After more deepening, re-focusing, re-planning, the work will be moving forwards.

L:S:D: works for designing, making and writing. Skills of selection don't always come fully formed – they can take time. However they will improve and often subtly, until you surprise yourself at how you can make, or are making, decisions about your own work, so that you don't need someone else to make those suggestions for you.

But this is not instant. It takes practice.

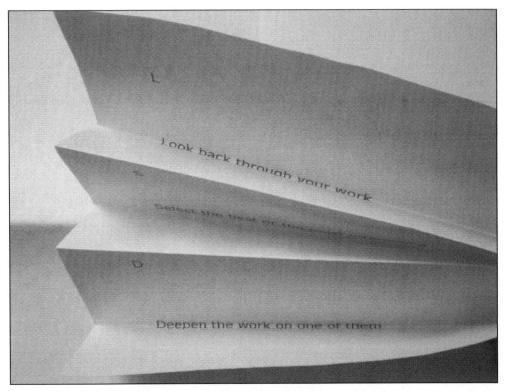

Fig. 37: L:S:D: a handout in the shape of a fan – to unfold its principles.

Making a Selection

Often you are asked to choose something, make a selection from many choices on offer. This can be very hard and we often feel that it is an impossible task.

So we have to create a strategy to help us.

This might help.

Think of a chocolate selection box. It is made up of dark, milk and white chocolates; there are hard and soft centres; chewy ones, crumbly ones; fruity, nutty and plain.

You go through the selection and mentally tick off each one:

It will get stuck   this will crack my teeth
        I like it, but it doesn't like me   can't stand
                                                                         coconut
        squidgy   even squidgier
                sticky   too sweet
                    this one makes me dribble

But although you now have a shortlist, which one do you choose?

Well, the situation is: you are wearing a clean tidy suit or blouse – you are just going for an interview, you have been offered the sweet and it will be good luck.

So the situation can also dictate what choice you make. If you risk the squidgy one and get it down your front: bye bye job. If you take one that is going to last ages, you might get caught with your mouth full. You don't want one that is too strong tasting, as that might stay with you when you have to speak. The highly coloured one will make your tongue look strange ...

(Probably you should save the sweet till after the interview.)

The point in all this mouth-watering preamble is that it is the **criteria** (in this case it was the situation of being prepared for a job interview) that you always have to bear in mind when you are making a selection. We usually do have, or can focus on, the criteria for each circumstance, and this will help make the selection. Some choices will be automatically ruled out in one situation, whereas they will be strong contenders in another.

So whenever there is a selection to be made:
first focus on the criteria to be met.

Structuring

Labels

As a way of sorting out areas of work in order to construct a structure, I often suggest the use of labels – to clump people, movements, events, artefacts, etc., together.

The idea of labelling throws up a range of questions or points to be considered:

- *Do we restrict something when we label it?*
- *Is it hard to break free of a label and try something else?*
- *If an artist is labelled an '…ist' does, or can this, inhibit their work, or the reception of it?*
- *Do we give credence to someone or something when we give them, or it, a label – do they become more recognized? (This might have implications for prices if work is sold. If a piece is attached, however loosely, to 'x' movement it receives the kudos of that reputation and the price rises.)*
- *If the label is negative, then, by association, can someone's work be de-valued?*
- *Will changes in fashion or taste also colour the label?*
- *A name can become a label. (This is particularly so in fashion and a name becomes synonymous with a desire, a pretension, a cult, a must-have …)*
- *Labels can lead to stereotypes which, while having a use in areas of satire perhaps, never reveal the whole picture.*
- *Generalizations can occur with labels, masking the specific qualities of someone or something.*

If we see a work and are told it is by Picasso, we approach it with a mindset that is informed by what we know of Picasso. We can never approach it entirely neutrally. If informed that a film is 'post modernist', we have certain expectations, and on occasions, this label is deliberately given to it before anyone views it, so the director ensures that it is approached with that frame of mind.

At Tate Modern there is a Time Line about artists and art movements, which uses labels, but as there are no lines or borders around the names, visually there appears to be a looseness which transcends the confines of a label. The way the illustrator, Sara Fanelli, has written some of the names implies that they only toyed with the ideas encompassed in some of the labels.

Labels can affect the sorts of written work you might have to do. Something handed in as 'an essay' might get low marks, as an essay, but high marks as a report or as an evaluation. Same piece: different label, different intention.

The methods in this book often state that creative writing techniques are being used to help the writing of other forms or categories. In stating this, I am using the idea of a creative writing label which is different from other techniques.

Awareness of labels, styles and outcomes can help your organization of work and also contribute to analysis. So the use of labels in the planning of a written piece of work is not meant to be an end in itself. It is a method to be used with care, and with this care, creative links can be made. Labels can be created solely for the purpose of planning – an essay, a statement, an evaluation, a report, etc. But labels can also be removed from something – they are not permanent fixtures.

Also it may be helpful to cross-reference with the paintings on postcards exercise, earlier in this section, where I suggest that you look and write about the visual before knowing the artist or title (the labels).

Use real paper labels, such as luggage labels or price tags, to help sort areas of work: or use Post-its or index cards. But remember that these are all made from paper – they are not set in stone. So they can be changed, altered, torn up …

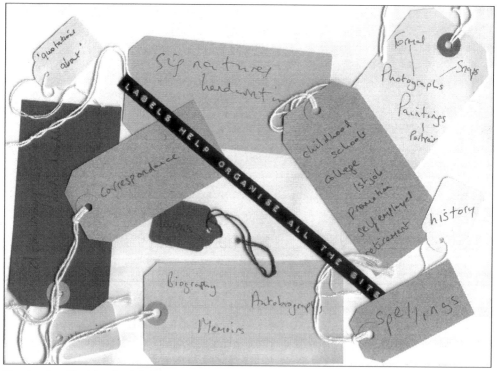

Fig. 38: 'No libel in the label.'

Classifying and Clumping

With many writing tasks it is necessary to sort out an order, decide on the way information is to be gathered, and presented. Decisions have to be made as to how connections and links are to be revealed. Lots of decisions, lots of possibilities. For many tasks there is more than one way of doing something.

The secret is in the planning: the background work – sometimes carried out before the writing even starts, or sometimes on reflection, when viewing and editing a script.

■ *It is often useful to try to classify the material in some **visual** way, in order to stand back and view the whole. Words alone are difficult to see in this wholistic way.*

■ *So ideas come down to just **key words** – which can represent a lot of material, but which help simplify and therefore aid the way the structure is arrived at.*

■ *Likening a structure to a **family tree**, or a **mind map** is one particular way. Families of information come together. An order is created: what has to come first, or who comes first; whose idea leads to whose actions?*

■ ***Colour*** *can help classify some things. All blue for one area, all green for another, yellow for another. And crossovers can even be a colour combination or a new colour.*

■ *Key words on a large piece of paper aid the overview. **Clumps and clouds** can be rearranged and lines connect the families.*

■ ***Post-its*** *can be created for sections and then they can be moved around to create different orders, until decisions are made.*

Classifying something means that decisions are being made about what are appropriate groups and what links things with one another. Sometimes this is easy, but on many occasions it can be complex. And there are no rules that apply to everything. This is so even in the ruled-based Dewey system in library classification, which is, in theory, straightforward. There might be logic in putting a book in a particular category. But it can end up with a mighty number, which takes account of all the aspects of the book, but is almost impossible to find on the shelves. There is a logic to the long numbers: countries have the same number, whether the book is about geography or flora and fauna of that country, for example. In different types of library it is more useful to arrange books in 'Dewically incorrect clumps'. An example of this might be to have all artists filed alphabetically under their name, rather than by country, and/or time period. Everyone knows their name, but not necessarily their country of origin or date. (There are counter arguments about this, which could rumble on indefinitely …)

In some ways the brain is one giant Dewey system, but it is a unique classification system: unique to us and what information we put into it. Our brains all make different connections, and one of the definitions of dyslexia could be that the connections can be different from the usual ones, and these can often be wonderfully creative, even if not logically correct or usual.

The answer to what the classification is, or how to clump material, is always to consider the **use, the purpose, or the idea behind** the grouping.

- *For an essay, the **question** needs to be considered, and then how **evidence** is produced and presented.*
- *In a reflective journal, there could be a **description of a process**, and then an **evaluation of the process** – not the other way round.*
- *For a letter of application, **skills** need to be clumped together in varying ways: all technical skills together; personal skills; academic; and so on.*

Giving labels to these categories can also be very helpful before the main task of writing is commenced.

An example
When considering the writers who had influenced my work in this book, I evolved a range of labels that I had not identified before the planning of the book. I arrived at these as follows:

I wrote a list of all the main writers I had been either quoting or had influenced me through ideas, structures and so on.

This list initially came off the top of my head, and then was aided by a consultation of the ongoing bibliography and a look at my bookshelves. So the list was in no order, although one or two authors reminded me of others related to them. So my brain was already making connections, even if I was not consciously aware of them.

I then used a large piece of paper, put my name in the middle and then started putting initials of the writers from my list in various areas around me (see Fig. 39).

These began to clump together, and I then consciously evolved a label for the area of inspiration or effect they had had on me:

- *there were the writers who had written about **reflection, or written quotable reflective writing***
- *there were the playwrights who wrote on **observation** and/or **dramatic techniques** that I had found useful*
- *there were the poets on the **essence of poetry***
- *poets and others who used **word play***
- *diarists who had kept account of the **process** of work, generally or specifically*
- *there were the essayists whose **structure** inspired **new thoughts** about the idea of what essays can be, rather than what they are always taught to be*
- *writers who used **photographs** to inspire research or **stories** or the exploration of memories*
- *and some writers who **crossed categories** or were **multi-categoried.***

This process was enlightening, clarified my thinking, helped me make decisions about who to use and when. It made me think of other areas I needed to research.

> **Reflection:** There is great value in doing this activity with other people. There could be discussion about how we categorize things, and how each person approaches this differently. The sharing of methods can often be useful to those who have not identified how they work or how to work. Discussion on different categorizations for differing purposes is beneficial at a number of points in the process of a studio project and in many writing tasks. Closer analysis of the library system has benefits in many ways; getting to know what is there, and how it is organized and why, and then how that can make links to your own organization systems (or lack of).

The work of Georges Perec (1997) and Walter Benjamin (1969, 2007) can be used to stimulate analysis of their methods.

Reflective writing on the process is also an important part of the means of learning to classify.

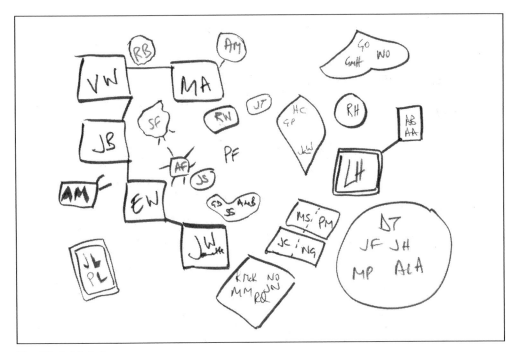

Fig. 39: Initial clumps.

Blobs

This non-academic word is the one I use when trying to explain the breaking down into parts of a big structure or work. If you have to produce a piece that is 1000 words, you cannot just do that straight off.

For most pieces there will be a requirement for certain bits of information, and there may be an expected structure that you have to follow.

For example, there may be guidelines, or conventions, that state that an essay needs an introduction, middle part and conclusion.

The middle part will be split into a number of sections – depending on the subject and size, but they might consist of:

- *background, current situation and future prospects*
- *or history, theories, two examples or arguments and conclusion*
- *or background, example one and conclusion, then example two and conclusion and then a comparison.*

It is quite difficult to generalize here but, broadly, you have to bear in mind what is required, the usual format/pattern, and then fit your subject into that.

The blob approach is when, having decided on the rough plan, you allocate the words, giving yourself small targets to achieve.

So, for an essay of 2000 words:

Introduction	250 words
Section 1	250
Section 2	300
Section 3	300
Section 4	500
Conclusion	400

Or, for a statement of 500 words about a piece of work you have been doing, you might plan that you need:

inspirations	point 1	50
	point 2	50
	point 3	50
process	techniques	100
	methods	100
	reflection	125
future ambitions		25

This might seem very mechanical – but when you actually do it, it can be an enormous relief. Psychologically, knowing that you have got to do x words or about a page on something becomes feasible, whereas the big blob, the whole, was insurmountable.

What often happens with the blob approach is that, having planned it, you frequently break it. In the writing, and as you build confidence, you adjust word counts in order to go with the flow of writing. But it helped you start and that is important.

The original blob allocation is often worth going back to when editing if you find you have drastically drifted off course, and you need to cut down.

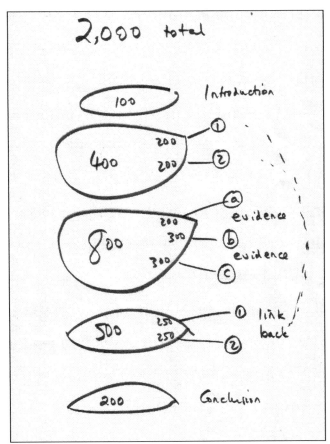

Fig. 40: The blob approach to breaking down the big task.

Structures

Structures are different for every piece of writing, just as building structures are dependent on land, materials, outlook, purpose, etc., or a garment which is dependent on size, fabric and so on. If a suit is tailor made – broad principles apply, but specifics alter.

One of the best ways of getting to know a repertoire of structures is to read and analyse others; to visualize the shapes of them; see how examples are integrated.

One generalization that I find useful is to think of a story: beginning, middle, and end (b,m,e). The beginning is the introduction, the middle is the development, and the end is when threads are drawn together. Some stories play with this convention and reveal the end first, then work back, but they are using our innate desire for the sequence b,m,e.

For essay writing, read the introductions of articles and books with an eye on how they say they are going to structure it. The context of the whole article or book and its subject and audience must be understood, and this then helps make the points that you need to follow.

The main function of the introduction is to give a route map so that the reader knows what is being done, which direction the piece is going in, a rough order and an idea of what to look out for. Then the writer can get on with it. The reader relaxes. If the reader is always wondering if the writer is going to do x or divert to y, it is not easy to completely concentrate on the points being made. The more secure a reader feels, the more the author's argument will be followed. This does not mean that the writer cannot spring surprises, but the best surprises are sprung when the reader is really with you. The writer is in control.

This is sound advice for most writers. Some well-practised creative writers can play with conventions, upset the norms, but if you are that good you probably wouldn't be consulting this book. Stick to simple devices until you are confident to overturn them.

Some metaphors for structures are *sandwiches* and *court cases*:

The middle part of the sandwich (what the sandwich is – the cheese, the jam) is the one that has to be planned so that it is presented in the best order:

■ *what the reader needs to know*
■ *what the order has to be*
■ *whether it has to be logical: background, what the problem is, the solution*
■ *the 'who', 'what', 'where', 'why' and 'how'*
■ *what you have got to show/prove/analyse in this piece of work*
■ *what back up you need*
■ *which examples you are going to use (and which not)*
■ *who you are going to cite (your expert witnesses).*

For many essays, a good structure is reminiscent of a court case:

■ *Introduction – what the case is, who is involved, what happened.*
■ *Prosecution and defence are the Middle – first one puts the case and introduces all the evidence and witnesses, then the other does the same and then they both sum up.*
■ *Conclusion is the judge summing up, and the verdict.*

Ping pong

This is a shorthand image which refers to thinking about structure and how to present material. If you have two artists to compare, for example:

- *do you do all the bits (medium, subject area of work, colour, etc.) for one artist*
- *and then do all the bits for the other artist?*

This then might seem like two separate blobs and they might seem unconnected. So you could do:

- *all of 'the colour' for one*
- *then all the colour for the other*
- *then all the medium for one*
- *medium for the other*
- *and so on.*

This can seem to go back and forward and is the ping pong effect.

Often in such works of comparison, you need to find another way or some fusion of the two devices. You need to avoid big blobs and ping pongs.

One possible solution is:

- *write about all the aspects of one artist*
- *then when you do the second artist you go through all the parts – but at various times, you compare that second one with the first.*

You don't leave all the comparisons to later: you mix the two devices.

Some of the phrases that prove useful in this sort of writing are:

- *whereas 'a' did this, 'b' developed …*
- *so while 'a' knew this, 'b' did not*
- *in contrast …*
- *however.*

I have made a strong point about bme's – the story approach, and that is the image that is most important to remember. Whatever your content, you are telling a story – that is what your reader will relate to. Telling a story doesn't mean that it is fiction when you should be dealing in fact. Story can be about form: it is the way all human beings will react to any sort of information – they want to go on a journey, and the story is the form that helps both writer and reader travel.

Shapes

All writing has a shape: whether it is just the mental picture we have of the form it has, or a physical shape – perhaps as in concrete poetry. It can help the process of constructing a piece of writing to think about its shape.

Triangles:

- *lots of ideas introduced which are whittled down to a few or one*
- *or it is the other way round – one idea which grows to many*
- *triangles can be top to bottom or left to right or right to left.*

Silhouette:

- *the writing goes in and out – expanding and contracting*
- *this shape is square and blocky, or smooth and sinuous.*

Three dimensional:

- *it could be a road or path that winds and has byways, bypaths and bypasses, or a river with tributaries and an estuary*
- *it can be very symmetrical and conform to conventions*
- *or asymmetrical with interjections, and the breaking of conventions*
- *it can be a scarecrow.*

Writing is rarely shapeless. It isn't just a single straight non-veering line going from left to right. It has dimensions: two or three, or more (see Fig. 41).

When you reach the writing-up stage, stop and think about possible shapes that will aid the planning and ordering of material.

Sometimes you know, or feel, what this may be in advance, sometimes not, but when there are difficulties in construction, this visualizing of the form may help.

Learning from the past
Look back at pieces of writing you have done and find an overall shape or internal shapes. How did they work, or not work – could visualizing a shape have helped?

The design of writing and reading
Writing is written to make the reader think – therefore there can be asides, surprises, prompts, explanations, excursions and retreats.

The best writing has a shape that the reader will respond to and take delight in. The writer is in control and has *designed* the writing. Many times a reader may not be aware of this: as with much good design, it is quietly there but does not get in the way of the function. Conversely a shape may manipulate the writing. Propaganda will utilize familiar shapes and forms and lull the reader into trusting the message. Thus, as well as helping with ways of writing, this approach may inform ways of analysing other written material.

It is in this dimension that writing can be so closely linked to art and design practices. A visual form for the piece becomes the solution to how to write and order the material.

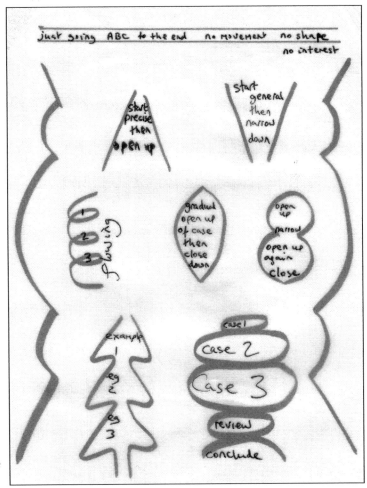

Fig. 41: Visualizing the shape of the writing.

It might not purely be shape.

One of my students talked about visualizing her piece. It would be bold, busy and densely typed at first, then calming down, slowing down and being more spaced out. She was making a comment on the speed of life and lack of time to do things carefully and thoughtfully, but wanted to take the reader on a journey where she could help them slow down and savour the ideas as she developed them.

Lots of wordslotsofwords SOUNDS NOISElotsofwordslotsofwords
Opinion, chatterclatterchatter words whizzing in and out
Yakyakyak I THINKTHIS andTHATthis and that
I THINK that and in my opinionopinionopinionopinion
Aren't you listening??? I'm talkingtalking talking talking
Listen up   steady on
Slow
Down   Calm down
Wind down

THAT WINDS ME UP!!!!!
.....unravel......

drift off   **day** dream   let it go
see where it goes

time   slows   down

stop and stare

step back and watch

step aside and ponder

take thoughts for a wander

and   wonder

let
the

words

go

Viewpoints

How to deal with opinions
This is an exaggerated activity to help 'over-opinionation'.

Take the subject you are writing about – then list your opinions:

- *I think …*
- *I think …*
- *I feel …*
- *I feel …*
- *I love …*
- *I love …*
- *In my opinion …*
- *In my opinion …*
- *In my view …*
- *I believe …*
- *I believe …*

This really makes the point how personal your opinions can be.

By doing this in such an exaggerated way, you may find that you need to do some research to find out more in order to back-up your opinions, or to challenge your opinions. Visualize yourself standing, hands on hips, saying this. This will help you get through that first stage of 'sounding off' about something. You may have been criticized in essays for just writing about your opinions. So **start** with them, then **move on** – deepen, research, back up.

Then when you come to write you may need to use some alternative phrases which are more neutral, such as:

- *It might be thought that …*
- *It can be seen that …*
- *X states that …*
- *Y believes …*
- *In Z's opinion … (then you can paraphrase their words)*
- *While A suggests … B prefers to put it as …*
- *H recounts that … This could be seen as …*
- *J is reported as feeling … This might seem to suggest that …*

What you can see from these phrases is that you are using other opinions, which should be informed views, to put over your material.

Another version of the 'I think that …' is to do the same with someone who tends to express their opinion a lot.

So you might have:

- *J's opinion is … J's opinion is …*

A couple of minutes doing this will soon help pick out the superficial opinion from something that is worth listening to.

What you always do need are contexts:

- *the circumstances in which something happened or was said*
- *background of person/event*
- *when it happened – what social situation there was, the politics, education, role of men/ women, and so on*
- *why something was done/said.*

And you need to continually ask questions and try to find answers: not just your own conclusions, but, from research, what others have thought or said.

Always start from the premise that you may not know the whole picture – therefore generalizations are dangerous or unwise. Specific evidence makes your argument stronger.

So when you have written out a list of opinions:

- *go through each point and make an evidence column*
- *what evidence do you have to prove your opinion*
- *if you cannot find an immediate piece of evidence, then indicate how you could find evidence*
- *what research could be done.*

The evidence has to be serious and/or substantiated.

Fig. 42: 'I am right and you are wrong or you are right and I am wrong.'

What If ...?

One of the standard exercises in creative writing courses is to set up a scenario, or present a range of characters and then ask 'what if ...?' The writer then has to leap into possibilities outside the conventions and norms.

This device could be used in many areas of writing that you have to do, either as a warm-up to generate ideas, or in order to seek alternative views.

Just write: bullet points, flowing sentences, whatever comes – let the writing hand fly.

- *What if all the serious newspapers stopped being published?*
- *What if M&S stopped selling underwear?*
- *What if the colour red was banned from use?*
- *What if plagiarism was encouraged?*
- *What if the Internet crashed?*
- *What if we had dress up Monday (not dress down Friday)?*

Take this further: think of your own 'what ifs ...' Be crazy, be serious; just push ideas as far as you can take them.

'What if ...' is:

- *divergent thinking – spreading out, not honing in*
- *thinking outside the box*
- *lateral thinking.*

It is creative because it allows the brain to make unusual connections, dig deep into its recesses, and have fun. This is relaxing, and when relaxing, the brain makes connections more fruitfully. This loosens up your writing.

- *'what if ...' is sometimes a good **strategy** in arguments – putting other sides and viewpoints*
- *'what if ...' is an **invitation** to do something creative, not an **instruction** which you might want to resist*
- *'what if ...' sounds like the chance to **dream** and **invent** and **hope**, as well as think about the consequences of an action*
- *'what if ...' is the thought that springs to mind: as with the **chain reaction** caused by the butterfly flapping its wings on one side of the world, which causes a hurricane to happen on the other side of the world.*

Heroes and Villains

This was inspired by an exhibition at the National Portrait Gallery (2003).

The purpose of this exercise is to reveal the problems of **hagiography**. This is where the subject of someone's essay is treated as being the 'bee's knees': idolized, and with no critical reflection and no perspective. The resulting writing is weak and so coloured and biased that it can alienate the reader. Often we do not realize that this is happening when we are writing. This exercise, while it can be very funny, helps to make the point, as well as providing practice in thinking of the questions to ask to avoid the hagiography effect.

Select two figures – one you really like or whose views you admire, and the other who you really dislike or whose stance you repudiate.

Firstly, write, discursively or in notes or bullet points, about your hero as a hero.

Some prompt questions are:

- *How did they get to where they are?*
- *Did they work hard at a skill?*
- *Did they go with the flow or stand out of the crowd?*
- *Did they manipulate their followers?*
- *Have they justified their behaviour?*
- *Have others lionized them?*

Then do the same with your villain.

Then reverse this, so that you write about your hero as if they were the villain, and then your villain as a hero.

Do this seriously: at first it can be funny, but then the thinking starts. It is hard to villainize your hero, and it is hard to find the good points in someone you do not like; but this can be done.

It might help to draw or caricature your figures, as Gerald Scarfe did in the exhibition. If you are stuck, the work of other caricaturists might help. Think about cartoons and caricatures and how they influence our views, or how they are so important in society in bringing someone down to size.

Variations include working on this activity with someone else, so that each of you selects a hero and a villain, but here you have to do the writing first, followed by then justifying your words in discussion with the other person.

Alternatively, one will take somebody like Madonna as hero, and the other will take her as villain. This is good for thinking about viewpoints.

This is also how the exhibition worked – each subject was written about by two different people. Some of these were definitely the victims of hagiography.

Using visuals such as caricatures to help stimulate ideas is another example of the visual arts and writing working closely together, both in process and outcome.

> **Reflection:** This is a seemingly simple exercise, but it has much depth. The ability to see other points of view, the reasons behind reputations and questioning your heroes is crucial in academic writing. Vocabulary is deepened, as it is very difficult to write glowingly about someone without repeating the same few words; therefore the thesaurus needs to come out. Finding the serious words, the ones appropriate to an academic appreciation, is vital. Taking the subject away from being just the focus of an essay, and turning it into a fun exercise, helps make the point, but also enables deeper work to be done.

Fig. 43: Hero or villain?

Scenarios and Viewpoints

The purpose of this is to explore ideas of different views about the same subject.

Look at the situation given, then react as if you were each of the characters in turn. Jot down the different view(s) that each character might have had. You will begin to invent things but you also have to think what that person might have seen or experienced.

Alternatively, this can be done with other people and each person takes on a different character. After noting down ideas, you can then discuss with the others and see how each character saw the scene.

This may seem like a party game or just play, but it is working on the idea that, with any one situation, there are different points of view. Even if the facts seem the same, we all see things differently. This is very useful in many forms of writing.

This sort of exercise is often done in creative writing groups. But if you move from fictional situations into more academic ones, the same principles apply.

Examples of fictional situations and characters:

A. Situation: A fire alarm goes off in the middle of a Visual Theory lecture at college. Everyone goes out. Fire engine arrives. Turns out to be a false alarm. You are interviewed by a reporter.

Characters:

1. Lecturer giving the lecture
2. Student attending lecture
3. Caretaker – you have to check the college
4. Fire officer – you had to attend the call out.

B. Situation: A town hall where they are counting the vote in an election. It is being televised. The camera breaks down and the lights go out. Sound can continue.

The broadcast continues ...

Characters:

1. Presenter of programme
2. Producer of programme
3. Protestor against the electoral system
4. One of potential MPs.

C. Situation: A tour bus is stuck in traffic in London. It is very hot. The windows are jammed closed.

You are telling someone what it was like.

Characters:

1. The driver
2. The commentator of the tour
3. Elderly visitor
4. A child forced to come on the trip.

D. Situation: A picket line outside a striking newspaper printing works. A car arrives with workers trying to get in. The police try to intervene. You appear on television with your version of what happens.

Characters:

1. Policeman on picket duty
2. Reporter for national television
3. A striker on the picket line
4. One of those attempting to get into work.

Particularly with the last situation, there is an obvious link to more serious events in terms of analysis and the research needed in order to develop an understanding of why different viewpoints come about.

The following are examples where there are more obvious direct applications to the writing of an essay, or the discussion of issues in a seminar:

E. Situation: An art gallery. Visitors are crowding near to a masterpiece. There is jostling and someone lunges towards the art work. Guards rush forward. Someone is arrested for causing damage.

You are being interviewed about your version of events.

Characters:

1. The security guard
2. Professor of art
3. An art student
4. A reluctant visitor, who is part of a coach party.

F. Situation: A catwalk show. A model falls off the catwalk and is mobbed.

You are interviewed by a journalist for *Dazed and Confused*.

Characters:

1. The model
2. The collection's fashion designer
3. A Vogue journalist
4. A paparazzi photographer.

> **Reflection**: This is a deceptively simple exercise but has the potential to be deepened and broadened into many subject areas for debate.
>
> Some preparation is needed as the situations have to be written up and characters invented.

Viewpoints in old photographs

The purpose here is to consider different perspectives or viewpoints using, as the starting point, the occasion of the taking of the photograph. Although photographs are used, the principles apply to many other subjects and the underlying ideas are at the core of most art and design subjects.

You will need a number of old photographs, featuring people. These can be found in books, although for my workshop session I find the use of actual old photographs that can be handled the best way of doing this, partly because of the tactile nature, but also because they are the original photographs, with all that that implies.

This list of questions will need to be adapted to each particular photograph:

- *Who is in the photograph, who is the photographer?*
- *What is the relationship of photographer to subject?*
- *What was said by photographer to the subject before and after the taking of the photograph?*
- *Who else was there (off camera)?*
- *What was the occasion?*
- *Why was the photograph being taken?*
- *What did the photographer feel?*
- *What did the subject feel?*
- *What did they say about it to other people sometime after the photograph was taken?*
- *Where did the photograph go – was it put in an album (and if so, who by), was it framed, sent to someone … (who and why)?*

In a way this exercise could be thought of as role play:

- *put yourself as the subject and then answer the questions relevant to that*
- *put yourself as the photographer and answer the questions*
- *as someone off camera observing the event*
- *as you, now, looking at the photograph, looking for clues, possible interpretations.*

There are lots of issues that arise in this activity and many can relate to your writing: about the act of photography; how we analyse this material; memoirs; autobiography; the differences between oral history and written history, and so forth.

Viewpoints of those in the photograph can be explored, although they are probably unverifiable. This, in itself, is a useful reflection:

- *how we can never know the truth and how that alters what we see or think*
- *how we should look at photographs, anonymous or known.*

Context of the occasion:

- *the date – is it known*
- *the sort of camera being used and the impact of this*
- *is it a formal professional camera with a professional photographer taking the photograph*
- *or is it informal, belonging to the participants, and perhaps a Box Brownie; therefore what is familiar or unfamiliar*
- *social events*
- *social mores*
- *costumes worn – and why this garment on this occasion, etc.*

In creative writing, an exercise might be to take one photograph and write a paragraph about the person, from a number of different perspectives – it is surprisingly interesting, difficult, but very rewarding.

- Write as yourself: *'I wonder why this girl, who looks as if she were pretty, looks so cross?'*
- Write as if you were the person in the photograph: *'I sat for 10 minutes waiting for them to get the lighting sorted out. I got so hot.'*
- Then, the same person, but written as 'she': *'She had to wait for 10 minutes while the photographer and his assistant experimented with the position of the lights.'*
- As if you were someone else there at the time but outside the frame: *'Elsa got so fidgety, and I was afraid she would crease her dress …'*
- Write in the present tense, personal: *'How long are they going to be – I want to go and play with Freddie.'*
- Write in the past tense, impersonal: *'She had waited with increasing impatience until they were ready. Her face in the final photograph showed the strain.'*

All these provide fascinating insights into the photograph and the people and our relationship with photography.

Maybe talk to someone else, and consider their opinions:

- *How do their viewpoints differ from your own?*
- *Why is this? Is their background being brought to it, are they more imaginative, more perceptive, more knowledgeable of context?*

As with many other exercises, the questions are purely meant as starting points, and alternative questions will arise and lead in all directions.

Other areas to be explored include costume, cameras, albums, snapshot photography, family relationships and writers on photography (both in fiction and academic writing).

All the ideas in this work link to our own situations and thoughts about it. This personal inspiration leads to the writing, and the writing can be personal and reflective and just for ourselves, or it can be shared.

Fig. 44: Anon.

Reflection: The ideas in this section encapsulate much of the value of the workshop experience. The use of actual objects, the encouragement of the use of imagination and enquiry, the requirement for back-up research, are all found there.

The collection of old photographs is the only preparation needed, and variations could include participants bringing in their own family photographs, or ones they have collected; and work on the ideas of what is verifiable and what is not.

The ideas from this sort of workshop can develop into creative writing with stories, exploration of social eras and the writing of poetry. The work done here can enhance academic writing, in part because it often leads to further reading and questioning and the paralleling of experiences. It can greatly aid the depth of our reflective writing, and writing in journals after a workshop is often found to be prolific and thoughtful, and the ideas prove lasting in their influence on future work.

The issues of the private and the public, the known and the anonymous, are valid for all areas of visual art practice. Valuable discussion naturally sparks out of sessions such as these, and they go way beyond the planned activity.

Patchwork Writing

This term has been used by a number of writers, but I was inspired by Richard Winter's statement: 'Regular writing tasks would aid learning far better than the last-minute essay' (2003: 15). In advocating the idea of regular writing, Winter also supports the writing of a number of pieces of work, in differing styles. This encapsulates the concept behind patchwork writing – exploring differing styles by writing for differing purposes. It can take a number of forms. The patchwork analogy shows the common theme: patterns or colours in fabric patchwork; differing styles and outcomes in writing. The communal aspect of making patchwork is another layer of meaning that can also apply.

One student tackles one subject from a number of different perspectives through a range of varying styles of writing, which might include:

- *a review of an exhibition for two different publications*
- *a description of layout*
- *an observation of the viewers at the exhibition*
- *a piece of publicity blurb written as if by the gallery promoter*
- *a personal musing on the opportunities for future exhibitions in that space*
- *an art/design history putting the subject of the exhibition in the context of the art and design world*
- *putting the subject in its social context.*

The alternative is for a group of students to take the same subject and each do one piece of writing on it, as set by the group. Then the pieces can be discussed and edited by the group.

Each alternative, and there can be more, is valuable for the writer and helps with individual work because of its appreciation of styles, the practice in doing them and also the contribution of feedback, and, in the second example, experience of editing.

This patchwork approach to writing styles is very closely linked with the idea of building a Folio of writing.

An extended example of Patchwork writing, entitled Women Travellers, is given in Part 3.

General to Specific

Frequently a criticism of essays is that they are too generalized and not specific enough. The same often applies to design projects. It is very difficult to do a project or an essay on 'world poverty' or 'global migration' – they are so huge and often out of our experience. But if we can relate to something concrete within it, or we can hook ourselves to a specific point or angle or story within it, then both creator and audience can identify with it.

The television news programmes frequently cover a large story, then hone in on a particular 'human angle story'. That attracts attention. We cannot always cope with, or assimilate, the wide picture, but we can empathize with the individual or the family. This does not mean that we have to lose perspective and only see one part, which is perhaps as lopsided as only seeing the whole.

In writing, we have to be able to blend the general and the specific. Frequently the specific is where we can work from. It can be our starting point. The detail of a person, of an object, of a situation is what we can more easily write about and more readily read about. In creative writing, emphasis is put on the specific – the detail.

In starting the writing for an essay, it is often far easier to start writing notes about specific ideas and objects, or people, and then move to the bigger general picture. Otherwise it is possible to get lost in the big morass of information.

In personal statements, detail is more important than generalities. In publicity blurbs, detail makes something stand out from other broad general pieces. In essays the specific has to be seen within the more general, but the specific is the most important. It is foregrounded and detailed, but clearly located in its setting and against its background.

The analogy might be a photograph of a landscape. If all is in focus, our eye probably will not linger for too long. A real landscape would keep our attention longer because we ourselves can focus in on a detail within it and then broaden out. So maybe we also need a specific focus in the photograph of the landscape. It might be a tree from which the landscape pans out; or it might be an animal or a building. Our eye goes from the specific to the general. This is one of the reasons for the creation of architectural 'follies'. The folly, not a real functioning building, gives a focus to the designed landscape surrounding it.

In a general picture of a crowd of people we will look to the individuals within it in order to understand the crowd's mood or purpose: are they unified or fragmented?

Thus specific detail is the key. Much of the work I propose is about this, with the important word 'context' coming after the primary focus on the subject.

Maybe a good visual to explain this is the spiral, in the form of the nautilus shell. This starts as one cell and then, as the cells increase, it whorls out, round and round, getting broader and broader, but with the starting point still clearly visible.

There are some contradictions, however. In some forms of writing we have to paint the background before focusing in on the specific.

So as soon as one rule is made, I break it.

The point here is that you have to be conscious of what is the best solution for what you are doing.

- Is it – *start with the specific and then give the context?*
- Or is it – *give the background and then come down into the detail?*

Each task requires a different journey.

But this still emphasizes the primacy of the specific.

Wherever it is located.

'What discoveries I've made in the course of writing stories all begin with the particular, never the general' (Welty 1995: 98).

Generalizations

This is a weakness in much writing:

> *'All women wear make up.'*
> *'All men love sport.'*
> *'All babies are cute.'*
> *'All pets are pampered.'*
> *'All art is for the privileged.'*

These statements are all nonsense. OK, that statement too is a generalization, but it makes the point.

As soon as you say 'all' or 'everyone' you are into dangerous territory. Can you back up these generalizations?

When you have written something look for these generalities and make decisions:

- *If you have to say 'all' – prove it.*
- *Can you say 'most' instead and be justified in doing so?*
- *Can you make it more specific?*

Make a list of things you often say, in the style of the generalizations made above.

Which can you prove, or which are crazy when you stop and think about them?

Look out for some in magazines, or in the news or in adverts. Let yourself get stroppy about those you do not agree with. This exaggeration will help you see them.

Go back through past work and see where you have used generalizations, and think about alternative ways as to how you could have presented these: as verified facts; or as generalized opinions, belonging to specific people?

Becoming aware of these tendencies in your own work is the best advice, as well as learning to look out for their existence in others.

Practice with Little Arguments

An argument might start with a statement which you then have to convincingly unravel, back up and expand on.

Before tackling the argument for an essay, a task which is probably daunting and not easy to identify at the beginning, *practice with small arguments*. Plan out what you might do, even if you are not going to go the whole way. The following is one argument related to writing, and it is good to take ones not in your specialized area in order to clearly see what you are doing. Later, when the ways of working are clearer, you can invent small ones for your subject.

It is easier to put something down as a statement rather than a question, at least initially. For example:

Good writing depends on extensive reading.

- First jot down your immediate gut reaction to this statement – do you agree, disagree, think yes but ..., no but ...
- Then try re-wording the sentence. Find alternative words for each main word, and/ or expand on them:

  - *Good: this is a value judgment – what is good, what is bad? It depends on context. Effective is another possible word – but then effective for the reader or the writer?*
  - *Writing: published/unpublished – informal/ formal ...*
  - *Depends: relies, or is benefited by ...*
  - *Extensive: wide ranging (breadth) or lots of (quantity) ...*
  - *Reading: what is its quality – and who defines the quality?*

This already begins to unravel the layers that are possible in this sentence and will also give ideas that you might follow. It will also probably begin to give you your deeper view which might not be the first one you thought of.

Link back to that first view – jot down some reactions about what has changed.

These will give you some ideas if or when you get stuck with what to do.

Then list:

- *What back-up might you need to find in order to follow up certain points?*
- *Who could give you this evidence – is it going to be lecturers, authors, critics, other students, etc?*
- *Where do you need to go to get this material? List areas of possible research (always remember that this will not be complete – one area of research will lead to another: at the beginning you do not always know what you do not know – yet).*
- *When should points be introduced and in what order?*

This is rough at this point, and the order would not be set in stone – but it does help to clarify the sequencing of the argument.

List 'for' and 'against' – put yourself in other shoes. This will help you consider other points of view, and also see why people say what they do, and also if there are changing contexts for saying something. If someone is marking an essay (they are the critical reader), they might have one viewpoint, but when they become a writer, and are having to think about how to express and structure an argument for an article, they might feel differently.

You might jot down something like:

I think reading is essential to writing, but it shouldn't inhibit it. It should be parallel: the more you do, the more you want to do. So often we read what we feel we should read and not what we want to read. But it is about reading with a questioning about:

who is writing

why they are writing this – whether they are paid to do it, the view of the newspaper/ journal, book, etc.

and if the writer is having to fit into this, or are able to go against it

who the intended reader is

what the purpose is – perhaps to sell something, persuade government, etc.

Pick up specific points and delve more deeply using your own experience and also see what happens to your views when you research.

The exercise on **adverts** (see activity earlier in Part 2, p. 142) explores the languages of advertising and how we entice or appeal. I am not advocating or supporting the methods of advertising – just highlighting what is done. This is where reading and writing come closely together: the more we can analyse how this language of persuasion works and how we are sold something, conned into buying something, or alienated from something, the more we realize that when we write, we too can use certain tools. Do we want to con, persuade, pull the wool over eyes, or awaken a spirit of enquiry, inform, etc?

Think about your argument **Shapes** (see Fig. 41):
Triangles – either way up or horizontal
Christmas trees – as in a child's simplistic shape – going in and out, with points
Onion layers
Russian dolls

The Final Points in the Writing Process

Titles

We are often busy getting on with the writing, answering the question, fulfilling the brief, but, suddenly we become concerned that we have no title for the work.

Sometimes a title is given to us and we have to remember to relate to it.

And in this sentence there is the key for those times when we have created something, but not given it its title.

It has to *relate*.

- *it has to set a tone*
- *it has to reflect what we are doing*
- *it is a label: it is a signpost for the reader*
- *the tone of the title will give the reader a lot of clues.*

So, I have now made it into a really important, and therefore scary, task.

There are a number of strategies to use to help getting a title.

- *Probably one of the best is to **talk** to someone about it – sometimes explaining what you are doing, or have done, or what you are intending to put over, might give you the nugget of a title. If they are really listening to you, they might be able to help (so: cultivate titled friends).*
- *Making a **list of key words** from your piece will also help.*
  - ☐ *Look at the list.*
  - ☐ *Join some words together – create new words.*
- *Look at any **quotations** you have used, particularly important ones that sum up what you have been doing. Can you use two or three words from the quotation and then frame your own words around them?*
- *Think of a **clever** title and a **serious** sub title:*
  - ☐ *Write the serious sub title first: this is what you have done: 'an analysis, a report on, a discussion of ...' – collect these phrases, these words and know which ones suit what you are doing. The sub title can go on a bit (you might be able to edit it down later – but always start wordy).*
  - ☐ *Then you think of the headline: the attention grabber. Play with your key words, look at the quotations, make it active.*

The key points to remember in creating titles:

- they often don't come to mind at the start – at that point we don't really know where the writing journey will go, and so the inspired titles are not yet born
- you will never get a title by staring at a blank page

- generate titles in the same way as you generate ideas
  - ☐ brainstorm
  - ☐ list
  - ☐ play around with words
- list possible titles
- leave them
- go back later
- ruminate on them.

Then you may get the blinding flash of inspiration.

If not – phone a friend.

> **Reflection:** As mentioned above, it is frequently other people who can help us most with this task and therefore there is some justification in making this a workshop activity to encourage the listening and talking to others. This helps us see how others see what we have put: we know what we meant, but do they?

Fig. 45: Talking titles.

Mini Sagas

For years *The Daily Telegraph* ran a competition called 'Mini sagas'. Pieces of writing, of no more and no less than 50 words were sought – written by amateurs and professionals.

Some are extremely clever, others facile, some so laboured they are painful. Some have vast truths; others document the minutiae of domesticity.

While fun, the practice of these can help with editing.

Start by telling a story or explaining or describing something. Just free-write.

- *it comes out at 75 words – set yourself to do it in 50 words*
- *if you first write 100, cut it down to 70 and then 50*
- *you make the decision*
- *but the point is to see what you could cut*
- *what you could amalgamate*
- *where you can use punctuation to cover several words*
- *what you can drop.*

Here is an example.

1st version:

The Fall of the Roman Empire

This took place in the British countryside, in the field of a rich farmer. One day, while digging, he found some Roman pottery.

Archaeologists came to see what he had got and trenches were dug. After a while they discovered a palace. Amongst the finds and rooms a complete bath and drainage system was excavated. The press wanted a scoop story about this. They got the farmer's daughter to slowly pour some water down the ancient pipe. The headline they used was: How the Romans went down the plughole.

This version comes to 95 words. Some of it is loose and woolly, and it needs dynamism and variety.

2nd version:

Fall of Roman Empire

In a country field, a farmer found Roman pottery. Archaeologists came; trenches were dug; a palace was excavated. A bath was discovered. Local press sought a scoop, picturing the farmer's daughter pouring water down the ancient pipe.

Headline caption: How Roman Civilization drained down the plughole.

This is exactly 50 words.

This 'editing' exercise helps:

- find the important points
- reveal where you do need the extra adjective
- what will work as a sentence without being one
- what can be left unsaid
- where one word will cover three
- exchange one word for another that says more.

Make words work – justify their place.

It is also a very good way of understanding how punctuation can be used:

- the semi colon often does away with the need for 'and'
- the colon delivers consequences
- the comma helps give a pause for emphasis and meaning.

This doesn't mean you write all the time in such an intense way – but it helps develop the editorial eye and helps you see what words can do, or do do.

Reflection: This is a fun task to do in a workshop. Encourage a piece of free writing in a set amount of time. Count the number of words, and then working with someone else, find ways to cut it down. The idea of working in pairs is very useful to build up confidence in editing. Four eyes are often better than two.

Blurbs

This is linked to the preceding section on Mini Sagas. It is very useful to take stock every now and then in a project and crystallize for yourself what you are doing.

Think of it as being the blurb on a book.

The blurb is the small piece of writing on the book jacket – usually on the back of the book, so that when you take it off the shelves, you look at the front cover, and then immediately turn over to see what is written on the back. There may be a few quotes from reviews, a short biography of the author, but there is also, usually, a blurb.

This succinctly sums up what the book is about. It sells the book to you. It is couched in words that appeal to its intended audience; it uses the buzz words that will draw a reader/purchaser in. By using 'buzz' I don't mean that it is all jargon, or shallow. But if you are looking for a book on making money – you will look for those buzz words – 'making money'. If the book is about giving away wealth, then you quickly see it is not for you.

So this device makes you think a bit like a salesperson. You have to sell your work – but if you are selling it to a tutor, you must avoid too much showing-off, or false claims. You need to hook the other person, but not alienate them. You must sum up the whole scope of your project in a few words.

The effort required to do such a task is great – but extraordinarily well worth it. It can actually help you see what you are doing: it makes you summarize and crystallize and focus.

You can do this task two weeks into the project – to help you make decisions as to the direction you are going in.

You can do it half way through a long project – to get you on track.

You can use it at the end – when you are having to think of captions, statements, etc. for the display of work.

It is also related to abstracts which are written for long and academic pieces of writing. There is a particular style required in these, which is not about sales, but frequently they have to be a limited number of words and they have to capture the essence of the bigger piece. The writing of the abstract can make you realize the precise nature of what you have written. It is sometimes asked for before you have written the main piece. In this case it is more like a proposal and it focuses you on what you are doing – and also what you are not doing at this moment, in this piece.

Set yourself 50 words as a target:

- so start by writing a list of the key points – brainstorm them
- then look at these – put them in order of importance
- then cut some out – or amalgamate some
- reduce each bullet point to 3 or 4 words
- then write about 100 words – making these bullet points into sentences
- then look at this piece of 100 words
- see where grammar can help
- see if you can use a colon(:) to give dramatic effect
- see if you can use commas or semicolons to make lists
- try to cut down your adjectives and make the nouns speak for themselves
- see if you can emphasize the energy of what you are doing in your verbs

Now you have to cut the 100 words down to 50 – so really find the most important points, and ones that are implied, or are not as important, can go.

Practice and lots and lots of drafts are the only way in the end. But the task is worth it as it brings you face to face with what you are trying to do. If you weren't sure about what you were doing, by the time you have written your blurb, you will be.

Fig. 46: Widel.

Edit Later – Not as you Go

Sometimes writing is hard to do because you are trying to polish it, sort it out – *as you go.*

If you were out sketching or capturing a scene, photographing an event as it was happening, you would just draw, get it down, warts, splashes and blots and all, or shoot lots of pictures – to make sure you encapsulated as much as possible.

Then you would go back to the studio or dark room and look at, select, focus in, draw, rub out and … then edit.

You do, then edit.

The same applies to writing.

Collect your raw material, write notes, get thoughts down, write chunks, leave spaces, but capture the energy, the drive of the idea (see Fig. 46).

Then later, reflecting on it, standing back from it, you can see that a word doesn't work, so you find another, better one. A sentence has gone on too long – you split it up.

The principle is:

Do it now, edit later
Get it down, edit later
Write it down, edit later (this has a mnemonic of 'widel' – pronounced widdle)

Maybe that rather crude mnemonic will help remind you of this hugely important and serious point. Remember to widdle. (sorry)

Editing

It can be harder to edit than it is to write in the first place. This is how many of us feel, and editing then becomes the thing that we do not do at all. What is handed in or sent off is often a first draft.

It seems tedious to read through what we've done. But if we feel it might be tedious, this is probably an acknowledgement that we know it isn't perfect. But we are scared of having to try to improve it, or lazy at the thought of the work it will involve.

But if we can't be bothered with it, why should our readers? We have to respect our readers and we have to bother.

Possibly the main reasons for prevarication and putting off the editing process are lack of strategies to call on. But when you do have a go, the rewards are encouraging. You recognize, in your own work, an improvement.

Here are a few strategies:

A. *Leave a gap.*

■ *You must go and do something else.*

This is just like giving your eyes a rest. You don't always have to close your eyes to rest them: you can change focus. If you have been doing close work, then do something where you are looking further away. This is the same as with the physical: if you have been doing something tight and close, then you need to stretch and loosen up.

So too
With editing.
  Do something else
    Then come back
      Then put on different hats

Have a purpose to the editing. You are not simply just checking and looking out for certain things; you need to interact with the writing. Checking can be boring and I think that this is where it also goes wrong. It seems like a production line and you are just doing the boring checking of how many baked beans there are in a tin, or whether all the peas are round, or if every cup cake has a cherry on it. Reading and writing are NOT like this.

The proofreading stage also needs to come after a space: leave a gap between writing and proofreading. Therefore your planning needs to allow for this time. The night before hand-in is not sufficient. If we read as soon as we have written, we read what we think we have put, not what we have actually put down.

B. *Look back at the requirements for this piece.*

■ *Is there a specific question to be answered?*
■ *What is the title?* – or do you need to decide on one which the written piece will then answer or develop? This helps focus the writing, and allows you to prune what is not really necessary. So, focusing on the purpose before you read through alerts you to what the point is.

C. *Look back at original brainstorms, mind maps, plannings, lists, etc.*

■ *Find the original energy and purpose behind the writing.*

This might also remind you of important points that actually have been missed out of your writing. Then, as you read, you are actively thinking about where these parts need to be inserted.

D. *Read out loud, slowly.*

■ *We hear repetitions, mistakes, if we really read what we have written.*

Long sentences, without any pauses or too many clauses, become impossible to read out, without taking breath. That is a key sign for action: split sentences up into smaller units. Sentences which are not sentences are revealed because we do try to read out loud with meaning and we are left hanging in space when we come to the full stop. If you change tenses, it is much easier to hear this than see this.

■ *Ramblings are revealed.*

We go off the point or do not make a point. Colloquialisms occur when they are not 'allowed'. The reading out loud picks up the chattiness and the slang more clearly than if we read silently.

E. *Read through several times – each time looking for different things. This helps focus on one problem at a time.*

■ *Repetitions of words (then find the thesaurus). Brainstorm alternative words.*
■ *Spellings (do not look too closely at sense – you are doing more of a proofreading task). Know your problem words: this is also one area where you might need others to help, as you do not always know that you do not know how to spell certain words.*
■ *Read for flow – does your piece tell a story?*
■ *Paragraphs – too few or too many?*
■ *Split up sentences – where, grammatically, things don't work. Maybe the subject of the sentence doesn't match the verb or the beginning doesn't match the ending, etc.*

F. Paragraphs

■ *Many grammar books give definitions of paragraphs which make each sound like a mini essay. This is a pattern that can work for many occasions.*

So the paragraph will have:

■ *an introductory sentence or two presenting what it is about*
■ *then there will be a presentation of facts*
■ *then a discussion and development of the argument*
■ *a production of evidence*
■ *and a conclusion.*

But there are occasions when a paragraph is very small and succinct and to the point. You are deliberately making a dramatic effect and you will not follow all those conventions. (I often use this device.)

Paragraphs also need variety – if you followed the rules every time, the writing would become boring and predictable and the reader would switch off.

So, on a paragraph edit, you are looking at:

■ *the possible structure*
■ *flow*
■ *variety*
■ *length*
■ *links back to the planning.*

In your planning you might have made a list of the key points to be made – it may be that these points could each form a paragraph.

■ *The rule of one key subject per paragraph is quite a useful one.*

G. Read and note key words.

■ *For each paragraph, write one or two key words – no more than three or the point is lost. You will end up with a list of key words which will help you stand back from the piece and see where repetitions occur, where an order could be changed, or needs to be altered to help the flow of an argument.*

If I am given a piece of writing by someone else and, on an initial read through, I cannot make sense of it, this is what I do. It gives me a hold on the piece and the list then begins to give me the solutions to fix the piece.

Related to key words is the issue of the title.

■ Do **words from the title** constantly **weave in and out** of what you are writing?

H. Shape

■ What shape or shapes does the piece have?

Does it need to have some shape, if it is shapeless?

Draw the shape of:

■ what you want your written work to be
■ what you think it is
■ when you have read it – what it is.

I. Cutting down

■ Identify parts which seem to go on a bit, or are waffling.

Are there repetitions? You have written a good word, and then written the meaning of it in other words: hedging your bets, labouring the point. Think in design terms of 'less is more': a brief, to the point, line has more of an impact.

Could one good word do the job of several roundabout words?

J. Difficult explanations

■ If you have a complex point – say it with simple words.

Do you get stuck trying to explain something difficult, and do it with long words: ones which you are not really confident using?

There is nothing more revealing of lack of knowledge or confidence than saying something difficult in difficult words and not succeeding. The rule might be 'Complex idea? Use simple, short sentences.'

K. Balance

■ Good writing ebbs and flows.

Good writing should have the:

■ long and short
■ precise and discursive
■ statement and explanation
■ quotation and discussion ...

Not all in pairs – but there is variety and drama: there is the expected and, suddenly, the unexpected insight and unusual expression. This will keep the reader's attention, and also gives you, as the writer, something interesting to aim for.

L. Conflate

■ *Blend or fuse together (especially making two different texts into one).*

This is the dictionary definition of conflate and is a really apt description for a lot of writing activities. And 'activities' is the right word: it is active, blending, and it is physical: with the mixing and melding, the seasoning, the to-ing and fro-ing, and the cut and paste.

It is tricky: to have two pieces with their own identities, written at different times and as part of different missions, and then to have to bring them together – it is very tricky. Sometimes I feel like leaving both and doing a new one, and sometimes this is what I do. But often the time is not there, the deadline is imminent, or I want to have a go because the two pieces have in them bits that are good, and I am pleased with.

So I have a go:

mix and match
meld
mould
collate
conflate
confuse
configure
reconfigure
etc.
etc.
then leave
and stand back
and then fuse together –
it is physical
and keeping this physical idea in mind
helps with the process.

M. The Abstract

■ *Writing the abstract should always come after writing the paper.*

There are a number of ways of approaching it:

- *Write one sentence per section of the paper.*
- *List the key words and write a sentence on each.*
- *Consider the essence of your introduction and your conclusion and then write two or three connecting sentences in between.*

Writing an Abstract, even if you do not have to hand one in, can be useful as a focusing exercise:

- *Practice by looking at Mini Sagas.*
- *Write a light hearted Blurb as a warm up to the serious Abstract.*

N. Drafts

- *Drafts are the rough sketches of writing and give the foundations for the finished piece.*

Drafts are an important aspect of writing. Ideally a piece of writing goes through a number of drafts – from the rough and ready splurge of ideas to something that is honed and crafted. This can take a number of drafts. So in the management of a writing project, time has to be allowed for these stages.

We all know the feeling when getting a piece of work back that is covered in red pen: how could we have missed this or that? The answer is that, if you do not allow yourself the time, you see what you *think* you have written. It is not that we cannot do something: that is not the real reason.

The spelling checks on computers create a tendency for us to become lazy and think that they will do it for us. Personally, I cannot stand them: it doesn't allow me some of my combinations of words, nor does it like my grammar, which is appropriate to the style of the piece I am writing. I do acknowledge that these checks are useful for many people – but they are NOT the TOTAL answer.

One example of how spell check can mislead is in not identifying when a typing mistake creates another word. Often, when I am typing, my fingers are sometimes going so fast that I get letters in the wrong order: just like Eric Morecambe in the André Previn (or Preview) sketch ('Morecambe and Wise Show' 1971) – all the right letters, but not necessarily in the right order. Or, in my case, *most* of the right letters. One word that I am using rather a lot is 'writing' – but invariably when I type it, it comes out as 'wiring', and the spell check doesn't show it up, as it is a correct word. This book would have to be re-classified in the electronics section if I hadn't proofread it.

How to Connect 'I' to the Academic

This is a short section on considering how to develop some work from the first, personal voice, to the more objective, academic voice.

There might be a passage:

> *I really like the smooth feel of the plastic – Bakelite, and the mottled pattern of rusty colours. It feels warm and is a comforting shape – it nestles in my hand.*

Or

> *I think the photograph is wonderful. There are these two young women dressed up – they're identically dressed, with plus fours, I think they're called (trousers gathered below the knees), fitted jackets opened up, waistcoats, cravats and hats. One is looking out – seems to be looking straight at me. The other looks off to her left. They look spirited, tomboyish. I feel they were a bit rebellious for their time. But their names are Ethel and Hilda! Now they sound so old fashioned, yet then they were challenging fashions – women just didn't dress up in trousers. This was daring for their day (see Fig. 47).*

Go through similar passages you might have written and create two columns:

on the left
list the opinions

on the right
list the facts and the evidence and back-up

So then what you have is the separation of what is opinion and what is fact, with notes about what will constitute back-up evidence.

Then it is a matter of re-phrasing some phrases to:

- *it could be that …*
- *it appears that …*
- *it could be seen that.*

So where I originally wrote:

> 'One is looking out – seems to …'

this could be followed by the phrase

> 'This could indicate …'

or

> 'By the way they are dressed it looks as if …'

> 'The trousers are evidence of …'

Where there are opinions that still seem important, but are lacking in evidence, consider other ways of presenting the information.

Above I have suggested the use of 'it could be that' and 'it might be thought that'. There are varying opinions about this 'indirect' style of writing. Another strategy is to put the statements more directly, and use questions:

> *The young women were dressed up as young men. This is apparent by the wearing of trousers in a period when women did not – so this was not their normal attire. Why might they have dressed like this? Maybe they were theatrical performers ... or ... or ...*

With research it might be possible to back up these opinions.

> *'At that time there were ...'*

And back this up with a quote from an authority of that period.

These are the stages in this writing:

Fig. 47: Hilda and Ethel.

- *firstly describe, using senses, own feelings, own memories and associations, thoughts, imaginary ideas ...*
- *then make columns and separate the opinion from the evidence*
- *then find the links*
- *from this, decide where research is needed to back up opinion*
- *decide what can be dropped – perhaps some things are still just too personal*
- *after research, analyse further by working out what questions to ask and how to answer them.*

The only way to be able to write in the personal as well as the academic voice, is through practice. Working from one to the other is a much more manageable task than trying to strangle your personal voice early on, and sound like someone you are not.

Specific Pieces of Writing

Personal Statements

This can be a very hard piece of writing to do as it may sound big-headed, can seem false, showing off, blowing your own trumpet and all the other clichés.

But it is also a very important piece of writing as it might be what attracts a potential employer or curator, to your work.

Therefore –

do not plunge straight in.

Planning is vital for this task. This is partly because the rough preparations can help get the false claims, the feeble language, and the cloying cliché, out of the way.

Try any, or some, of the following as warm-ups:

A. *Branching out*

- *Profile metaphor (see Part 2: Using Metaphors … to find out …).*
- *List inspirers – those who inspire you, or what inspires you.*
- *Do lists and then clump them into categories.*
- *Brainstorm technical skills, personal qualities, interests.*
- *Draw a caricature of yourself – concentrating more on the qualities than on the physical: e.g. if you are a good listener give yourself big ears; a good talker: big, open mouth; observant: big eyes. Do you smile/frown? Are you a warm colour/cool? Are you tidy/messy? This will help make you look at yourself as you see yourself, and also as others see you.*
- *What makes you tick or shout Eureka?*

B. *Closing in*

- *Look at the reasons for the statement: whether it is for a job, an exhibition, blurb, book, article, catalogue …*
- *Do some research about the post, the gallery, etc. – so that you will be able to gear your writing to this.*
- *Ask yourself what the criteria are.*

C. *Number of words*

- *split this down into headings – blobs*
- *inspirations*
- *skills: technical*
- *skills: personal*

- *what makes me, me*
- *the work done for this piece*
- *the research*
- *the future – ambitions or ideas.*

Read other pieces, but read with a questioning eye – not a copying eye:

'What were they trying to get over, or sell, why did they put it like that?'

instead of

'Oh, no, its GOT to be like that.'

Read as if you were the prospective employer, reader, exhibition-goer.

D. *Write from other viewpoints.*

Do a few lines (can be bullet points or fully written out):

- *wacky – over the top*
- *very personal: lots of 'I's and 'me's*
- *very academic*
- *very show-off*
- *very lowly*
- *one that your best friend would write about you*
- *one that your tutor would write about you*
- *one that someone else would write about you.*

Write a reference for yourself as if you were your tutor (or employer):

- *What points would they pick out?*
- *What would they cover up?*

The point of doing all the different voices is partly to get them out of your system and to see yourself from different perspectives.

Practice writing in certain ways and begin to find what works and what doesn't.

The eventual statement might be an amalgam or a composite of all these styles.

If you write a statement about yourself, but in another voice, it helps you see what you can and cannot say:

> T. is very thoughtful, although this can sometimes come over as not very involved. She does not readily speak up in group situations, but she is certainly listening to others. She is reluctant to voice her opinions, but has usually researched widely into the topic and has thorough research notebooks. Her presentations are very quiet and low key and might give the appearance of being a bit off hand. This however is due to chronic nerves and not lack of preparation.

Immediately you can see that you have to put the positive side of this in your statement, emphasizing the research and the good listening skills. Perhaps you might want to write that, although you are not confident about presentations, you are working on vocal skills. This would then give a positive colouring to something that is otherwise deemed a weakness. For a prospective job application this would be a good point, but it would be unnecessary in a personal artist's statement.

Writing a Summary

For the assessment of many projects you might be asked to keep some sort of Reflective Learning Journal and then produce a typed **Summary** of what you have got out of the project.

The following are an initial list of points and **questions** that you can use as a starting point. Some of them will lead to other points, and different projects will suggest their own directions.

The Reflective Journal will help you reflect on:

- *the changes the project went through*
- *what worked and what didn't*
- *what inspired you*
- *what caused blocks and how you did or did not get out of that block*
- *it will also reflect on the tutorials or advice you received*
- *how you managed your time*
- *what ideas it has given you for the future.*

Going back through your Reflective Learning Journal will remind you of how you worked and ideas you had. If you have not kept any sort of note, you are often inventing what happened and also miss some good ideas.

This is all really important for the project, as it will set you up with ideas about how future projects can be managed.

Other questions to ask yourself and to write about in the summary:

- *Did you allow enough time for research and development and experimenting with ideas?*
- *How do you cope with contrary advice?*
- *Have you made the most of the advice available?*
- *Have you experimented enough and gained any technical skills?*
- *Have you discovered particular strengths in your work, or areas that you can identify as needing more practice?*
- *Have you changed in this project – in terms of attitude, ideas, ways of working, etc?*

The Summary is about reflecting on you and your work and being honest with yourself, whilst also presenting a professional view to someone else.

Writing from an Exhibition Visit

This is an idea that you can adapt for your journal, as practice in styles of writing, and as a generator of ideas for many projects. It is based around an activity that you will be constantly doing anyway – visiting exhibitions.

Find something – an exhibit, a display, a themed room or other aspect of the collection and the way it presents material – and record this in your sketchbook or notebook.

Your work can be drawn and written and needs to represent a period of recording and reflection on a particular idea. This item or theme could link to your project idea – however loosely.

- *It may be, for instance, that you are particularly intrigued by how the themes of one room are displayed, or how they tell a story and you might want to sketch the layout of the room and the way the narrative unfolds.*
- *You might find one painting or a sculpture or installation that is particularly inspiring and relates to your own ideas. Record your response to this work in some way.*
- *It might be that you want to watch the way people approach certain works of art and this might relate to your research or interests. Again record, by some means, your observations.*

If you are working on a project and the idea is very vague at the moment, then find something that really inspires you and that you are intrigued by, and/or want to find out more about.

- *What is it about this artist/art movement that is special?*
- *What was the social situation that brought that piece (or works) into being?*

Then produce a range of short pieces of writing such as:

- *personal reflections as indicated above*
- *a review of the art work/exhibition in the style of a particular journal or magazine – e.g.* The Guardian, Art Review, Time Out, *etc.*
- *the publicity blurb for promoting the exhibition*
- *a voice-over for a documentary*
- *a piece of creative writing e.g. a poem, dialogue of viewer and artist …*
- *a spoof documentary.*

(These are just some ideas – the point is to write in a few particular styles)

For your journal, you could find some related pieces of text and comment on them. These help you to analyse writing styles, and then help you with what is suitable for your own writing.

> **Reflection:** this can be adapted to work with group visits to exhibitions and set pieces can be required, or groups set to develop specific ideas – such as the range of writing used in exhibitions: labels, information boards, catalogues, posters, reviews.

3

Examples

Fig. 48: When the writing meets the visual.

IV
Caught   Crack before the beak   Only spike shows contempt
             Crooked fingers pointing   Cocked his leg.
             Croaking cries of guilt   And for the year
             Carted off to clink   Spike would wait

Introduction

This section is very varied in style, voice and content.

- I have written some examples to amplify what I have suggested in a number of the practical exercises, and have annotated some of these to clarify points.
- Some pieces are pure reflective writing, which are then commented on in order to show how they can be developed into other areas of writing.
- Others are working pieces for this book – where I have tried to show the journey of a germ of an idea to its fruition.

There is also some creative writing to underpin the argument of this book: that the creative writing approach may yield much potential for the development of skills in a range of writing tasks, including the academic and the promotional and personal.

The reason for all these very different pieces is to help emphasize another of the mainstays of this book. This is that writing is about experimentation and letting ideas pour out: you can only turn out a polished piece when you have done the rough groundwork. It is by trying, by pushing, and by having a go, that skills develop, and the eye is trained, the voice is matured and the thoughts are fired.

I do not claim that all the pieces are 'good' pieces of writing – they are being offered in order to give the idea of the first-draft notes which are still raw.

In using my own pieces of writing which informed the writing for this book, I aim to show the rough thought-pictures that I used to help me extend the ideas. I have not written any of the pieces to order; it is rather the other way round. I have found pieces that I have written and then shown how they link with the ideas which I have been suggesting about process and development. So there is no false writing here. It is all genuinely about the process and stages of writing – rough, raw, inspirational, contradictory and questioning.

For each piece I have made a short introduction (in brackets) as to what the piece is. The piece then follows, largely unedited. (Sometimes I have put in some punctuation to make the meaning clear. In my own notes, punctuation is not always consistent – I use a lot of dashes.) And then follows a **Comment** on the writing, which will relate the piece to the rest of the book.

Rain

(This is in the nature of a brainstorm and word play – pushing one word to an extreme.)

How many clichés are there about the British obsession with the weather?
I love the variety – don't know what it will be
As a gardener I love the rain –
When it comes after a dry spell.

Relentless rain
Rain drops – millions – all different like snowflakes
All the sorts of rain – gentle, cloud, misty, torrential, drizzle, downpour, driving, thundering.
We have so many words for it.

The word rain – add letters: brain, train, strain, drain, refrain

Corrupt the 'r' – pain, vain, main

Other end of word rain – change n to l
Rail – wrong sort of rain on the railway – becomes a cliché and term of derision

Mnemonic:

Rain
Always
In
News

'The Rain in Spain'… is a rhyme in elocution

The word is used not just for water/weather:

Bombs raining down

Possibles:

Word play
Quotations – first thought is of 'Still Falls the Rain' (Edith Sitwell poem from 1942)
Metaphors
Pictures of
Design, product, fashion, architecture
Photography: rain drop – micro photos.
Environment
Feelings – associations

Memories – associations
Experimental work – dyes affected by rain, paper and other materials out in rain

One word – infinite number of ways to take it.

Why do it? – mental limbering, making connections.

Comments
This is an example of a brainstorm – triggered by seeing a postcard in the shop, Paperchase, with the word 'rain' repeated on it in various blues, and with differing qualities of printing, as if affected by the rain.

At the time of writing this, Britain was experiencing excessive rainfall, and extensive flooding affected parts of the country – but not where I was writing, hence my liking it for the garden and not praying for it to cease.

I play with the word. I think of other 'literary' connections, but also link to the visual potential with work being subjected to weathering.

The word play activities relate back to several Practicals.

This is personal and idiosyncratic, but even if I didn't follow this up immediately, there are clues here that can be picked up on later.

It is also an example of the sort of writing that could go in a Thought Book, or in terms of the Daily Detail – a reflection on the weather.

Mobiles

(An observation while out on a walk led to this reflective writing.)

Mobile phones might be said to be one of the problems of the modern world and the reason for our increasing panic.

So, although for many people they were thought to be a safety essential and to be used for emergencies, they have become a prop and are now used all the time. It is very difficult to escape from them.

I have just seen a woman driving a car, using her mobile (now illegal – but that is another issue). The point here is that she was having a furious argument with her partner. She was off to do the shopping: he should have been doing something and was not.

Before mobiles she would have left the house, driven off, cooled off and then gone back later and the argument may never have happened. Now she can drive off to do her thing, but instead of cooling off, she will phone her other half and pick a fight.

This little scene, which I may have embroidered slightly, led to the thought that time is now being wasted because we fill it so much. What do we fill it with? Rubbish – literally in the case of waste material, but also wasted thoughts, and arguments.

The world is connected so instantly – but we are not always the better for it. Sometimes we need to slow down; sometimes need to pause, and consider, and reflect.

We could walk off our anger. But if we drive everywhere we will arrive before we have fully worked off our wrath, and then we carry it on – either by then talking to someone else about it and working ourselves up again, or by picking the fight, because we have not got rid of the adrenalin.

And linked to the *mobility* of driving – *automobiles*.

Hang all mobiles!

Let mobiles be made into mobiles, hanging in the air: connected, but also not.

Thinking of this, I hear the wind chimes hanging near my door – a tinkling sound, they are only set off when the wind is in a certain direction. Kinetic mobiles are visual, and yet they can also make sounds. I look up to the chimes and then above them see the clouds in the sky: racing. All things are connected, and sometimes very fast.

A thought chain, triggered by observation of one thing, has taken me off into the stratosphere.

Comments

This piece is virtually unedited. It is writing from a thought, making links, being open to imagery, playing with the words (mobiles in particular), but then broadening the idea out into other themes. It is this sort of creative, opinionated but thoughtful writing that could fill a reflective journal: it may not be academic, there are no references or footnotes, no formal structure, but it is pursuing other ideas that could lead to connections being made for further research, a project or for an essay.

Metaphors: Flies in Amber

(Reflective writing inspired by reading a very kinaesthetic metaphor, which, in the early stages, transformed my thoughts and plans for this book.)

I first came across a quotation from Margaret Atwood, in Alberto Manguel's A *Reading Diary* (2004) where he is talking about time. I then went to the original Atwood, in the introduction to her book on writing:

> ... we are all stuck in time, less like flies in amber – nothing so hard and clear – but like mice in molasses (Atwood 2002: xv).

This image resonated very strongly with me. It also reminded me of someone I had once worked with who collected amber. I had not known anything about this 'gem' before meeting her. It always struck me as rather macabre – wearing a necklace or pendant next to your skin that contained a dead fly or, for me, the horror – a spider!!

But the image that Atwood presents is so clear. Amber is a natural resin that in time sets hard. Living things were trapped in it and have been preserved for thousands of years. Her contrast – like mice in molasses – is funny and so visual and tactile that you can imagine little paws laboriously being lifted out of the sticky treacle-like morass.

I worked on this in my mind and actually, instead of it just being about time, it became more and more to be a description of the difficulty of writing – so writing is as difficult as mice clawing their way in molasses.

I returned to Atwood's introduction to her lectures on writing. The quotation not just embedded itself further in my mind, but also led on to reading what she said about the process of writing and the slog and the graft, and how writers struggle with the craft of writing. Also how they use metaphors to describe their work.

Intrigued with Atwood's metaphor, I even bought a piece of amber. It is very expensive and to get a recognizable insect, you would pay quite a lot of money. Not having much money, the piece I purchased had some little flakes in it (quite unidentifiable); maybe just specks of dust or debris – but the entrapment is clear.

Then, in the way of serendipity, I was listening to a programme on the playwright, Bertolt Brecht, and the use of music in his plays. In the conclusion there were a few of Brecht's thoughts about the fact that he felt that his words, when placed in music, might last, like flies in amber, for all time.

This set off echoes of the Atwood quote, and again a whole series of images were brought into my mind. I then looked in the dictionary of quotations and two quotes stood out, neither modern: Bacon and Pope:

Whence we see spiders, flies, or ants, entombed and preserved for ever in amber, a more than royal tomb (Bacon).

Pretty! in amber to observe the forms
Of hairs, or straws, or dirt, or grubs, or worms!
The things we know are neither rich nor rare,
But wonder how the devil they got there. (Pope)

The use of amber in all these analogies reverberated for me: I think that I may talk and show this in a workshop. What I would hope to do is set off ideas in others and encourage them to find and become aware of what niggles at them. What grit continually rubs away at their imaginations and recurs in their work?

In a workshop, this could lead to discussion of metaphors and similes, of visuals and tactile memories, of inspirations, of quotations, or following trails, of going off at tangents.

And it is not easy – I will never forget that image of mice in molasses, which has now become **my** image of mice in molasses. When writers, or any other artists, give you these morsels, you could be trapped on a desert island without books, or paper to write on, but you have that richness in your brain, forever, to play with.

Comments

This piece of writing might seem to meander off in many directions – but that is what reflective writing should do. It is a way of working that allows the brain to make connections and then relate what is heard and seen to ideas that are bubbling under the surface. There are a number of references in this piece that could lead to further research if I was going to transform the idea into a more polished and finished article.

It reveals my own inspirations – what fires me. And that is what I am trying to encourage in the development of reflective writing – which might appear in journals, and therefore be rather private, or could be shared with others.

This is about the encouragement of the raw writing, and the focus on idea generation, rather than setting the writing in amber too soon.

Fig. 49: Writing is like mice in molasses.

Dialogue – Inspired by Beethoven

(This is a piece of writing inspired by hearing a piece of music and relating it to something I was working on at the time. It was noted in my journal, and then later I came back to it. The second column represents the subsequent layers of thoughts and reflections, two weeks later.)

In the slow movement of Beethoven's 4th Piano Concerto the orchestra has loud, decisive, precise passages, interspersed by the piano in a conciliatory, subtle, flowing manner. There is a backwards and forwards of interactions as in a conversation.

The piano 'wins' – and develops a song: there are other interruptions later, but the whole movement is in the form of the conversation: listening, talking, proposing, answering, evolving new ideas. The final part ends questioningly – there is no end to this conversation.

Sometimes it is good to take or think about something that is not what you are meant to be doing at that moment. Then make a parallel to what you are doing. It is part of the stepping back from something, looking at it differently, re-focusing and re-viewing it. Making analogies. This is also where metaphors come in.

I wrote this 2 weeks ago. I have not read it since – although I remember writing it and it will have informed what I have done since. I now see other ideas.

For all sorts of writing, thinking of it as dialogue can be useful to gain perspective, point of view, etc.

Conversations explore issues and feelings; they wander off in different directions. The speakers make links both in subject ideas, and emotionally.

It has given me bits to use in other parts. It reaffirms the underlying thread of dialogue in all my work – whether it is my own dialogue, or dialogue of writer and reader, or writer and others.

Talking out loud, as in a conversation – this links to talk write.

You hear other voices, just as you hear your own, but objectively.

(Need to think of other music where this happens)

Also whether dialogue is written or spoken or drawn.

I have also used this to play around with the ideas of writing a reflective comment on the side of text. Have used italics – to resemble handwriting – but it is difficult to read on screen – may need to reconsider.

Comments

This is an example of double entry in journals, an idea particularly promoted by Moon (1999), who has done so much to encourage the use of secondary reflection. There is the immediacy of a thought and then the later, more objective, thinking about the ideas and actions. The final comment brings it into relationship with this book and the ongoing reflection about how to relate it to what I am doing now. Layers of time, layers of thought, and thoughts changing and adapting as a result. New connections made – some to practical issues, others to concepts.

An Internal Dialogue – On the Evening of a 'Wasted' Day

(This is a reflective, but very active piece of writing – to show that even when you are stuck you can write something and it makes connections. This is raw, rough and free writing and is very personal.)

I have an inner voice – or voices.

At times I can have a spirited debate: I solve problems; see other points of view; I ask questions; answer them; decide on further research; or further action on future works.

But I have voices which have attitudes.

'I need to do something …'

"Why?"

'Because …'

"So what?"

'But …'

"I can't be bothered. Am I bothered?"

In a way (and to date the writing of this book), this is like the teenage creation of the actress Catherine Tate, who asks in the most infuriating way, but so recognizably, 'Am I bothered?', over and over again.

This is exactly the voice I get when I am trying to galvanize myself – trying to do the work I actually do want to do.

But …

And there is always that but

But I'd better just water the garden

Put the washing away

Read the paper

Just this

Just that

But I want to do a bit more, write another section of the article, or sort out a bit of the book

Well??…

But …

I day dream another 10 minutes.

Lounging, uncomfortably after a few minutes, staring at the clear evening sky and observing the flitting dappling of leaves in the wind or the lashing of the rambling rose on the wall, occasionally rattling at the window and making me jump

And so …

I can ramble off

I haven't written for the article or the book

I want to

But …

I'll just make a coffee, then I'll get going.

But …

then I'll just read that article in the paper – it might be the key I've been waiting for

……….

It was a stupid column, a waste of space – why do they print such drivel? Why do they pay someone to do that? Why does someone write that?

And still I don't do what I want to.

But of course – I actually wrote.

I did mnemonics:

Prevaricate
reflects
evades
vacillates
and
ruminates
interminably
causing
another
time
evasion

And I did 'essay':

essays	essays
sometimes	suggest
strain	starting
and	arguments
yet	you'd
surprise	stopped

So …

I actually was writing – not what I planned, but as I wrote I was trying to reflect what so many writers feel when they procrastinate and prevaricate (although my dictionary says that these words are often confused – prevaricate is used when it should really be procrastinate) but the meaning of prevaricate is actually very interesting with its 'evasion, go away, transgress' and its origin in the Latin *praevaricari* – 'walk crookedly'.

Having written this on my lap in the growing gloom, I am now bent double over the page trying to see it, and my prevarication has turned into a true crooked posture.

But at least I did another mnemonic.

And I might use this piece to share with everyone.

We all procrastinate and prevaricate.

Don't lose sleep over it.

It won't last.

Find the tricks to get you started.

Tonight I must decide what I will write first thing tomorrow and then I will write.

Last night I didn't decide exactly what to start with today and I've had excuses all day.

That is my way.

But maybe give it a try.

If not, another good tactic is to take a small piece of paper – perhaps a blank postcard. Just write on it – fill it – first thing that comes into your head – what you can see, what you feel like. Stream-of-consciousness stuff. Take one word from what you hope to do. Anything – but write, don't stop – hardly let your pen/pencil lift away from the page – scribble, don't check spelling or punctuate.

It is a warm up – after you've filled the piece of paper, you will probably be readier to start.

If the blank page frightens – draw on it – draw the shape of what you might do; draw a line that reflects the journey of the writing/project/research so far.

Write a list – top to bottom, left to right, diagonally – a list of words for what you are doing – let one word lead to another – go off at tangents – it doesn't matter – but sometimes good links are revealed.

Use Post-its – a good way of brainstorming – can be moved round, added to, re-organized.

The blank sheet in front of you is NOT the final piece – it is rough – so treat it roughly. Show it who's boss – it's your paper, to be covered in your way. Blank does not imply or enforce blank.

Blank is just a vacuum to be filled

By you

Comments
This piece has been typed with almost no alterations – only punctuation to make it easier to read.

This is as I wrote it one evening. It is stream-of-consciousness writing but leads to energy, ideas being generated and a better feeling about my work. I started really grumpily and I ended up focused again. This is what reflective writing can do.

In later entries in my notes, I refer to this piece as being a landmark in thinking about voice and tone in writing. It also reveals the point, which works for me, about knowing the night before what I want to tackle in the morning. I had not *consciously* thought of this strategy before. Now it is conscious, I can really use it to motivate and organize my work.

Talk write is a term used throughout this book. And it is not just talking with someone else – you can talk to yourself most productively, as this piece revealed. When I am stuck, I often interview myself – and the mixture of subjective and objective voice often clarifies what I am trying to do.

On proof-reading this piece, I was struck by my emphasis on the writing on the page – the hand filling the space of the blankness. For those who write straight onto the computer, there is a slightly different sensation. However the principle is still the same. The blank screen can be filled with odd words, rambles, and plays with typography and layout. That is not the final piece, but the *play* might get the writing brain more focused, and the appearance of the words on the screen may generate action.

The writing in this Comments section is also now an example of the secondary reflection, mentioned in the previous piece about a dialogue inspired by Beethoven.

My Process of Writing

(A personal piece of writing which is descriptive of my own process of writing, but written to share with others in order to generate discussion about everyone's preferred ways and methods into writing.)

My writing gesture has to be very free and flowing, and loose and spaced out – allowing time and space for thoughts. Not being cramped.

Some of the practical exercises in this book are to help with this free and loose and unfettered writing. Forget rules, don't worry about spelling, punctuation or grammar – let the thoughts take the line for a walk. Be distracted. Leave spaces if you feel you might want to come back to something.

Writing is a physical activity and I find that I am quite active in the process of writing. When searching for a word, or getting excited at how something is coming out, I will gesture, emphasize with my arm or hand movement. I nod, I wriggle, I tap.

Often, having written a piece, I have to get up and move around – there is some energy that has been generated and it can't all come out on paper. I walk and pace around and then often can come back to the sitting-down part of the writing. This is also probably why my writing is loose and flowing – I cannot write neatly and tightly and firmly while the thoughts are writing.

After a morning of writing, I need to go for a walk. And that walk, is sometimes quite fast, as the ideas are still buzzing and dictating a pace. I will often put the work in context – think of conclusions; think of references; see a structure; come up with alternative words; evolve a title; and make links to other things.

This is my way: my own gesture; a voice; an activity. It is up to everyone to find their own. Some know what and how; others, frequently the worried writers, those lacking in confidence, do not realize that all of this goes to make up the writing.

Some need noise (I need peace), or music, and they may need to drive, or draw, in between drafts. But that is their voice; their method. By sharing mine I hope to encourage thoughts about your own.

Comments

Understanding the way you work and how you need to do things is vital in any process. Sometimes we feel we are being homogenized or standardized, and that we all should be the same. In the studio we are encouraged to find our own methods of evolving projects, and I think that writing should receive the same attention. This is the reason for this short piece – to act as a stimulant for discussion. That is why it is personal, but is also objective. It should not alienate a reader because it is too subjective. I have written elsewhere (Francis 2005) about the starting point for writing. Here there are reflective comments to put my process in a context – as with, for example 'there is some energy that has been generated and it can't all come out on paper', and my comments about the physicality of writing.

An Example of the Process of a Piece of Written Work – from Rough to Publication

(This is a descriptive and analytical piece showing how an article got to print.)

For an article, published in the educational magazine *Special Children* (Francis 2002), I started with brainstorms and lists. These were scrawled over a variety of pieces of paper at different times.

A handwritten version then followed. I use a very soft flowing pen or soft pencil; I am profligate with paper, and the writing is very stretched out, on one side only of the paper. I write continuously – if I can't think of a word, I leave a line; if I repeat a word and know I am, I don't stop to think of an alternative, I keep going with the flow. If there are any notes while working (e.g. find a reference) or a bit that I know is 'iffy', I make a mark in the margin. I just let it flow – I see where it goes. The thoughts take a turn I didn't anticipate: I let them. I can always edit, chop and change, cut and paste later, but the idea journey is important to follow. New aspects, new connections are made by letting the pen flow.

When putting this on the computer, I can copy exactly and/or change some bits as I go (not too much though). When it is printed is the time to start to stand back and consider, play, manipulate.

Although my own spelling is pretty reliable, I don't worry in this first scribbled draft, as long as I can read it. Checks can be done later. Some people cramp their own flow when they stop to look up a spelling in this very first draft.

I print up this version and leave it for a while. I then read it, fairly quickly and easily – following the ideas and seeing if it is doing what I had envisioned in my head.

I make a few pencil notes on this – any obvious mistakes, or more probably squiggles to indicate that something isn't right. I do *not* try to put it right at this stage.

Again I leave it for a bit.

I next work on the computer, going through looking at the notes and working on those. Tackling the problem bits.

I print up again.

This time the read through is more closely detailed. Certain parts are clumsy. There is some waffle, and that gets cut down. I have noticed the repetition of some words – I use a thesaurus to find alternatives.

Print again.

The next read through is about carefully looking at grammar, spelling and repeats of words. I read this out loud, as that nearly always finds the repeated words. Unbelievably, even at this stage I find three 'differents' in as many lines. They are worked on. The reading out loud has led to me wanting to emphasize various words – so that my points are clear. I decide to use italics in some places.

The next print-up requires a very objective review. I am reading as if I was a very serious critical reader. This finds the colloquialisms, the tub thumping (I am rather inclined to get on a soapbox and push the message). I make some things more subtle.

I cut the title and opening paragraph. This had been

Failures Favour Firsts

You can see the headline in the local rags – pupils who were labelled as failures at school achieve 1st Class Honours at University.

I cut this – as it was too sensational.

The next paragraph read:

This is the story of success despite all the odds. This is the saga of achievement which should inspire all those children who are put down, all the parents who despair and the teachers, some of whom are the ones who put down, and some who wonder what could happen.

This became:

This is a story of achievement to inspire all those children who are put down; all the parents who despair, and those teachers who wonder what could or might happen if young people were given appropriate opportunities to excel.

Gone was the phrase that might have alienated the teachers ('some of whom are the ones who put down').

The title became: **'Success against the odds'** with a subheading that the editor slightly rephrased in order to give the name of the author: *'Pat Francis finds that pupils who were labelled "failures" at school can go on to gain First Class Honours at University.'*

This last edit can be quite ruthless. The objectivity allows you to get rid of some of your favourite phrases. But the message put over by the article was clearer and stronger for the hard graft in editing.

Exactly the same process has been my method for this book:

- ideas – on an amazing number of bits of paper
- first long hand splurge
- onto computer
- several drafts
- pulling together
- drastic editing, several times.

The amount in the 'not-used' files is extraordinary. It is a hard lesson, but a necessary one, to be able to cut your own work. But as with so many other strategies, this is not an instant process, nor is it learned fast and easily. But the effort is worthwhile.

Comments

The tone of this piece is obviously addressed directly to the readers – showing and sharing with them the process undertaken. The author's voice is very clear and needs to be thus, if I am going to convince the readers that this is not made up. I break conventions of grammar in order to show what I mean. This is a piece for visual people and needs to look active and clear.

Editing a Few Words

(This is a practical piece of writing with precise examples that could be used as a handout.)

This is an example of editing and the thought process behind it. Obviously not every sentence you write will be as crafted as this. But when you want something to have impact, you do have to work it through in this sort of detail.

I had just written a couple of sentences in my rough notes:

> 'But the important thing is to **read** through with a questioning eye/mind what you have done.
>
> Not always looking for answers
>
> But looking for questions.'

I felt that this was unclear and a bit wordy. It needed to be snappier.

This is the process of changing this:

1. The first sentence is too long. This needs to just be an instruction.

Maybe: **We should be**. Firstly, I thought of *you must*, then, no, *you should*. I then decided to make it less of an order and make it something for all of us – i.e. *we*.)

2. Because there are two uses of 'looking for', I need something for difference and impact: **'seeking'** is one word. This is an improvement.

3. Now I am using the 'seeking answers', the 'looking for questions' sounds a bit as if it is hanging in space.

I add **'to ask'**.

I wonder if this is just repeating – obviously you ask questions. But the answer is yes. It needs this for rhythm and also emphasis.

Reading aloud gave me the definitive answer.

So the final bit is:

**We should be
Not always seeking answers
But looking for questions to ask.**

By not having a common grammatical form and being laid out to aid the reading, the writing has more impact.

Comments

I have really tried to convey my thought processes, so the writing is very colloquial. But this seems to be the best way to achieve the required effect: underlining how physical the process is, emphasizing the activity of reading out loud and the idea of rhythm.

The Puppeteer

(This is a reflective essay with a strong metaphor to intrigue and to attempt to throw light onto the writing process.)

Maybe the writing that is so often required of us could be equated to the 'work' of the puppeteer.

The puppeteer has to juggle lots of things at once; has to have a number of perspectives and viewpoints at any one time; awareness of surroundings – other puppeteers and their work; the puppets; the audience …

Imagine …

Puppeteers – using glove and rod puppets. The glove puppets go on the hand. When not in use, they are hung upside down inside the booth so that the puppeteers can plunge their hands in quickly, and get their fingers in the right places. Up comes the puppet facing the right way, fingers in the arms and head, ready to make an entrance. Maybe there is a different character on each hand.

A rod puppet has one rod for the body and head, and two rods attached to its two hands (one for right, one for left) so that the puppeteer takes the body rod in one hand, and manipulates the two rods for the puppet's hands, in the other hand.

The puppet might be quite heavy and invariably the costume is flowing and can engulf the puppeteer's head. The puppet is stored in a rack at the back – the principal rod going into a hole on the stand. To pick up the puppet, the puppeteer has to bend down to grasp the main rod, and quietly sort out the metal hand rods that are clashing around.

The script is written for two puppeteers, but ten characters. Much of the time some characters do not meet – how can they as the same puppeteer operates them? But the plot eventually requires a short scene, where, for example, a glove puppet meets a rod puppet. As both 'belong' to one puppeteer, the other puppeteer has to work one of the puppets – but the 'owner' puppeteer has to do both voices.

This takes some doing – and the subtext below the playboard of the puppet theatre is fascinating to observe. The facial expressions of the puppeteers, one to the other, could be deadly, but a sweet voice might be speaking. One puppeteer is mute but has the power, with the puppet they are manipulating, to throw or enrage or corpse their partner.

This will only be witnessed by a small boy on the front row who sneaks a look under the drapes of the puppet booth. Both puppeteers with their arms in the air can only kick at him and kill him with looks – but he is oblivious.

The puppet has to speak the text, using very different voices to distinguish characters – as the puppets' mouths do not move, this is important. The puppets have to move and react appropriately.

The operators' arms are held well above the head. No scene in a puppet script will last for too long – or collapsing puppeteers will occur. The playboard is at a height to hide the tallest puppeteer, so the shortest has to stretch even higher. Pairs of puppeteers rarely comprise a giant and a dwarf.

Entrances and exits are timed so that puppeteers can change puppets. A number of scripts have voices 'off stage' before a character enters.

Props are a nightmare. Picking something up from a narrow playboard when you cannot see what you are doing is dangerous (props falling on puppeteer's heads), excruciating (props slipping, sliding, missing), and disastrous (prop knocked into the audience so the puppeteer cannot then see what happens to it – a helpful child might offer it up, but the puppeteer cannot see this, and the child cannot understand that the puppet cannot see it – aarrgghh).

The puppeteer has to listen for whatever clues might penetrate their own noise, the muffle of the booth fabric and the sweat dripping in their ears. The close proximity to the other puppeteer, the slippy, but tappy, floor surfaces, the doors behind the booth, the sudden ad libs of the other puppeteer, the sinking feeling that you've already done this bit (but actually it was the previous performance).

Why do they do it?

Because they have to. They love it/hate it.

Like so many creative jobs it has extreme highs and extreme lows; is hard graft; is about multi-tasking; incomprehensible, at times, to yourself and others, yet magical. It calls for an all-round performance – 360 degree awareness; physical stamina; mental alertness; creative sparks; endurance; and an ability to laugh at yourself and a need for the sound of laughter in others.

Most of these qualities are probably also needed by other creative artists – particularly performers. But it is also the case with the writer, though this might not seem immediately obvious.

Here I will attempt to prove the links …
Writers also juggle with a number of perspectives and viewpoints at one time. They have to have an acute awareness of who the audience is – who their reader is. There is a parallel between the words and the puppets – both are the tools of the trade. From this follows the preparation – how words/puppets work.

And technical things in writing have to be understood and used, but not so that they get in the way of the message. This might include use of quotations or footnotes, perhaps in the same way that the puppeteer learns a script, works out how to use props, make movements and find a voice which is right for the character.

There is a subtext in both forms – the writer may talk in one voice while feeling another thought or emotion, and the puppeteer might 'do' another character.

Both writer and puppeteer have to move and react and be aware of what is said or written and how a balance must be created in causing effects on an audience.

Props and actions are like examples or quotes in that they are difficult to handle and to contextualize. The reader might misunderstand and put the idea into another context. You do not know how an audience will react.

The major difference is that a puppet show is a live performance with a live audience and the puppeteer knows what the reactions are and can try to vary what they do accordingly. The writer is not usually present with the reader. Therefore writing has to be clearer in intent and layout. A live performance can react intuitively and be varied. Writing, once printed, is more concrete. This is probably the main fear for most writers, whether experienced or not: 'Have I written what I mean? Do I really mean what is down on the page?'

Comments
This is not intended as an academic piece, but it follows some of those conventions in that:

- *it has to describe some things in order for the reader to understand the concepts presented*
- *it has to select what points to use as examples*
- *it has to make these points clearly*
- *it must present arguments*
- *– and draw conclusions.*

The ideas that came out through this writing underlined other ideas presented in the book about the physicality of text. But it also draws attention to the differences between active performance of language and written text.

I wrote this particular example as I used to be a puppeteer and so can speak from experience. I am also a writer and so I am proposing the link based on my own knowledge. By using the puppeteer I hope to intrigue the reader – there are insights presented which are not necessarily known, and they can hook the reader. The proposal of the parallel is set as a bit of challenge – so the reader keeps going with the idea in order to see if it works and if I can pull it off.

Extended metaphors can sometimes be very useful – they might be pieces of writing that are worked through in rough, and not used in their entirety in a finished piece, but the process is useful.

Sometimes you have to take metaphors for a walk and see where they go.

Fig. 50: LIVE – the puppet show.

White

(This is a piece of reflective and creative writing. It is very personal, but was written in order to get down the ideas sparked in response to reading a chapter of a book.)

I'm always much more interested in the process, in the journey of a project.

Where there is the finished piece, the exhibition, I'm vaguely disappointed.

Trying to put my finger on this disappointment, I realized that, *for me*, what is displayed can be only a part of the piece. It is finished; it is final. It is hanging in a clean white space. It has a label, which is sometimes pretentious.

But when I know the story: the paths; the ups and downs; the *Eureka* moments; the trial and error; when mistakes become the key – this is much more exciting. The messy sketchbook, the scrappy notes and research, the thoughts, lists and reflections – these are the journey made.

The final piece in its clean white state is beautiful in its aesthetics, but sometimes it has lost its owner.

White is worrying.

White is neat.

I cannot be neat: I never could be neat.

As soon as I learnt to write, my infants' teacher told me I would have to learn to write neatly as otherwise I would lose marks in texts and exams.

Luckily I never took notice of that or it might have inhibited or deadened my thoughts.

My face cannot be neat. My glasses are always lopsided.

My house has never been tidy. I try, but I never succeed.

The dust has dust.

I collect and hoard
And everything is stored
Haphazardly.

I was a librarian for a while. I had to catalogue and classify – but I broke the rules.

I could never tally/marry how it should be with what it could be.

I like dysfunction, I like disorder.
I need things to be skew-whiff.
That is the way connections and links are made.

I like the patina of use:
It is the patina of life.
Patina it is
Neat it ain't.

(This last couplet is a bit of word play on my name and patina and neat.)

Comments
This whole piece was inspired by reading the first essay in David Batchelor's book *Chromophobia* (2000).

This collection of essays is a wonderful example of writing – a mixture of the erudite and the personal; the analytical and the emotional. He has asides and thoughts that are not what would be expected. And it was this tone and style of writing that inspired my own notes. It led me off at tangents.

But my first thoughts about the exhibition space, inspired by Batchelor's writing, made me go on to think about other issues of display. The personal details were a bit of light-hearted reflection, which could be extended into more serious writing. I am certainly not saying that the personal piece of writing is what should be handed in for an essay, for example. But it maybe that pieces like this abound in a journal. They reveal the starting points for ideas.

Many of the authors quoted in this book, particularly Atwood, Welty, Woolf, Bennett and Walter, have sections of very personal material which they share as a way of communicating ideas and showing the *sources* of an inspiration, a reflection or an analysis. I share this piece in order to encourage the writing of the personal. In this book the personal has become public, but most of this sort of writing that you will do will not become public. But it may get you going, break the blocks, and give you ideas beyond what you have put down,

> *As emphasized before, this book proposes that the personal is the way into the objective, and the detail of the specific is the way into the specific thought, that will underpin the academic piece of writing. This is not about generalities, but details.*

How We Are

(Some notes on an exhibition – but more about word play than the exhibition itself.)

This is the title of a photography exhibition at Tate Britain, 2007.

But the **play on words** in the title is interesting ...

Who we are: this is just rearranging letters of 'how' to 'who'.

Who are we? This is achieved by just rearranging the order of these words and leads to a big change: statement moves to question.

This leads back to the original words and different order:

How are we ...? Again, a question, but with different implications.

This deceptively simple title can lead to questions about layers that relate to the exhibition and beyond.

This helps you engage with the ideas being presented and your own reactions.

At the same time there is an exhibition entitled 'Learn to Read' at Tate Modern.

This is not what you would think from the title: it is not about reading systems, etc.

It is about the way artists have used words in their work: their play with words; words in layers; and erasures and erosion.

Again, this is a stimulant to thought – because you immediately challenge it.

This all links to creating titles and how important they are and what they set off – and how they can mislead, which might or might not be wanted.

But sometimes this is also just about the use and play of words, not taking anything as if spoon fed, but questioning it; rearranging it. As soon as you start to do this, you engage with it. It doesn't necessarily matter if what you do is incorrect: it is an active interaction.

Comments

This is just a short piece which is very clear in its playing with words and showing what that play can lead to. It is the sort of writing that could inspire discussion. So sometimes it is good to write thoughts down, so that someone else can read them, and then you can talk.

'Learn to Read' Exhibition: Tate Modern. Opening day 19 June 2007

(These are notes written shortly after the visit to the exhibition – so there are all sorts of odd thoughts flitting in and out – but this underlines the principle of getting the thoughts down, there and then.)

I must have been one of the first in – in fact one of the guards was having a good look and someone else was checking the exhibits – something was missing or else they had a check list as to how something should look – not clear to him or anyone else – bit of eyebrow raising, I think. Lot of security intercom babble – which was fitting – words incoherent.

Some pieces just seemed clever-clever – not very deep, or I didn't get it. Others resonated.

In some, the aesthetics were wonderful. Some had so much text you physically couldn't stand and read.

The opening exhibit – laid out like a mind map, so parts were upside down – so couldn't read all. It was like a handwritten brainstorm – so was hard to read, as it was an individual's piece of work – as if for that person alone.

The more you look – the more you get the overall idea; read a few bits and then move on.

Eight pieces I think – all different. Will need to look again – when I have thought about it. Lia Perjovschi (artist). One of the brainstorms is reproduced in leaflet which will enable me to look at it later and really see what it is about. Also it was done in relation to exhibition.

Looking at this example in the leaflet – cannot read all the handwriting and I am fairly good at doing that. Don't think everyone would be able to? Are you meant to read all of it? – is it done for aesthetics? – actually the content is all relevant – not gibberish – but still not meant to be read through, word for word. Is this one just the 'briefing' one? What are the others? – need to look.

Aesthetically the cigarette burns one was fascinating – visually stunning and then individual bits that you could pick out to read – very legible. Would go back to time and again. (Simon Evans)

Also his piece on tree rings – pencil shavings – again visually stunning and then links to life.

I tried to read some fully – but couldn't physically. One was done on an old typewriter, with very dense lines – single line spacing and very long. Standing up, and at a slight distance, it was very difficult to get to the correct next line. In a book this is easier – though this is a problem dyslexics have (therefore this could represent a *simulation* of difficulties).

In this thought there is a link to the title – many might misinterpret it – take it very literally. But this is about questioning what we see, mistakes, misinterpretations, play, doodling with words, making it, or them, visual.

As always, for me, reading the notes to the exhibition, makes sense of it. Some pieces become clearer. This is an area that I can never understand with other people – do they fully get it without notes? (What do I mean – get what? And does it matter – is it for each person to get something – but what about those who definitely go away quickly because they don't get it, dismiss it? So many people say it should speak for itself, doesn't need notes, etc. But – this is sometimes laziness, or they don't like the statement, etc. – because it is difficult to do, or they have difficulty reading it.)

In an exhibition you often see people spending more time on caption/explanation than on work.

With this one – only name, date, medium and location. The notes are in the leaflet.

Could I use this one as an example for the book? – because it is word related – title multi-layered – words associated with exhibition. Lack of notes with pieces, short notes in leaflet.

Leaflet notes: approx. 100 words for each artist – who they are and what they do, and the work in exhibition – very dense piece – in that way a good example.

If I did something on this, might be a good idea to contact the curator(s).

In the leaflet, the use of lists helps put over a lot. In the three paragraphs, it has:

what the exhibition is (1st para)

where it comes from – predecessors (2nd para)

and links coming up to current day (3rd para).

Comments
These are my notes written on the train coming home after the exhibition. I have left them pretty well as they were written – with only one or two words changed to make it clear for this book.

This sort of reflective, questioning, dialogue with self is very important as the sort of record for an exhibition or event. There are enough reactions in it to pick up on later and to act as springboards. The asking of questions means that I will follow up on them – not just go home and forget it.

The questioning of the work and the content and the possible meanings also begs dialogue with others and discussion of their interpretations.

This sort of writing could exist in reflective journals and also contribute to areas of patchwork writing either individually generated, or in a group.

The brief analysis of the leaflet and captioning is also a good habit to get into, helping with ideas of structures and how material is presented, so that when you have to do a similar piece yourself, you have more knowledge of what works and what doesn't.

Brass Prom: Combining Senses

(I attended a concert at the BBC Proms 2007 as part of a Brass Day. The concert I went to had pieces played by a vast range of brass instruments. I sat high up in the circle and had a brilliant view over the whole experience. I later talked to people who had listened to the concert on the radio. This made me think of the difference, particularly with a concert, of being there live or just listening to it. We might think of music as appealing to the auditory sense alone. We listen to music. But the live concert uses other senses.)

The brass concert needed to be viewed as well as listened to.

The prime example was the music from Uzbekistan. The men blew down long brass ceremonial trumpets called *karnays* which were about seven feet long. The performers moved them around so the sound changed, and in the Albert Hall the acoustics made it amazing. It was a summoning call, and how that was revealed! They moved together like synchronized swimmers (although that image debases it a bit). It was choreographed and both the sight of this, and the amazement that the men could both blow sufficiently to fill the hall, and then move these *karnays*, which were bigger than them, and carry on, non-stop, for about fifteen minutes, was awe-inspiring.

If heard on the radio, you could not get this and, apparently, the piece seemed to go on a bit. The acoustics are so balanced in the radio broadcast that the effect we got in the concert hall was lost.

Those listening to the radio were surprised at the amount and scale of the applause – but those in the audience at the Prom were 'gobsmacked' and really showed their excitement. The performers were brought back a few times. They gave an encore – just one phrase, which seemed like a thank you.

So any one art form is not just about one sense – music is not just auditory; visual art is not just visual – it is emotional and it might be auditory and tactile.

Poetry usually thought of as just auditory, is not: it can be visual – if you see someone read it, or look at the typographic layout – but it is also tactile: the hairs can go up on the back of your neck and you *feel* the rhythm.

There is the auditory from the page (hearing it in your head), and the auditory when you physically hear it. We all have different levels of being able to hear the printed word. The more you are able to read out loud, the better, perhaps, you might get of the physicality of the text.

All these ideas relate to the emotions: emotional memory, significance, relationships, etc.

All this applies to writing, too.

Comments
These are a few notes written, later, on the day of the concert, and again thoughts have gone off in other directions, particularly when I heard other reactions. I had written about the importance of senses in writing, and this Proms experience seemed to underline it in an unexpected way. What it brought out were things that I already knew, but had not voiced before. This is about the constant open-mindedness to connections and links.

Analysis of Words to Help Inform Work and Generate Research

(This is part of a handout for a project introducing the idea of keeping a journal.)

Documenting the journey

Document

- Late Middle English
- This is from an Old French word, from Latin *documentum* 'lesson' 'proof', which became in medieval Latin 'written instruction, official paper'. The base is the Latin verb *docere, 'teach'* (Chantrell 2004);
- a piece of written or printed matter that provides a record or evidence of events, an agreement, ownership, identification, etc;
- prove by or provide with documents or evidence;
- record in a document (Thompson 1995: 398).

Journey

- Middle English
- Journey is from Old French *journée, 'day, a day's travel, a day's work'*:
- These were the earliest senses in English. Latin *diurnum* 'daily portion' is the base, from *diurnus* 'daily', from *dies* 'day' (Chantrell 2004).

Loosely then, these words taken together, imply teaching about the journey – therefore also learning from the journey, passing on evidence of the journey as some sort of document or record. There is also the written element and, in the roots of journey, the regularity or daily nature of this. We never insist on daily entries, but they do need to be regular, as otherwise things happen and they are not reflected on, and then in later notes they become victims of hindsight, or mis-memory.

Comments

Looking into word histories is nearly always a fruitful activity in early research and also something to do if you ever get stuck. The story of a word and its history and changing context may give ideas that deepen and contextualize your experience and reactions to the word.

This example of trying to convince others of the usefulness of keeping a journal and providing evidence reveals the good practice of referring to the roots of words. You can often give yourself back-up, just in this investigation alone. But it can also alert you, the writer, to other meanings that you hadn't seen.

Some of this material has also appeared elsewhere in this book.

Words in Arguments

(This follows other principles in the book – looking at words in detail to help you understand the task and give yourself clues as to how to go about something.)

The following are some words that it is helpful to analyse when thinking about creating an argument. A greater understanding of the root of a word may give an insight into how to present something or what is relevant or what is implied.

Sometimes word play can give important insights.

Argument
In Middle English, 'argument' had the sense of 'process of reasoning' and this is the best way of thinking of it. Reasoning is about being measured – seeing different sides, not being one-sided. It is about giving reasons/statements/facts, and implies that you have considered/worked through something.

So if you are late handing something in you might say: 'the reasons that this essay is late are because':

- my computer crashed and I couldn't print it out
- I misjudged how long it would take me to do
- my dog ate my essay.

Some of these sound like excuses, while some take more responsibility for actions. When reasons become excuses, they are not taken seriously.

In an argument, they have to be serious or considered. Constantly look at how your list of evidence is coming along. Think about the reasons that we give for something and this might help separate the serious from the silly; or the strong from the weak.

Argy-bargy is a common phrase to represent an argument. It even sounds like the to and fro of debate. Just as the 'b' is added to 'argy', so in an argument can one word be added to, or developed by the other person, and carried on backwards and forwards, cutting down, building up, etc.

Fallacy
Think of this as a **fault** or as the argument **fall**ing down.

Something is **false** about it – the evidence doesn't stack up, it is opinion that is very subjective.

This is like saying:

- 'Everyone reads about celebrities – so, everyone wants to be famous and rich like them.'

Apart from the unsupportable idea that 'everyone' does these things, the little word 'so' is the give away. One thing is this – so something else must be that.

She is fat, so she must be unhappy.

He is strong, so he must be brave.

Often statements come about like this from generalizations. Apart from needing to breathe, eat and defecate, and the fact that we are all born and die, there are probably very few other things that *all* human beings truly have in common. (There's an argument to use as practice.)

Evidence
This is the idea of available facts to support something.

But the word 'evident', when we usually use it, is in the way of, 'it is plain or obvious' – you can see something. The root of the word comes from the Latin *videre* –'see'.

So something becomes clear and visual through the evidence presented.

Back-up
There is a funny visual idea here.

If your back is playing up, you often have a bolster – a big fat cushion to support it.

So back-up material – is just that: cushions/bolsters to support what you say.

Quote
This comes from the Medieval Latin *quot* – 'how many?' We often use it if we are getting an estimate for something: 'I was given a quote of … for mending this.'

So maybe link this with what you need to do if you use quotes or quotations in your argument – you need to give it value:

- you need to discuss what the value is of your quotation
- what evidence it is giving
- but also whether it has a value – the person being quoted is an expert and therefore their words are of great value, or it is some ill-informed opinion and therefore not of great value in terms of facts, but might be of value in terms of the feelings of many people, or is representative of a time.

Chains
Dictionary definitions include:

- connected flexible series of … links
- a sequence.

Sometimes this might link with the word 'logic', in the sense of a logical sequence, which is where one thing leads to another, then on to another, and has to be in that sequence.

Think of the lyrics for the song known as 'Chain Reaction' which is also a scientific expression – and this leads to the idea of cause and effect, very important in arguments. If one thing happens, then another thing might, then another. These 'chain reactions' need to be shown clearly to build the argument.

There is also the popular scientific belief that when a butterfly flaps its wings on one side of the world, on the other a hurricane happens.

Cause and effect are two words that can help to see where arguments might progress.

Absurd
An argument can be said to be absurd when something that does not relate to the argument is put forward as being relevant. The dictionary meaning of absurd is 'wildly unreasonable, illogical or inappropriate' – and the links with the words above help clarify this. It is un**reason**able – il**logic**al.

Titles – Examples

(This is short piece to expand the ideas of generating titles, and using my own work as examples.)

Writing a book is slightly different from most of the activities you might have to do at college. When you propose a book to a publisher you have to suggest a possible title – and you haven't even written it yet.

My answer was to generate a lot of different ones – all fairly loose and abstract, some clever-clever, some so obscure only I know what I meant. I submitted them all to give the flavour of what I hoped to do.

Inspiring Writing/Soft Pencil on Off White Paper/A sense of Writing/Drawing on Writing/Making a mark/Drawing on a sense of writing/Drawing on the Writing Hand/A feel for writing/Writing Reflects/Writing Traces/Taking a Line for a Write

With two possible subtitles:

Encouraging students in art and design into writing.

Visual and Practical ways into inspiring writing in art and design

I constantly played with ideas, and jotted them down and looked at them from all angles. That is one of the things you have to do – look from a number of different directions, thinking of the number of different sorts of reader you might have. You have to think of your audience – and if that is broad, then the title has to appeal to all, and not alienate a significant number of the potential readers.

I will explain the genesis of two other pieces that I have written in the past.

Content in Writing (Francis 2005)
This was a discussion paper for an organization made up of writers and academics in art and design education who are all interested in the process of writing, and how to promote the pleasures and techniques of writing. I was proposing a hands-on approach; an engagement with the subject and starting from the personal, rather than from some point outside the potential writer's experience. I used word-play. At the beginning of the paper, the word 'content' is about the subject, the focus of what is being written about. It is the 'what'.

By the end I had moved towards the idea of writers being 'content' with their writing – being 'happy' with it. So I have played on the same word, same spelling, but different meaning, and often different pronunciation. I built towards this, and the readers followed my argument. This was inspired by the writer, Jeanette Winterson, in her book of essays, *Art Objects* (1996). Here, the word 'objects' is understood as 'things', but in one essay she used the idea of art objecting or disagreeing with aspects of the modern world.

I loved that idea and copied it from her, but I am sure she would not object.

A paper for college was entitled 'Finding the I in assessment' (le Marquand and Francis 2006). This again is a bit of word play: there is no letter 'i' in the word assessment. But what the paper was about was the individual, and their role and understanding of the process of assessment, and how that individual journey is more important than the tick-box criteria of many assessment procedures.

Looking at the Blurb for Geoff Dyer's *The Ongoing Moment*

(This is an example of some notes taken on a book's blurb, showing the use of key words – italics mark particular points.)

The blurb on the back of the book (Dyer 2006) reads:

> How Dyer has mastered the art of the essay, understood as a *piece of discursive, personal writing* in which great, often melancholy themes are raised with lightness and very dry humour (Alain de Botton).

Another quoted review talks of:

'*Graceful ruminations*'

I am particularly taken with the '*piece of discursive personal writing*', as that seems to sum up exactly what I am trying to promote in my book as a valuable form: keeping the personal, but spinning off, widening out, and following up on details.

Alain de Botton is also a writer who is erudite and yet readable, who links the knowledgeable with the personal. I think of the section he has on 'word paint' (de Botton 2003: 230) as written about by John Ruskin, and his explanation is anecdotal, detailed, inspirational and comprehensible, where the original Ruskin is difficult.

The review comment, 'graceful ruminations', is just brilliant. 'Graceful', meaning well-written, flowing, beautiful writing. But, ruminate – isn't that what cows do? They chew the cud, over and over again – going over material in great detail and with thoroughness, yet at the same time a very natural process, gently done.

The blurb on this book has made me want to read it. All blurbs are meant to sell something, and this has done.

Comments

This piece is highly personal but there are clear points that link to what I am doing in this book – and that really is the importance of it. The key words are the connections to your own project: you are picking out the things that sing to you and they will remind you of ideas and reaffirm your directions. Reflections on the small details pay dividends.

Blurbs on books are a good initial way into seeing if a book is going to be useful to consult, and when other writers give comments, this can also give you a store of information about the probable pedigree of it.

Reflections on an Article

(Reflective and analytical writing about ideas and language, with notes for further reading.)

The article is by Jeanette Winterson in *The Times* Saturday 19 May 2007

> 'The strength of art is a private moment between individuals'

> 'Reading is a private dialogue between you and the book'

Two key words in these lines are 'between' (which is in both sentences) and 'dialogue'.

It is between you and the work of art, whatever that is; the ideas it speaks to you, whether intended by the creator or not. The questions it asks of you and the answers you try to form, or the thought explosions it gives you. That is the value of art – not its monetary value, but the resonance and richness it has for individuals.

She then talks about language and words, relating the words a writer creates, to the babble and corruption of language in the everyday.

> *I believe that a good book – fiction, poetry, nonfiction – does more than ask questions, or offer different realities; by using language honestly and accurately, literature keeps us alive to the slippage so common in media-babble and newspeak. Real language, like real feeling, shows up its counterfeit. The spin merchants and speechwriters of political life have made ordinary people distrust language as much as we distrust politics. But our mistrust of language is only our misuse of language. The integrity of literature restores our sense of what language can do, and indeed reminds us of why human beings invented language at all; not to ask directions, or even to call a spade a spade, but to handle all the difficulty and complexity of life and love. We owe it to ourselves to read a good book; it gives us back human experience as a spectrum, not as a soundbite.*

This part about language reminds us that it is not just about directions or labelling, but is about trying to cope with, interpret, express, play, explore, and more, and that is why it is important to work at our writing – for ourselves to understand, and for others to read. But it is also why writing is about exploring – it does not come ready-made, it is **not instant**, it is not in the form of soundbites.

Winterson also writes that art is not mass culture and that not everyone responds to all areas of art: but it doesn't matter which areas you do, and do not, respond to: it is just important that you find what you can respond to.

> *The strength of art, wherever you find it – Shakespeare, Verdi, Carol Ann Duffy, Antony Gormley – is a private moment between individuals. It is always a one-to-one experience and, while that experience can be shared, its effect is personal.*

Note to follow up: How does this link with Walter Benjamin's essay 'The Work of Art in the Age of Mechanical Reproduction' and 'aura'? ([1936]1969)?

Comments

By taking two extended quotations and again picking up key words, the first reflections on the essay provide notes for the future. Also noting the idea that I need to think about how this links with another standard text that is often offered to students in art and design: Benjamin's 1936 essay 'The Work of Art in the Age of Mechanical Reproduction' (Benjamin 1969). This is making the reading into an active linking to further work. The reflective research journal which accompanies preparations for an essay or dissertation might contain notes such as these: the noting of things to think about, look up and read, indicate the journey being taken.

Benjamin's work is not easy for many students who do not always know the context, the period and how it can relate to their circumstances today. Because of this, it is sometimes helpful to start with something contemporary and then make a link back to the past: as in archaeology, work from the known to the unknown.

In terms of archaeology, Benjamin's words about his *Archives* (Benjamin 2007) may merit some exploration to show how writing was used to classify, as well as reflect on its contents.

This also is an occasion where the development of time lines is very beneficial. The time line would reveal the birth, and development of, photography, silent film, sound film, printing presses, newspapers, television, the Internet, etc., all of which relate to the ideas being offered by Winterson and by Benjamin.

In addition, the exercises I have written about the use of postcards and some of the questions posited may link in here, making the reading relate to practical thoughts, and also relating to writing experiments.

Patchwork Text: Women Travellers

(The following pieces of text all constitute ideas for patchwork text: with differing views, styles, lengths and the exploration of a range of voices. The common theme is the inspirations from a visit to a specific exhibition. I briefly introduce each piece, and make comment on some of the sections.)

'Off the Beaten Track: Three Centuries of Women Travellers'
An exhibition at the National Portrait Gallery, 2004

Description of layout
(It is good to start with pure description of something, to immerse yourself into the subject. For the exhibition, the layout and arrangement and the type of visitors, are all aspects that can be considered.)

The exhibition is displayed in the Porter Gallery, which is shaped a bit like a clover leaf – without the curves. There are sections on the British women from the three centuries covered, with photographs or paintings or drawings of them, and examples of their own paintings or photographs. Display cases, in the middle of these rooms, contain artefacts that some travellers brought back with them. In the third, and smallest, section are various women from other countries who travelled to England. A subsection of this part has activities in it for children, a book/gift stall and examples of books on sale downstairs in the bookshop.

The exhibition is split into sections, not chronologically, but by subject, such as: Starting Out, The Americas, Russia, Turkey and Eastern Europe, Africa, etc.

There are two short videos running throughout. At weekends there are showings of films relevant to the subject.

In addition to the children's activity area (building different sorts of architecture from building blocks), there are suitcases which contain items such as a headscarf and a hat, which can be tried on, or ancient pottery that has to be pieced together.

There are large print captions in the form of a book/folder which can be carried around. Available for a suggested donation of £1 is a fold-out guide to the overall theme of the exhibition. There are also audio guides.

The shop sells a few postcards of key figures, the exhibition book, and a range of contemporary copies of artefacts, or imported items from countries featured. These items include jewellery, scarves, lanterns and an elephant puppet. A survey is being carried out by the curators to ascertain its success, and how people access it.

On the Saturday morning I visited there were, at first, mainly middle-aged females, singly or in pairs. Later in the morning there was a more mixed audience – still predominantly female, but of all ages. Only one child was seen in the two hours I was there. Some people looked around very briefly, but a substantial number were spending a lot of time reading the captions and studying the artefacts.

Comments

In a formal analysis of the exhibition itself, or its display aesthetics, it is necessary to start with description. It is good to practice this, as otherwise you have a lot of inconsequential information and you can get bogged down in minutiae. Selecting and ordering material to use is a part of the planning. Each paragraph here covers a different aspect of the exhibition.

Description of content

(This description is moving more towards providing a background to an analysis of the content of the exhibition.)

The exhibition is principally about key women from the last three centuries who have travelled, for a variety of reasons, and who recorded their travels in a number of ways. Their principal method of recording was writing. Therefore this exhibition is, in a way, quite a literary display. There is a lot of reading. The visuals are portraits – paintings, drawings and photographs of the women travellers – some made by themselves, but mostly by others. However, as the catalogue remarks, these were often taken or completed out of the context of their travels: that is, in the comforts of the home. The portraits are principally from the National Portrait Gallery collection and this has dictated who is represented in the exhibition.

The portraits vary enormously in size – from a small ambrotype to large oil paintings dominating a wall. There is also a sculpture of one of the women. In the case of two women, Aphra Benn, and Pocohontas, the portraits are not authenticated, but are most probably of them.

These portraits are accompanied by maps, so that the themes of the exhibition become clear: the destinations of the women, or the purpose of their travels.

The exhibition is made more visual and less literary by display cases housing artefacts from their travels, which have frequently been loaned by other museums. There are the masks, rattles, wood carvings and pottery that were collected, and also the personal belongings of some of the travellers, such as Mary Kingsley's hat or Freya Stark's passports. There are originals and some copies of the actual writings, notebooks or annotations of many of the women.

The reason that the exhibition is about women travellers is to point out to today's women, who now have almost unfettered access to travel, that these early figures were

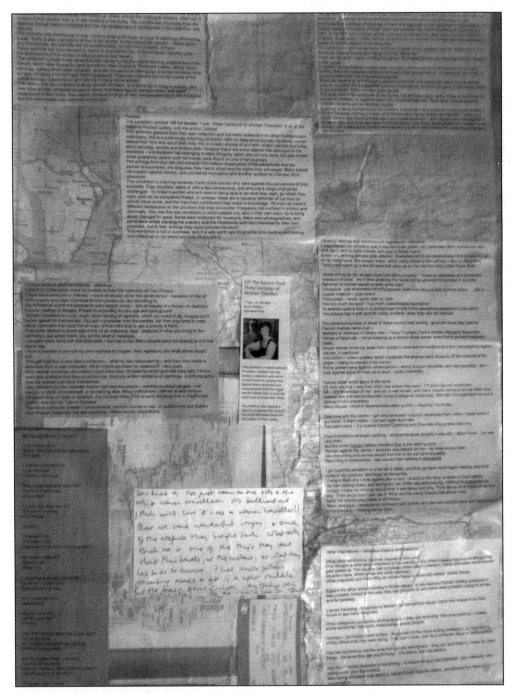

Fig. 51: Patchwork text for 'Women Travellers'.

pioneers, and were exceptional in their times. Today's visitors will bring a range of their own experiences to the exhibition, and this encourages very personal encounters.

Comments

This description is enhanced by the specific details used: the sorts of pictures – oils, watercolours, ambrotype, etc; and the artefacts – masks, passports, etc. If it had just said pictures and objects, the reader would not have had any real sense of the variety of forms the exhibition presented, and it might have been perceived as very two dimensional, as there had been a comment about it being a 'literary display'. Inevitably, some analysis creeps in with the comments about today's visitors and their very different attitudes to travel, but that is totally in keeping with the slant of the exhibition.

Personal feelings and reactions and inspirations – reflective writing and notes

(This passage is in the form of notes – many taken at the time, and consisting of a lot of quotations that particularly struck me.)

I was pleased the exhibition was in this particular gallery, as I have seen other exhibitions here and like it: it is more intimate and easy to follow round. Some very striking pictures grab attention. Overwhelmed by the determination that shows through on so many faces. Not always 'pretty', which really makes a link with me – but so interesting.

Taken particularly by a few phrases that come up on the captions and I jotted these down:

'chose writing as her escape route from family poverty' 'icicles on eyebrows and eyelashes'

'pleasure of ruins' 'don't wear anything that would not be ashamed to be seen in at home'

'Believed no woman equals a really great man'!

Screwpine: 'odd sketchable bit of foreground. Had roots like a cluster of white pillars ... – like a puppet creature – goat beard

On a photograph the photographer had written: 'spoilt alas' on the back

'had too much too soon. Too much unassimilated experience'

'to awaken quite alone in a strange town is one of the pleasantest sensations in the world'

'she always had a soft spot for needy students, stray dogs and old vehicles'

The adventurousness of some of these women was striking – given the times they lived in.

Certain themes came over:

- mothers or relatives of literary men – Fanny Trollope; Fanny Kemble; Margaret Stevenson
- wives of diplomats – some keeping up a certain dress sense, some doing as their husbands bade ...
- single women breaking away from society's rules and conventions and then campaigning against slavery, in particular
- inoculation – letters pirated, which explained the strange word dropping off the bottoms of the pages – being squeezed in by copyist
- some women were against emancipation – which is quite incredible, and very puzzling – and I took against some of them as a result – quite irrationally.

Human detail which stays in the mind:

- EE took her dog – and they didn't mind where they went
- FT didn't like the Americans
- BB – tiny ambrotype of her, and yet is well known, and many visitors honing in on her when they realized that she had co-founded Girton College at Cambridge. Was also the inspiration for one of George Eliot's characters
- Marie Stopes – lived in Swanscombe when a child – inspiring link for me.

Odd thing with the names – got very confused – couldn't remember them, and when I made notes, it got better. This didn't matter – but was quite dominant.

Two particularly – Constance Gordon Cumming and Charlotte, Viscountess Canning

> Found exhibition strangely exciting – strange because actually it was odd – about travel – yet was very static.

But this is the *Portrait* Gallery therefore *that* is the starting point.

Women against the norms – personal inspirations for me – as have always been.

Also the writing and journal aspect and that is my own preoccupation.

Recording of experiences – key quotes from catalogue *afterwards*.

I go round the exhibition in a fair bit of detail, and then go back round again making very brief notes in my notebook and linger on favourites.

Trying to think why I took against one or two – a look on the face, or some of their beliefs.

On train coming home and during the rest of the day and evening – looking through material bought, and:

- I make up my mind as to what it was about and why
- think on what inspired me and why
- think around how I can use it
- think what the visual images are that are so clear
- I need the sketchnotes made at exhibition
- I need catalogue – because of confusion with names and also who people were and deepening of understanding – making sense later.

Comments

There is a wealth of detail and thought in here. Some of the reactions are irrational, but make me think about why, and that is useful in writing: to know your niggles and how to deal with them.

I have documented how I go round the exhibition, and what has taken my eye there.

Fig. 52: Journeys into writing.

Then there is a note about ideas that strike later – the standing back and reflecting on it.

Also about the importance of the catalogue in an exhibition like this, where there is so much detail that you cannot possibly remember it all.

What has stood out for me are some key words – usually in the form of quotations, and the look of people, or details of their attitudes or behaviours.

Use of the word 'sketchnotes' – which really sums up the importance of recording.

Comparisons to other exhibitions – reflective
(It is good to reflect back on other exhibitions. Comparisons can enhance writing, because they make thoughts more specific, and they make your writing more objective. Good practice for essays.)

Exhibition in the same place as postcards from the collection of Tom Phillips.

His display was arranged in themes – and some obviously cover the same period, because of rise of photography and idea of postcards from places you are travelling to.

Big difference is that his postcards were largely visual – lots of images in a frame, no captions, humour, pathos of images. You relate to them according to your age and background.

Women travellers is much, much, more reading of captions, which you need to do. Images don't purely speak for themselves. You get a character from the portrait, but then you need to read about them and also read the writings of that individual to get a picture of them.

Postcards related in some way more on an individual level, because of what you bring to the exhibition, but works more, too, on the level of nostalgia.

I needed some facts with the postcards – but that is me. Many people were not looking at it in the same way. I almost wanted to provide my own captions to images. Also wanted to see what others would put. I thought that this is one man's collection – what he has responded to – and then has also made a selection from a vast collection. What criteria are there for selection? **key point**.

With Women Travellers, the criteria might have been dictated by which portraits they had, or if there were any artefacts that they could borrow. Also any written evidence or paintings, or photographs that the women had done themselves.

Very different exhibitions, but the common theme I felt was the people – exhibitions about people – not design, or style or movement, or something else. About individuals – names or anonymous. Whatever time or date, or location, the common links. This is partly because this is the Portrait Gallery and not the Tate or National.

Therefore particular images from postcards: comical scenes or sad, or questioning and quotes from Women Travellers that are revealing – these are my inspirations.

Fig. 53: Taking a dog for a walk.

Comments

These are just notes that could build towards a formal comparison of the two exhibitions. It is thinking through writing. As I wrote certain phrases, I understood more. An example of this is the part about Tom Phillips making a selection – he collected them, then he selected them and organized them in frames.

And also the point about individuals, anonymous or known, as compared to many exhibitions at other galleries.

Creative Writing: a poem

(This is fairly self explanatory. Finding something in the exhibition that sparks off pure fantasy, memory, humour ...)

My Muddy Brown Elephant

The notice said
Black, white and brown elephants
For sale
I wanted a brown one
One who had
Rolled in the mud

They searched and searched
But only black ones
Abounded

Finally she dug one out
But out of the bag
Fell his ear

Broken

I rescued him
Will mend him
Restore him to roll in the mud again

My brown elephant
Symbolizes
What I do

I could have turned him down
Gone for a black one
Abandoned the idea

But I became more
determined

Had to have him
Had to give him
a home

Like the traveller who had a soft spot
For stray dogs
An ordinary, extraordinary woman
(With a lovely smile)

So my muddy brown elephant
Has found his home
With an ordinary, extraordinary woman
(On the banks of the Nile*!)

*Thames didn't rhyme, and I had wanted to keep the emphasis on 'smile' and could only achieve this if made a rhyme for it.

Notes. Inspired by an experience in the exhibition shop on 21 August 2004.

Some of the details about travellers had emerged in the exhibition – for example, the photograph of the woman traveller, who loved animals, and who had a beautiful smile.

Review

(Meeting the challenge of a specified word count, and a newspaper or magazine style, this is a difficult but valuable exercise.)

The exhibition entitled 'Off the Beaten Track: Three Centuries of Women Travellers' is on at the National Portrait Gallery until the end of October.

With portraits gleaned from their own collection and borrowed artefacts from other museums and collections, this is a surprisingly inspiring exhibition. With a theme of pioneer travellers, women before their time and out of their time, this is a static display of portraits, written extracts and a few wood carvings, textiles and broken pots. However there are some objects that belonged to the travellers, such as a threadbare hat belonging to Mary Kingsley which she not only wore, but also held some gruesome objects, such as human parts found on one of her journeys.

The writings from journals and extracts from letters reveal some of the adventures that the women encountered, the disguises they had to adopt and the sights they witnessed. Many started campaigns against slavery, one pioneered inoculation and another worked for Chinese blind education.

This exhibition is inspiring because it tells of the women who went against the conventions of their societies. They travelled, alone or with few companions, and endured a range of physical challenges. To today's women, who are used to being able to do what they want, go where they want, and not be considered freaks, or outlaws, these examples are a valuable reminder of just how far women have come, and the important contribution they made to knowledge. Women can have a different perspective on the societies that they encounter. Frequently not involved in politics and diplomacy, they see the real conditions in which people live and, in their own ways, try to bring about changes for good. Some were collectors for museums; there were photographers; others who were artists painting the scenery and the inhabitants; and many who travelled for their own purposes. However, in their writings, they have pictured the world.

This exhibition is full of surprises, and it's well worth spending some time reading and looking and reflecting on our world, and how others saw it in the past, and how we see it today.

Comments

Using a brief of 350 words, the challenge is to whet the appetite of the readers of a newspaper such as *The Guardian* or *The Independent*. There is a specific audience and they are drawn in by specific details – hence the mention of the threadbare hat, and the list of pioneers and their deeds. Lists are a useful device for getting in lots of information, and, in other places, adjectives and adverbs can add quickly and economically to the amount of information being conveyed. This is one particular technique that would vary for different papers or journals. Each has their house style, so the writer needs to know what that is. Part of a newspaper's brief might be to encourage their readers to go to the events that they cover in their papers, so there have to be enticing remarks and the phrases which prepare a reader for what to expect. This is seen in 'it is well worth spending some time ... and reflecting on our world ...'

Other inspirations – reflective, creative and analytical

Ideas for research
(It is not just about the task you have to do now; it is always about thinking ahead, and filling the compost heap of creativity. Therefore reflective notes and inspirations kept in a journal, will act as a treasure trove at other times. The act of writing, also lodges ideas more securely in the compost.)

What other exhibitions could be inspired by this one?

- First thought is what about travellers in this country – why does it always have to be abroad that gets looked at? This country has not always been easy to travel in.
- the difficulties women travellers would have
- areas that are rarely explored
- the prejudices that there are
- why women have to travel with others
- safety issues.

Expand the aspect about other women coming to Britain. In the National Portrait Gallery exhibition it was probably limited to the ones they had portraits of, and these were probably going to be few and far between.

Literary travelling – imaginary or factual: did the authors always travel and research for their books or are many journeys imaginary?

Other categories of occupations that have travel as part of the job: journalists, photographers – they are recording material.

The occupations that demand travel for other reasons: nurses, airline personnel, reporters, missionaries, sports people.

Holidays – journalists, travel writers: the growth of the travel writing profession as opposed to writing about what they were doing. This didn't come over as a particular issue in the exhibition.

The best exhibitions are the ones that get you asking:

- why or why not
- what if …
- ideas for other things
- linking to other areas
- how to make it active, and not passive.

The personal response to something – this is based on your own character, your interests, your background, your experience.

Telling someone else about it makes things become clearer; you develop the ideas in conversation.

Comments
Even in the form of a scrappy list, this will lodge enough ideas to be picked up on again later. If combined with some of the other areas of writing, it means that you can recall the things that struck you, stirred you, at another time. Where the sketchbook mainly captures the visuals and feelings, the sketchnotes and reflections make non-visual links, or reminders, and log some curious thoughts.

Reflective notes, particularly on the element of time and writing
(This writing came out of doing all the other pieces of writing, and is meant to read as a reflection on *when* you write – at the time, or later, etc.)

A. Thinking and Writing:

- at exhibition
- over a coffee
- travelling home
- later that day
- next day
- few days later
- re-read and write more,

B. Writing:

- after telling someone – immediately
- fairly soon after
- much later,

C. Reflecting and Writing:

- after someone has looked at what you have written,

D. Thinking and Writing:

- after you have read what others wrote about the exhibition – either reviews or colleagues,

E. Layers of Writing:

- going back to own writing at different times – reflective layers.

Comments

This may look like a very simple list. Yet it has various stages that reflect the processes and stages of writing that were expounded at the beginning of this book. Referring to the reflective notes above:

A. is about the early, raw, rough, bits of writing and is dominated by feelings
B. is the idea of talk write, and the early standing back, reflecting
C. sharing with others and seeing their points of view on your work
D. taking on board other viewpoints
E. constant returning to your work, and expanding, and also going off in new directions.

The words and the ideas epitomize many of the pairings of words which I used as a poem on the title page of the book. For example: talk write, think write, write about, doodle write, write re-write, etc.

Photos from an Album

(This is an extended piece of creative writing, but which relates to almost all areas of writing proposed in this book. I have used five photographs from an old photo album, found in a flea market.)

There are three parts:

- the facts
- a story
- the reflection.

The facts

The album has photographs, mainly from holidays, from the period 1928–1931.

There are two from 1928 – a group on a beach at Luccombe, near Shanklin on the Isle of Wight, and the other of five seated people with walking sticks.

There are two from 1929 – a woman and a boy on a country road, and a group of four – two older women and two boys on Lovers Seat, at Hastings.

The last one is of Polly parrot in a cage in a garden in 1931. This has some colour in it.

At first I thought the older ladies must be grandmothers of the boy who appears quite a lot throughout the album. But it becomes clear, from the very occasional labels, that one of these is his mother.

The photographer is not in many shots but would appear to be the younger boy's older brother. There is a studio shot of him to open the album. The final few pictures are of him and his wife and a young baby in 1931. There are garden scenes with Polly parrot and Jane, a young dalmatian dog.

The camera could have been a No. 1 Pocket Kodak Special which was produced between 1926 and 1934, or the No. 2 Brownie introduced in 1901 and discontinued in 1933. The picture sizes of both these cameras match those in the album. The camera case does not appear in any pictures or this would have been a clue.

A story

Lillian was born in 1880. She married Stan in 1900. Stan was an engine fitter on the railway. In 1905 Gerald was born. Stan went off to fight in France in 1916. He came back on leave early in 1918 and Freddy was conceived. Stan returned to France and was killed 11 days before the 11th hour of the 11th day. Freddy was born the day Lillian heard the news of Stan's death.

Lillian coped. You had to cope. She took in washing, and a lodger. Gerald studied hard and was soon working at a local bank as a clerk, with prospects. Freddy was a happy child, often in his own world, reading books, and making things. He was no trouble to Lillian and they were close.

In 1928 they all went to the Isle of Wight for a holiday. Gerald brought his fiancée, and her sister and her husband, and her mother Enid.

Gerald had just bought his first camera.

On the beach

They didn't all go to the beach that day. Lillian went with Freddy despite the cool breeze. Enid stayed indoors. Not comfortable sitting on the sand, nevertheless, Lillian tried to join in with the hilarity. Gerald was being a clown, showing off in front of his fiancée, Clarissa, and Sophie laughed at him too, which egged him on more. Freddy buried his feet in the sand. John took the photograph. Clarissa always thought Gerald was funny. Freddy thought that he was becoming a bit of a twerp. That's what love does.

The beach was busy with everyone enjoying the brief sunshine of that chilly summer.

The next day, on a walk inland, they came across a long seat and it was decided to have a picture of the couple-to-be, their mothers and Freddy. A distance seems to separate the mothers – a distance of class and aspiration. But the similarities of the toughness of their situations unites them far more clearly now.

The next year, at Hastings, Lillian and Freddy and Gerald went to stay with Lillian's younger sister Kathleen and her son Ronnie. There's a rivalry between Freddy and Ronnie. Ronnie, not so clever, tried to sabotage Freddy and tells tales, but it wouldn't ever spoil Freddy's holiday.

The picture at Lover's Seat is ironic – the sisters not that close, and cousins competing.

Later, on a walk away from the town with just Gerald, Lillian and Freddy, they are more relaxed. Gerald takes the picture and his family cheerfully pose. It's another chilly day and Freddy has his coat on – it's had to last a few years and is no longer a full length coat. But he has a camera too – and soon will rival Gerald for taking snaps.

1930 sees the marriage of Gerald and Clarissa and so there is no holiday. Every penny went into the wedding, as Lillian did not want to let her son down. In 1931 there is the birth of a baby girl, Lucy. Gerald now has a full family, with Polly parrot and Jane, the dalmatian. Freddy and Lillian come to stay and help.

The album ends.

There would be an album all for Lucy and the brothers and sisters-to-be. Freddy had his own camera and rarely appeared in pictures again. Lillian stalwartly, solidly helping out; not allowing any help for herself. She died in 1939, broken at the onset of another war. She'd lost her love to the war to end all wars, and that was in vain.

Gerald, now a bank manager, became part of the Home Guard.

Freddy joined the RAF and learnt to fly Spitfires, and was shot down in the Battle of Britain. He was 23.

The Reflection

This is all speculation: I don't know the names – apart from the parrot and the dog. The dates and places are labelled, but not the people.

These facts alone are poignant, but if we relate this to our own albums – we rarely put names down, after all we know who they are, so we put down places, as we might forget those, and animals because we have different relationships to them and are less self conscious at writing their names. But the people remain anonymous to others.

How did the album come into my hands? It was on a stall in a flea market; one item in a house clearance. I 'rescued' it – somehow the horror of a photograph album being finally scooped up into a black bin liner when it did not sell, was too much for me. Not just any old photograph album – this one, with these people.

I have invented a story for them – probably not at all true, but that does not matter.

Some might question me using this material in the teaching. There may be some who are most uncomfortable in using other people's stories. Others are absorbed. I do not force this on anyone. But it will always elicit a response. It will raise issues that stir thoughts.

What this sort of writing produces is questions – it needs research into what could be going on; what technology there is – in cameras, etc; but also in what they are doing; the nature of the holidays; the details of what they are wearing. This is before the Welfare State, so assumptions are made as to their circumstances. The relationships between people being photographed, and then between them and the photographer, also gives us so many insights into society and its structures.

This, I believe, is an important way to look at history. It is the history of ordinary people, but they are affected by what is happening around them and the clues are there in so many ways. So imagination leads into facts. And as so many writers have proved, we learn more through stories than through bald statements of fact.

Life doesn't hold still
A good snapshot stopped a moment from running away.
(Welty 1995: 84)

Above all I wanted – in a single image – to seize the essence of a situation arising before me.
(Cartier-Bresson, in Cartier-Bresson and Giacometti 2005: 66)

Comments
This piece encapsulates what I have tried to put over in this book – the use of creative writing techniques to inform a range of writing, thoughts and concerns.

The writing says all that I want to express.

Fig. 54: Five photos from an album.

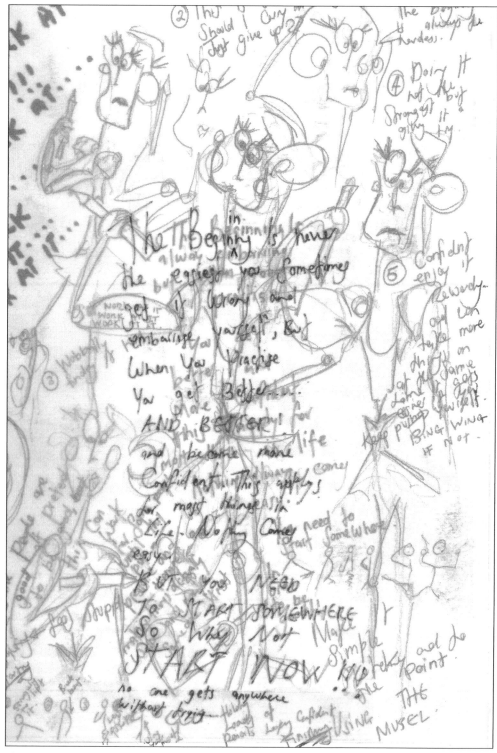

Fig. 55: Layers of thoughts from a student's journal – a palimpsest of inspirations.

CONCLUSION

This conclusion is short and sweet because in a book like this it is difficult to end.

Before I had finished writing all the sections, I was having more ideas for further work, so volume two may follow.

But what is more important is that this book is about stimulating ideas *for* writing and *into* writing. The metaphor here might be a relay race – I hold the baton, and you, passing me, take it and run, and then pass it to someone else. The difference is that, having held the baton, you pass it on, but you don't stop running yourself. I would also add that I picked up the baton from many other people.

You carry on in your own ways – and perhaps in different directions to the race.

Take your writing on journeys: for walks, for runs, for climbs, for swims, for jaunts and jollies, for stopping and staring, for doodling and dreaming …

This book might act as a palimpsest. A palimpsest is a manuscript, written on a surface from which an earlier text has been partly or wholly erased.

So you might scribble over what I have written: take odd words from it, extend some, manipulate, transform or revise others. You may take the writing you have done earlier and then rub out parts, write over other parts, substitute one word for another, and create new writing. But writing which springs from earlier sketches (see Fig. 55).

So there is no end …

And when it is hard to end something yourself, get someone else to do it for you.

And T.S. Eliot, in 1944, in 'Little Gidding', one of *The Four Quartets*, gave us words that exactly match this thought:

> *What we call the beginning is often the end*
> *And to make an end is to make a beginning.*
> *The end is where we start from.*

Appendix

Writing PAD

Writing PAD (Writing Purposefully in Art and Design) was an HEFCE FDTL Phase 4 project which began in October 2002. Led by Goldsmiths College, Central Saint Martins College of Art and Design and the Royal College of Art, its Project Director was Julia Lockheart.

The initial phase brought together a number of institutions to create discussions and dissemination of ideas about the role of writing, the nature of writing work going on in art and design colleges and to open up debates about new forms and methods. A website was set up and conferences were held that extended these networks of participants. The spread of its influence encouraged performing arts to join as well.

After funding ended, having already been extended because of the excellent work it was doing, the still very active Writing PAD community launched its own journal, *Journal of Writing in Creative Practice*, under the editorship of Julia Lockheart and John Wood, published by Intellect Journals.

Regional networks have now been established and exploratory themes, debates, and collaborative projects are still developing.

It is, in part, my involvement with Writing PAD that led to the writing of this book. The encouragement, support and exchange of ideas is what will enable change to happen in institutions where writing is still bolted on to studio practice. It also encourages those working in places where exploration is happening, to extend and embed writing in all practice.

The website contains discussion papers and case studies and a range of other information and links.

www.writing-pad.ac.uk

The *Journal of Writing in Creative Practice* is published three times a year.

The Illustrations

This book is about journeys into writing: I emphasize the rough, experimental, first impulses of writing which capture the energy of the thought. This can then be worked on and edited and tweaked, but with care being taken not to lose the creative spark. As the writing styles are eclectic, varied and oscillating between the very personal and the formal, so too with the illustrations and visuals.

I asked friends and colleagues, tutors, students and ex-students to contribute and I am thrilled with the range of work that has been included.

Finished and published work includes *Inertia Wall* and *Girl Reading* by Pilar Muñoz del Castillo. *Inertia Wall*, screen printed faces on wooden blocks, won the *Printmaking Today* award at the 2008 RE Annual Exhibition, and I am grateful to Pilar for allowing me to use it. Her work is seen in Illustrations 1 and 3. See her website for more details: www. artpilarmunoz.com

Fernando Feijoo's artist's books *Crack's Progress* and *Charlie's Progress*, which are contemporary workings of Hogarth's *Progresses*, contain reduced versions of the original creative text and lino cuts. The part-open book and one spread are featured in the opening page of Part 3. I asked Fernando for journey works to amplify the exploratory aspects of Part 1 and 2 and his two train illustrations graphically reveal this. The train for Part 2 is appropriately from his series entitled *The Journeyman*. The alphabet train, following this journey theme, is from the end papers of his *Contemporary Street Alphabet*. Fernando's works have won prizes, so, again, I am grateful to be able to reproduce them in my text. His work is seen in Illustrations 5, 21, 48 and 56. See his website for more details: www.fernandofeijoo.com

Alex Bunn is an artist, puppeteer and theatre designer. He met requests for specific illustrations for key pieces of my text, and created wonderful and characterful annotations to the texts. His work is seen in Illustrations 20, 49, 50 and 53.

Helen Ralston was fired to produce a range of figures in her sketchbook – characters who are scared of reading and writing, and daunted by words. Her work is seen throughout the book and reflects also the ways some of the exercises generated her own writing explorations. Her illustrations are: 15, 16, 17, 18, 30, 34, 42, 45, 46 and 55.

Sarah le Marquand provided inspiration for many visuals, and she was, as always, the guiding hand behind many of the pieces I produced.

All other visuals, diagrams and collages, are the work of the author. Many of these are included to show the sketchy and rough explanation of an idea which might happen in a one to one encounter, or in a workshop. Every reader is invited to adapt any that might be of use to them.

Bibliography

A Selection of Works on Writing and Inspirations

Alexenberg, M. (2008) *Educating Artists for the future*, Bristol: Intellect Books.

Alvarez, A. (2005) *The Writer's Voice*, London: Bloomsbury.

Arden, P. (2006) *Whatever you think, think the opposite*, London: Penguin.

Arizpe, E. & Styles, M. (2003) *Children Reading Pictures: interpreting visual texts*, London: Routledge Falmer.

Atwood, M. (2002) *Negotiating with the Dead: A Writer on Writing*, Cambridge: Cambridge University Press.

Atwood, M. (2006) *The Tent*, London: Bloomsbury.

Ayckbourn, A. (2002) *The Crafty Art of Playmaking*, London : Faber and Faber.

Baker, B. (2006) *The Way we Write*, London: Continuum.

Barker, C. (1977) *Theatre Games*, London: Methuen Drama.

Batchelor, D. (2000) *Chromophobia*, London: Reaktion Books.

Beadle, P. (2006) 'Mind your language – and know what it means' in *The Guardian* Education 16 May, p 6.

Beard, F. (2004) 'The poem that was really a list' in *Things* 17–18 Spring, pp 194–95.

Bell, R. (2005) *Pictures and Words*, London: Laurence King.

Benjamin, W. (1969) *Illuminations*, New York: Schocken Books.

Benjamin, W. (2007) *Walter Benjamin's Archive*, (translated by Esther Leslie) London: Verso.

Bennett, A. (2005) *Untold Stories*, London: Faber and Faber.

Berger, J. (1972) *Ways of Seeing*, London: Penguin.

Berger, J. (2002) *The Shape of a Pocket*, London: Bloomsbury.

Berger, J. (2005a) *and our faces, my heart, brief as photos*, London: Bloomsbury.

Berger, J. (2005b) *Berger on drawing* edited by Jim Savage Aghabullogue, Cork: Occasional Press.

Berger, J. and Christie, J. (nd) *I send you this Cadmium Red*, Barcelona: Actar in collaboration with MALM.

Birkett, D. (2004) *Off the Beaten Track: Three Centuries of Women Travellers*, London: National Portrait Gallery.

Blake, Q. (2002) *Magic Pencil*, London: British Council/British Library.

Blake, Q. (2000) *Words and Pictures*, London: Jonathan Cape.

Bolton, G. (2001) *Reflective Practice: Writing and professional development*, London: Paul Chapman.

Borg, E. (2004) 'Internally persuasive writing in Fine Arts Practice' in *Art Design and Communication in Higher Education* 3: 3 pp 193–210.

Borges, J.L. (2000) *The Craft of Verse*, New York: Harvard University Press.

Brigden, A. & McFall, C. (2000) *Dyslexia in Higher Education Art and Design: a creative opportunity: Conference Report*, UK: Surrey Institute of Art and Design University College.

Burns, C. (2008) *Off the Page: Writers talk about beginnings, endings, and everything in between*, New York: W.W. Norton and Company.

Cartier-Bresson, H. & Giacometti, A. (2005) *The Decision of the Eye*, Zurich: Kunsthaus.

Childers, P.B., Hobson, E.H. and Mullin, J.A. (1998) *ARTiculating: Teaching Writing in a Visual World*, Portsmouth NH: Boynton/Cook.

Cixous, H. (1997) *Rootprints: Memory and life writing*, London: Routledge.

Clark, J. (2004) *Spectres: When Fashion Turns Back*, London: Victoria and Albert Museum.

Clarke, M. (2007) *Verbalising the Visual: Translating art and design into words*, Lausanne: AVA Publishing.

Cox, B. (1998) *Literacy is Not Enough: Essays on the importance of Reading*, Manchester: Manchester University Press & Book Trust.

Crowe, D. (2007) *How I write: The Secret Lives of Authors*, New York: Rizzoli.

Crystal, D. (1998) *Language Play*, London: Penguin.

Crystal, D. and Crystal, H. (2000) *Words on Words*, London: Penguin.

Crystal, D. (2007) *Words, Words, Words*, Oxford: Oxford University Press.

De Bono, E. (1970) *Lateral Thinking*, London: Penguin.

De Bono, E. (1996) *Thinking Course*, Harlow: BBC ACTIVE.

De Botton, A. (2003) *The Art of Travel*, London: Penguin.

Dennis, F. (2006) *When Jack Sued Jill: Nursery Rhymes for Modern Times*, London: Ebury Press.

Drucker, J. (2004) *The Century of Artists' Books*, New York: Granary Books.

Duff, L. & Davies, J. (2005) *Drawing – The Process*, Bristol: Intellect Books.

Dyer, G. (2006) *The Ongoing Moment*, London: Abacus.

Edwards, B. (2001) The New *Drawing on the Right Side of the Brain*, London: Harper Collins.

Edwards, H. & Woolf, N. (2007) 'Design research by practice: modes of writing in a recent PH.D. from the RCA' in *Journal of Writing in Creative Practice* 1: 1 pp 53–67.

Elkins, J. (2002) *Stories of Art*, London: Routledge.

Elkins, J. (2001) *Why Art Cannot Be Taught*, Urbana and Chicago: University of Illinois.

Evans, C. (2003) *Fashion at the Edge*, New Haven and London: Yale University Press.

Evans, J. (1998) *What's in the Picture? Responding to illustration in picture books*, London: Paul Chapman.

Evans, M. (2007) 'Another kind of writing: reflective practice and creative journals in the performing arts' in *The Journal of Writing in Creative Practice* 1: 1 pp 69–76.

Fairbairn, G.J. and Winch, C. (1996) *Reading, Writing and Reasoning*, Maidenhead: Open University.

Fanelli, S. (2007) *Sometimes I Think, Sometimes I am*, London: Tate.

Fanelli, S. (2006) *Tate Artist Timeline: 20th Century*, London: Tate.

Feijoo, F. and Francis, P. (2006) *Contemporary Street Alphabet*, Cambridge: Feijoo. Artist's Book.

Feijoo, F. (2004) *Crack's Progress and Charlie's Progress, (a re-telling of Hogarth's Progresses)*, published as winner of The Olive Cook Library Award, Fables Competition, and as an Artist's Book.

Fishel, C. (2005) *401 design meditations: wisdom, insights and intriguing thoughts from 244 leading designers*, Gloucester, Massachusetts: Rockport.

Fletcher, A. (2001) *The Art of Looking Sideways*, London: Phaidon.

Fletcher, A. (2006) *Picturing and Poeting*, London: Phaidon.

Foer, J.S. (2006) *A Convergence of Birds: original fiction and poetry inspired by the work of Joseph Cornell*, London: Hamish Hamilton.

Foster, J. (1999) *Word Whirls*, Oxford: Oxford University Press.

Francis, P. (2005) *Content in Writing*, A Discussion Paper for Writing PAD www.writing-pad.ac.uk.

Francis, P. (2002) 'Success against the odds' in *Special Children* November–December, pp 20–23.

Gardner, H. (1993) *Frames of Mind*, London: Fontana.

Gaur, A. (2000) *Literacy and the Politics of Writing*, Bristol: Intellect Books.

Gompertz, W. (2007) 'A Month in the Life of a Client': diary of the activities of the director of Media at Tate Modern, in *Creative Review* December pp 35–52.

Gordon, J. (2004) 'The "wow" factors: the assessment of practical media and creative arts subjects' in *The Journal of Art Design and Communication in Higher Education* 3: 1 pp 61–72.

Grainger, T., Goouch, K. & Lambirth, A. (2005) *Creativity and Writing*, Abingdon, Oxon: Routledge.

Graves, J. (2007) 'Conversations heard and unheard: creativity in the studio and in writing' in *The Journal of Writing in Creative Practice* 1: 1 pp 13–18.

Gray, C. and Malins, J. (2004) *Visualizing Research*, Aldershot: Ashgate, 2004

Gregory, D. (2006) *The Creative License*, New York: Hyperion.

Hall, L. (2008a) *The Pitmen Painters*, London: Faber and Faber.

Hall, L. (2008b) quoted in 'The legacy of the pitmen' by Madeleine Bunting, *The Guardian* 7 June, p 32.

Hall, S. (2007) *This Means This, This Means That: A user's guide to semiotics*, London: Laurence King.

Hardy, C. (2004) 'The art of reflection: reflective practice in publishing education' in *The Journal of Art Design and Communication in Higher Education* 3: 1 pp 17–32.

Hegley, J. (2002) *My Dog is a Carrot*, London: Walker Books.

Herman, J. (1985) *Reflections on drawing*, London: Arts Council of Great Britain.

Hickman, R. (2005) *Why We Make Art and Why it is Taught*, Bristol: Intellect Books.

Hjerter, K.G. (1986) *Doubly Gifted: The Author as Visual Artist*, New York: Harry N. Abrams.

Howard, U. (2006) 'Reading is passive. Writing is where the action is', *The Guardian* Education, 30 May p 8.

Hughes, T. (1967) *Poetry in the Making*, London: Faber and Faber.

James, A. (2004) 'Autobiography and narrative in personal development planning in the creative arts' in *The Journal of Art Design and Communication in Higher Education* 3: 2 pp 103–11.

Jeffries, S. (2006) 'The Death of Handwriting' in *The Guardian* G2 14 February pp 1–11.

Kandinsky, W. (2006) *Sounds*: translated and with an introduction by Elizabeth R. Napier, New Haven: Yale University Press.

Klanten, R. & Hubner, M. (2008) '*Fully Booked*', *Cover Art and Design for Books*, Berlin: Gestalten.

Klee, P. (1925) *Pedagogical Sketchbook*, London: Faber and Faber.

Knight, P. & Yorke, M. (2003) *Assessment, Learning and Employability*, Maidenhead: SRHE/ Open University Press.

Kriegel, O. & McDevitt, M. (Illegal Art) (2005) *Suggestion*, San Francisco: Chronicle Books.

Le Marquand, S. and Francis, P. (2005) 'An integrated approach to the delivery of writing in the learning environment of the studio', unpublished paper for Kent Institute of Art and Design.

Le Marquand, S. & Francis, P. (2006) 'Finding the I in assessment: Reflection on a journey from assessment to evaluation: a discussion paper'. University College for the Creative Arts.

Lively, P. (2002) *A House Unlocked*, London: Penguin.

Lodge, D. (1997) *The Practice of Writing*, London: Penguin.

Lumley, J. (2004) *No Room for Secrets*, London: Michael Joseph.

McKee, R. (1999) *Story*, London: Methuen.

McGowan, K. (2007) *Key Issues in Critical and Cultural Theory*, Maidenhead: Open University Press/McGraw-Hill Education.

Madden, M. (2006) *99 Ways to Tell a Story: Exercises in Style*, London: Jonathan Cape.

Miller, A. (2007) *Reading Bande Dessinee*, Bristol: Intellect Books.

Mills, P. (1996) *Writing in Action*, London: Routledge.

Milner, A. (2005) *Inspirational Objects: a visual dictionary of simple, elegant forms*, London: A&C Black.

Moon, J. (1999) *Learning Journals*, London: Kogan Page.

Moon, J. (2004) *A Handbook of Reflective and Experiential Learning*, London: Routledge.

Moon, J. (2000) *Reflection in Learning and Professional Development*, London: Kogan Page.

Morley, S. (2003) *Writing on the Wall: Word and Image in Modern Art*, London: Thames and Hudson.

Mortimore, T. (2003) *Dyslexia and Learning Style*, London: Whurr.

National Portrait Gallery (2003) *Heroes and Villains at the National Portrait Gallery. Over 50 Celebrities, writers and experts debate famous Britons with the work of Gerald Scarfe*, London: National Portrait Gallery.

National Portrait Gallery (2004) *We are the People: postcards from the collection of Tom Phillips*, London: National Portrait Gallery.

Newlyn, L. & Lewis, J. (2003) *Synergies: Creative Writing in Academic Practice: Volume 1 Sea Sonnets*, Oxford: The St Edmund Hall Poetry Workshop: Chough Publications.

Nichols, G. (2004) *Paint me a Poem: New poems inspired by art in Tate*, London: A&C Black.

Nielsen, D. & Hartmann, K. (2005) *Inspired: how creative people think, work and find inspiration*, Amsterdam: BIS Publishers.

O'Reilly, J. (2002) *No Brief: Graphic Designers' Personal Projects*, Mies, Switzerland: Rotovision.

Owen, N. (2001) *The Magic of Metaphor: 77 Stories for Teachers, Trainers and Thinkers*, Carmarthen: Crown House.

Padgett, I. (1999) *Visual Spatial Ability and Dyslexia: A research project*, London: Central St Martin's College of Art and Design.

Palmer, Sue (2001) 'Meet the Glove Gang: Profile of Pat Francis' dyslexia teaching', *Primary* magazine for the *Times Educational Supplement*, January, pp 10–12.

Patt, L. (2007) *Searching for Sebald: photography after W.G. Sebald*, Los Angeles: The Institute of Cultural Inquiry.

Peake, M. (2001) *Letters from a Lost Uncle*, London: Methuen.

Pepper, R. (2006) *The Artist's Cut: The Compendium*, London: Artist's book. www.dailydrawingdiary. com

Perec, G. (1997) *Species of Spaces and Other Pieces* translated John Sturrock, London: Penguin.

Prose, F. (2006) *Reading Like a Writer*, New York: Harper Perennial.

Queneau, R. ([1947]1981), *Exercises in Style*, translated by Barbara Wright, London: John Calder.

Race, P. (2005) Making Learning Happen, London: Sage.

Raein, M. (2004) 'Integration of studio and theory in the teaching of graphic Design' in The Journal of Art Design and Communication in Higher Education 3: 3 pp 163–74.

Raien, M. (2003) 'Where is the "I"?': A Discussion Paper for Writing PAD. www.writing-pad. ac.uk

Riding, R. & Rayner, S. (1998) Cognitive Styles and Learning Strategies, London: David Fulton.

Salisbury, M. (2004) Illustrating Children's Books, London: A&C Black.

Schama, S. (2005) Hang-ups: Essays on painting (mostly), London: BBC Books.

Schon, D. (1991) The Reflective Practitioner, Aldershot: Ashgate.

Sharples, M. (1999) How we Write: Writing as Creative Design, London: Routledge.

Starr, R. (2004) Postcards from the Boys, London: Cassell Illustrated.

Thomas, D. (1954) Under Milk Wood, London: J.M. Dent and sons Ltd.

Tonfoni, G. (2000) Writing as a Visual Art, Bristol: Intellect Books.

Tusa, J. (2003) On Creativity: Interviews exploring the process, London: Methuen.

Tymorek, S. (2001) Clothes Lines: A collection of poetry and art, New York: Harry N. Abrams.

Virtue, J. (2005) John Virtue: London Paintings, London: National Gallery Company.

Wainwright, A. (1992) A Pictorial Guide to the Lakeland Fells: The Western Fells, London: Michael Joseph.

Walter, H. (2003) Other People's Shoes: Thoughts on Acting, London: Nick Hern Books.

Warren, F. (2006) Postsecret: extraordinary confessions from ordinary lives, London: Orion Books.

Welty, E. (1995) One Writer's Beginnings, Cambridge, Massachusetts: Harvard University Press.

Wigan, M. (2006) Thinking Visually, Lausanne: AVA Publishing.

Wilson, M. (2006) Storytelling and theatre: contemporary storytellers and their art, London: Palgrave.

Winter, R. (2003) 'Regular writing tasks would aid learning far better than the last-minute essay' in The Guardian Education, 10 June, p 15.

Winter, R., Buck, A. and Sobiechowska, P. (1999) Professional Experience and the Investigative Imagination: The ART of reflective writing, London: Routledge.

Winterson, J. (1996) Art Objects, London: Vintage.

Winterson, J. (2002) 'The Secret Life of Us' in The Guardian, Arts 25 November, pp 10–11.

Winterson, J. (2001) 'In a world that makes no sense, artists, writers and actors have a right to speak out against war' in The Guardian, 16 October G2 p 11.

Winterson, J. (2007) 'The strength of art is a private moment between individuals' in The Times, 19 May, Books p 3.

Wood, J. (2004) 'The tetrahedron can encourage designers to formalize more responsible strategies' in The Journal of Art Design and Communication in Higher Education 3: 3, pp 175–92.

Wood, J. (2005) 'An Evolutionary Purpose to Dyslexia?' in Fourth Door Review 7, pp 117–25.

Woolf, V. (1990) A Room of One's Own, London: Triad Grafton.

Books that are Facsimiles of Journals, Extracts on Journals or about Journal Writing

Allen, P. (2001) *art, not chance: nine artists' diaries*, London: Calouste Gulbenkian.

Atwood, M. & Pachter, C. (1997) *The Journals of Susanna Moodie*, Toronto: Macfarlane Walter & Ross. (This is more in the way of an artists' book collaboration between a verbal artist and a visual artist.)

Burnaby, G.V. (1994) *John owes me Sixpence (Uncle Geoffrey's Diary)*, London: Merlin Books. (A reprint of a schoolboy's diary from 1912 – with writings and sketches to help highlight what is diary, observation, reflection, etc. and also because of its date, and that the boy went to war and was killed in 1916, an example of learning about context.)

Cixous, H. (2004) *The Writing Notebooks* (edited and translated by Susan Sellars), London: Continuum.

Cobain, K. (2002) *Journals*, New York: Riverhead Books.

Dolphin, L. (1999) *Evidence: The Art of Candy Jernigan*, San Francisco: Chronicle Books.

Eldon, K. (1997) *The Journey is the Destination: The Journals of Dan Eldon*, Chronicle.

Fanelli, S. (2000) *Dear Diary*, London: Walker Books. (Note: this is a children's book, but is interesting in its layout of different perspectives, stimulating ideas about diaries and journals.)

Francis, P. (2004) *Reflective Journals in Studio Practice*, A Case Study for Writing PAD. www.writing-pad.ac.uk

Garcia, J. (1995) *Harrington Street*, New York: Delacorte Press.

Graphic 10 (2006) *Taking a Line for a walk: Diaries, notebooks and sketchbooks*, Amsterdam: BIS Publishers

Grenfell, J. (2004) *My Kind of Magic: A Scrapbook*, London: John Murray.

Guinness, A. (2001) *A Commonplace Book*, London: Hamish Hamilton.

Herman, J. (2002) *Related Twilights: Notes from an Artist's Diary*, Seren: Poetry Wales Press Ltd.

Kahlo, F. (1995) *The Diary of Frida Kahlo* (introduction by Carlos Fuentes), New York: Harry N. Abrams

Lambert, C. (2004) *Taking a line for a walk: 1000 miles on foot Le Havre to Rome*, London: Antique Collectors Books.

Lawrie, S. (2004) 'We have a lot to talk about: dialogue journals in graphic design.' *The Journal of Art, Design and Communication in Higher Education*. 3: 2, pp 81–87.

Manguel, A. (2004) *A Reading Diary: A Year of Favourite Books*, London: Cannongate.

Middas, S. (1990) *South of France: A Sketchbook*, New York: Workman Publishing. (Whilst principally a sketchbook, the use of words gives it more of a reflective quality.)

Moon, J. (2002) *Learning Journals*, London: Kogan Page. (See also books on reflection in main list.)

Mortimer, P. (2003) *Broke Through Britain*, London: Mainstream Publishing.

Nelson, B. (1999) *Postcards from the Basque Country*, New York: Stewart, Tabori and Chung.

New, J. (2005) *Drawing From Life: The Journal as Art*, New York: Princeton Architectural Press.

Peake, M. (2001) *Letters from a Lost Uncle*, London: Methuen. (A work of fiction, but brilliant in its use of creative reflective layout in its visuals and words.)

Penny, J., Fox, R. & Carey, M. (2002) *The Artful Journal: a Spiritual Quest*, New York: Watson-Guptill.

Pepper, R. (2006) *The Artist's Cut: The Compendium*, UK: Artist's book, 2006. www.dailydrawingdiary. com

Someguy (2007) *The 1000 Journals Project* (foreword by Kevin Kelly), San Francisco: Chronicle Books LLC.

Steinbeck, J. (2001) *Journal of a Novel: The East of Eden Letters*, London: Penguin Classics.

Thomas, G. (nd post-1996) *Nepal: an illustrated journal*, Attleborough: UK: Breckland Print.

Woolf, V. (1987) *A Writer's Diary*, London: Triad Grafton.

Books to Help with Writing Styles and Techniques

Aitchison, J. (1997) *The language web: The power and problem of words*, Cambridge: Cambridge University Press.

Alleva, A. d' (2006) *How to Write Art History*, London: Laurence King.

Armstrong, D., Stokoe, W. & Wilcox, S. (1995) *Gesture and the Nature of Language* Cambridge: Cambridge University Press.

Bell. J. & Magrs, P. (2001) *The Creative Writing Coursebook*, London: Macmillan.

Birch, C. (2005), *Awaken the Writer Within*, Oxford: How To Books.

Brayfield, C. (2008) *Arts Reviews ... and How to Write Them*, Harpenden: Creative Essentials, Kamera Books.

Cameron, J. (2005) *Letters to a Young Artist*, London: Rider/Random House.

Cameron, J. (1998) *The Right to Write*, London: Pan Books.

Cameron, J. (2004) *The Sound of Paper*, London: Michael Joseph.

Chambers, E. & Northedge, A. (2008) *The Arts Good Study Guide*, Milton Keynes: Open University.

Clark, R. (2006) *Writing Tools: 50 Essential strategies for every writer*, New York: Little, Brown and Company.

Cooper, S. & Patton, R. (2004) *Writing Logically, Thinking Critically*, London: Pearson.

Cottrell, S. (2003) *The Study Skills Handbook (2nd edition)*, London: Palgrave Macmillan.

Geraghty, M. (2006) *The five-minute writer* Oxford: How to books.

Goldberg, N. (1990) *Wild Mind: Living The Writer's Life*, New York: Bantam Books.

Goldberg, N. (1986) *Writing Down the Bones*, Boston: Shambhala.

Gurdon, M. (2007) *Write On! The No-Nonsense Guide to Professional Writing*, London: New Holland.

Hadfield, C. & Hadfield, J. (1990) *Writing games*, Walton on Thames: Nelson.

Hargreaves, S. (2007) *Study Skills for Dyslexic Students*, London: Sage.

Hicks, W. (1999) *Writing for Journalists*, London: Routledge.

Hughes, R. (2005) *Exploring Grammar in Writing*, Cambridge: Cambridge University Press.

Levin, P. (2004) *Write great essays! reading and essay writing for undergraduates and taught postgraduates*, Maidenhead: Open University Press.

McKane, A. (2006) *News Writing*, London: Sage.

Morgenstern, S. (2005) *The Aspiring Author's Journal*, New York: Harry N. Abrams.

Morley, D. (2007) *The Cambridge Introduction to Creative Writing*, Cambridge: Cambridge University Press.

Pears, R. & Shields, G. (2006) *"Cite them right": the essential guide to referencing and Plagiarism*, Newcastle upon Tyne: Pear Tree Books.

Fig. 56: Journeys through letters.

Price, G. & Skinner, J. (2007) *Support for Learning Differences in Higher Education*, Stoke on Trent: Trentham Books.

Schneider, M. & Killick, J. (2002) *Writing for Self Discovery: a personal approach to creative writing*, London: Vega.

Townend, J. & Walker, J. (2006) *Structure of Language: Spoken and Written English*, London: Whurr.

Ur, P. & Wright, A. (1992) *Five-Minute Activities*, Cambridge: Cambridge University Press.

Weston, A. (2000) *A Rulebook for Arguments*, Indianapolis: Hackett Publishing Company.

Wood, M. (2002) *The Pocket Muse: idea and inspirations for writing*, Ohio: Writer's Digest Books.

Zousmer, S. (2007) *You Don't have to be Famous*, Cincinnati: Writer's Digest Books.

A Selection of Key Reference Books

(These are just some of the main ones used to explore words, meanings, origins, devices, etc.)

Aesop's Fables: There are many versions of these: they are invaluable examples of morals or stories which inspire discussion and ideas.

Ayto, J. (2007) *A Century of New Words*, Oxford: Oxford University Press.

Baldick. C. (2004) *Oxford Concise Dictionary of Literary Terms*, Oxford: Oxford University Press.

Bierce, A. (2003) *The Devil's Dictionary*, London: Bloomsbury.

Brasch, R. (2001) *A Bee in Your Bonnet?* Australia: Angus and Robertson/Harper.

Brewer's Dictionary of Phrase and Fable (This is the best and there are many editions. However it is quite large, so there are paperback versions available, sometimes by other editors.)

Chantrell, G. (2004) *Oxford Dictionary of Word Histories*, Oxford: Oxford University Press.

Crystal, D. (2004) *A glossary of Netspeak and Textspeak*, Edinburgh: Edinburgh University Press.

Daily Telegraph, Mini Sagas: The Daily Telegraph have published many collections of these 50-word stories – great inspirations.

Flavell, L. and Flavell, R. (2001) *Dictionary of Proverbs and their Origins*, London: Kyle Carthie Ltd.

Green, J. (2002) *The Big Book of Rhyming Slang*, London: Cassell.

Kirkpatrick, B. (1996) *Dictionary of Clichés*, London: Bloomsbury.

McCunn, R.L. (2002) *Chinese Proverbs*, San Francisco: Chronicle Books.

Parkinson, J. (2003) *Catchphrase, Slogan and Cliché*, London: Michael O'Mara Books Ltd.

Parsons, D. (2002) *It Must be True: Classic Newspaper Howlers, Bloomers, and Misprints*, London: Ebury Press.

Quinion, M. (2000) *Port Out, Starboard Home and other language myths*, London: Penguin.

Thompson, D. (1995) *The Concise Oxford Dictionary of Current English*, Oxford: Oxford University Press.

Trask, R.L. (2001) *Mind the Gaffe: The Penguin Guide to Common Errors in English*, London: Penguin.

INDEX